Book of Poole High Street

Jenny Oliver

This volume is published by the Poole Historical Trust whose primary aims are the promotion of research into and the publication of works on the history and life of Poole and the surrounding area.

Trustees

Previous Publications

The Pride of Poole, 1688-1851
An Album of Old Poole
Mansions and Merchants of Poole and Dorset
Brownsea Islander
Poole and World War II
A Portfolio of Old Poole
Ebb-Tide at Poole
History of the Town of Poole, 1839 (facsimile)
The Sydenhams of Poole (booklet)
Art in Poole and Dorset
Victorian Poole
Poole after World War II 1945-1953
D-Day Poole (booklet)
The Spirit of Poole 1953-1963
Lifeboatmen Never Turn Back
Schools of Old Poole
Poole's Pride Regained 1964-1974
Poole Was My Oyster
Hengistbury Head - The Whole Story
I Was There
For Nature Not Humans
The Royal Motor Yacht Club 1905-2005 (private publication)
A Winsome Place
A Pint of Good Ale
Up On Hill
Brownsea Island (facsimile of Van Raalte 1906)

ISBN 978 – 1 – 873535 – 882
Production by Graphic Editions Ltd, Poole. Printed by Ashley Press, Poole, Dorset.

Cover picture: *The Level Crossing, Poole* by Henry Lamb. Courtesy of the National Railway Museum

Acknowledgements

Thanks are due to many people who helped to bring this book into existence. The first germ of the book was the BBC's Turn Back Time campaign on the history of the high street and the inspiring memories of the people who visited the pop-up shop in Poole in 2010. Following this, Katie Heaton of Poole Museum and I set up the Poole High Street Project which was carried forward by the enthusiasm and research of the Project supporters Christine Ballantine, Alison Dalton, Valerie Furter, Alan and Anita Hawkins, Julie Noble, John Strang, Margot Teasdale, Sylvia Tomkins, David Warhurst, Leanne and Andy Whiting and many others. Articles contributed to the High Street blog by Ann and Jack Bath, Catherine Beal, Geoff Cummings, Gary Edwards, Andrew Hawkes, Katie Heaton, Roger Hopkins, Lyn Hunt, Sylvia Tomkins and others were an invaluable source of information and ideas for the book.

I would also like to thank Alison Dalton for sharing her experience on community projects and Bryan Gambier for allowing me to use his research on World War I and on his ancestor, Councillor Evan Gambier. Margot Teasdale has been a great help discussing the Borough's past and current plans for the town centre and High Street and I am indebted to Andrew Hawkes as a major contributor to the blog, a source of ideas and facts, and for allowing me to use some of his superb collection of photographs.

Poole Museum has also been very generous in allowing me access to their resources and photographs. Many of the staff have contributed to the blog and helped me with research, particularly Dai Watkins who has provided lots of help and ideas. Thanks to Graham Smith for allowing me to use his drawing of Tudor Poole and to the Poole Historical Trust, especially Ian Andrews for his encouragement, advice and guidance. Most of all, Katie Heaton has been a cheerful sounding board and support through the whole process. We started the book together and although she had to withdraw from full participation, it was not before knocking the Victorian chapter into shape. She has come up with vital sources and contacts, listened to my ramblings when things were going well or badly, and been invaluable in bringing the project to its outcome. I apologise for any errors of fact, which are all my own.

Jenny Oliver

Contents

Chapter 1 Medieval Origins ... 1

Chapter 2 Tudor Times ... 9

Chapter 3 17th Century ... 21

Chapter 4 Age of Adventure ... 41

Chapter 5 The Later 18th Century ... 59

Chapter 6 The Early 19th Century ... 75

Chapter 7 Victorian Times ... 89

Chapter 8 The Edwardian Era and The Great War ... 109

Chapter 9 The 20th Century ... 127

Chapter 10 The Later 20th Century ... 147

Postscript ... 171

Index ... 173

Jenny Oliver

Chapter One

Medieval Origins

'The town and port of Poole are notably inhabited and . . a great multitude of people are there and . . the said port is secure and sufficient for ships.'

The route of Poole High Street may have existed before the town of Poole was even founded. When the sandy promontory where the town now stands was still bare, uninhabited heathland, it was probably already crossed by tracks used by people from the settlements at Hamworthy and Canford.

In the 10th and 11th centuries, the Poole and the Hamworthy shores were used to land and process oysters on a large scale. From the enormous quantities and the dating of harvested oyster shells found in excavations, it seems that this must have been a commercial operation which lasted at least 150 years, perhaps into the Norman period. The oyster operation was only a seasonal activity however and Domesday Book, written 20 years after the Norman invasion, does not mention Poole. At that period it was a remote coastal area of no particular value on the edge of the manor of Canford, one of the many manors belonging to Edward of Salisbury.

The change came in the late 12th century as a small settlement grew up on the Poole peninsula, probably starting as a small fishing village. One reason for its growth may well have been the destruction inflicted on Wareham, a port from Saxon times, in the civil wars between King Stephen and the Empress Matilda in the mid 12th century. Ships sailing to Wareham had to anchor near Poole to wait for the tide to take them further up the harbour and it must have seemed increasingly safer and more convenient to unload their goods in the pool, 'La Pole', rather than sailing all the way up the Frome. The lords of Canford undoubtedly supported the development of the town as a future source of revenue.

The peninsula of Poole was much smaller than it is today; in fact it has been estimated that forty five per cent of the present area of the old town is land reclaimed from the sea since late medieval days. The original shore line seems to have run as far back as where Strand Street, Salisbury Street, Thames Street and West Street now lie. The route that became High Street started near the water's edge by an inlet in the shoreline later known as 'Mesurer's gap' and probably followed the line of an old track up the peninsula.

One theory about the origin of Poole's street plan is that the first area used for mooring or beaching ships was on the sheltered west shore. This would account for the location of the church of St James and the development of Church Street and Market Street as a spinal route up the peninsular. If this was how the town first developed however, the focus for shipping soon shifted to the south shore where the Great Quay was built, and High Street became an equally or even more important route.

Excavations show that by the 1200s, the town extended at least as far as the corn market area of High Street and what is now the junction with Old Orchard. The earliest houses were probably like some known from Southampton and elsewhere, timber framed stone clad 'hall' houses with thatched roofs. The front part of the ground floor was often used as a workshop, store or shop, with family chambers above. Behind this was the hall, the main living area, rising through both storeys to the roof, sometimes with a counting house and store behind. The kitchen was usually a separate structure situated in the garden behind the house, which was also used to keep livestock and dispose of waste. Only a few traces of these 13th century High Street houses remain, a few pits, post holes and beam slots, with fragments of the local brown-striped cooking pots and green glazed jugs brought in on ships from France. Bones of cattle, sheep, pigs, geese and pigeons, fish bones and oyster, whelk and cockle shells have also been found as evidence of medieval meals.

By the end of the 13th century, Poole was prospering. It had acquired a church, originally built as a chapel of ease and a dependency of the main church at Canford. In 1248, the burgesses had received a charter of freedoms from William Longespee, Lord of the Manor of Canford in consideration of a sum of 70 marks (£46.66). The shoreline had been built forward as far as what is now Paradise Street, using the handy supply of oyster shells as hard core, to create a convenient berthing for ships. Around 1300, the town's growth and status merited the construction of two massive stone warehouses, one on the Great Quay (now known as the Town Cellars) and the other at right angles to it in Thames Street. At about the same time, a large stone house was constructed for some prominent citizen on High Street at the point where the eastern end of the Quay met Mesurer's gap. Its front range lay 3 to 4 metres back from the present street frontage and it was built parallel to the

Jenny Oliver

Rear wall of the Town Cellars c. 1300

street, probably only one of several such substantial houses built in this early period of prosperity.

Whoever lived on High Street and whatever trades were practised there, one constant was the passage of wagons, carts and pack horses up and down the street carrying goods to and from the port. All sorts of cargos passed through the town from materials for building works at Corfe Castle in the 1280s and 1290s to the imports mentioned in an inquisition of the 1340s: staves, poles, codfish, salt, hides, skins, wool, resin, corn and oil.

In 1348, however, a deadlier cargo was brought to England, the bacteria of the plague which had been causing devastation across Europe. Apparently entering in July through the port of Melcombe (Weymouth), it spread rapidly through Dorset and the rest of the country eventually killing an estimated third to a half of the population. According to the scanty evidence which remains, Dorset suffered badly and tradition has it that plague pits were dug in Poole at Baiter Green to bury the dead. Some survived this terrible event only to succumb to fresh outbreaks in 1361-2 and 1369 which also took enormous numbers of lives. The effect of the plague was devastating, with families wiped out, animals and crops left untended and buildings deserted and crumbling. In addition, England was at war with France throughout most of the 14th century, imposing a great burden on the country.

There were some who found ways of profiting from the disordered state of Europe. In the late 14th and early 15th century, the Poole pirate Henry (or Harry) Paye and others made fortunes from attacking ships and seizing cargos. A series of petitions from angry merchants to the king demanding restitution of their ships and goods shows that Poole had become a centre for these lawless activities and Harry Paye's name was frequently mentioned. That the pirates' activities brought wealth into the town is suggested by the 1396 will of John Paye (very likely a relative of Harry). He owned three properties in Poole, two of them next door to each other. These he left to his son, John junior, his wife, Joan and his daughter, Alice. He also left John a chest of silver and Alice a belt with silver and 40 shillings for a dowry. The will mentions some of John Paye's neighbours, Richard Fideler, Robert Kyng, Henry Colyns and Thomas Caneway and this last named might well be the 'Canewaye of Poole' who received the cargo of a ship stolen from Peter de Weye of Holland in 1403. These could well have been early residents of High Street.

The pirates of Poole did not have everything their own way. Along with other south coast ports, the town suffered a number of attacks from the sea by enemy raiders. There is an account of one attack of 1405 in *El Vitorial*, the chronicle of the life of Don Pero Nino, Count of Buelna who led the raid on behalf of the King of Castile. According to the chronicle, the raiders identified Poole as the home of Harry Paye whose depredations are listed as a reason for the attack, (although on the day he was actually absent from the town.)

In the account, Poole is described as being unwalled with *'a fair tower with a round leaden roof shaped like a cup'*, probably part of the church. After the initial surprise of the attack, the defenders rallied and there was fierce fighting during which, it was said that *'the town was altogether burnt, except for one fair and great dwelling'* found to contain arms and ships' stores (probably the Town Cellars). Then reinforcements for the defenders arrived on foot and on horseback and a further fierce battle took place before the local men were driven back and the Castilians were allowed to board their galleys without hindrance. Among those killed was a brother of Harry Paye. The people of Poole were left to tend their injured and dead and contemplate the smouldering ruins of their property. How much destruction the town suffered is hard to say, but it is likely that many buildings in the lower part of High Street were damaged or destroyed. The town had suffered a major set back and must have taken some time to recover.

Poole burning, from a plaque on the Civic Centre

By 1433 Poole merchants were petitioning King Henry VI for a change which would greatly enhance the status of the town. They requested Poole should become a Port of the Staple or custom port in place of Melcombe Regis and benefit by all the liberties enjoyed by the port of Southampton. The merchants argued that Melcombe was thinly inhabited and less able to withstand attack by the King's enemies than Poole, as shown by the losses suffered by a merchant called John Roger and others. They also requested the right to fortify the town. The Commons made a few amendments to the petition but seem to have largely accepted the arguments that *'the town and port of Poole are notably inhabited and that a great multitude of people are there and that the said port is secure and sufficient for ships.'* This reasoning was incorporated into the letters patent by which Henry VI duly granted the petition.

Poole became the local customs port through which staple goods such as wool, hides and leather had to pass, while Melcombe was reduced to the status of a 'creek'. The letters patent also licensed the people of Poole to *'wall, embattle and fortify . . . the said town and port for the safe-keeping of all the merchandise and other goods coming thither'.* This grant gave Poole an enormous commercial boost while the construction of the town defences would have a significant effect on High Street.

The people of Poole must have felt that the main threat came not from the sea but from inland. To protect the town from this direction, the obvious location to build fortifications was across the narrow neck of land joining the Poole peninsular to the mainland. Sometime in the middle of the 15th century, as soon as funds had been raised, teams of men with barrows and shovels started work in upper High Street, digging out a ditch right across the peninsular, from one bay of the sea to the other. Soon after, heavily loaded wagons began rumbling up High Street bringing stone from the port to build the town gate and walls. Perhaps because of the nature of the subsoil, the location chosen for the gate was 100 metres or so to the west of High Street. The gate itself consisted of a gate house with a draw bridge, flanked by two tall round towers. This was reached by a lane branching off from High Street at the present junction with Chapel Lane. For the next two and a half centuries, High Street itself would lead nowhere, but terminate at the town wall and ditch. The lower part of the street, however, was still the main link between the Quay and the town entrance.

Jenny Oliver

A surviving stretch of wall probably contemporary with the main defences

The location of the Poole's defences was dictated more by the local topography than by the extent of building and the area enclosed was quite large for the size of the population. As a result, there was plenty of open space for the town to develop and building frontages were not crowded along the main streets as in many medieval towns.

Aided by its status as a custom port, Poole was becoming prosperous after the destruction of the early years of the century. A further boost came in 1453 when Henry VI granted the town the right to hold a weekly market on Thursdays and two fairs annually on the Feast of the Apostles Phillip and James (1st May) and the Day of All Souls (2nd November). The fairs were each to last 8 days during which time the Mayor and Bailiffs had the right to settle any legal disputes at a specially convened local court. Unlike other medieval towns which had grown up around their markets,

Poole's growth had always been based upon its port. Now the town could benefit from local trading that the markets and fairs would bring.

While Market Street was the location for the general market, the corn market was set up on the north west side of High Street not far from the Quay. On market days, carts, wagons and pack horses would come trundling into the town from early morning with sacks of corn and meal to be stacked on stalls pitched around the market square. Then the buyers would start to arrive, ready to haggle and strike a profitable deal. Local shops were closed for the day and all the buying and selling was concentrated around the stalls, while local inns did a roaring trade.

In the second half of the 15th century, the country was wracked by the power struggles later dubbed the Wars of the Roses. As a reward for their services in the wars, King Edward gave sixteen Channel Island families six years exemption from all customs duties at one of the western ports, Exeter, Dartmouth or Poole. At least four families began to trade through Poole, the most influential being the de Havilands who sent a younger son, James to set up in business in the town. Through a combination of wealth and business acumen, James and his descendants were destined to play a major role in the town's story.

The prosperity of Poole in the late 15th century allowed the inhabitants to embark on new building projects. The Town Cellars had probably been damaged in the raid of 1405 but was now partially rebuilt with a new south wall and fine timber roof. In High Street a row of substantial stone houses was constructed on the south east side of the corn market. These were all built parallel rather than gable end on to the street, suggesting that space on Poole's main street was plentiful at the period.

Lower down High Street at its junction with the Quay, the large house built around 1300 was now replaced by a luxurious L-shaped mansion of Purbeck coursed rubble and Bath stone dressings. This mansion, known as Scaplen's Court, still stands today. Its front range, set 3 or 4 metres further forward than the older house, is over 18 metres long and the domestic range which runs backwards from its southern end, over 24 metres long.

Callers to the house would be admitted through a stone porch to a passageway which ran through the building to a courtyard at the back. To the right was a store room for business or domestic goods. To the left, a doorway opened on to the main hall, an impressive room probably open to the roof with a finely carved fireplace and windows looking out on Mesurer's gap, the shore and the comings and goings to and from the Quay. The floor was covered with whitish tiles with a green glaze imported from Normandy. A wall divided the hall from a small inner chamber. The domestic range of the house may also have been open from the ground floor to the roof when the house was first built, and was provided with a fireplace carved with a rich floral decoration. The fine timber roof was similar to the contemporary roof

Andrew Hawkes Poole Photo Archive

Medieval roof, Scaplen's Court

of the Town Cellars but more decorative in style. Behind the house was a courtyard, enclosed by a wall, containing the detached kitchen building.

This must have been one of the most impressive of several houses built at this time. They were built by men like John Bedford, James Haviland and William Mesurer who had made money in trade, served in the Corporation and as Mayor and acquired fine houses as a symbol of their success. As the country entered the Tudor age and what was to be a period of comparative stability, Poole with its new status as a custom port was set to benefit from any business opportunities which came along.

Chapter Two

Tudor Times

'It is in hominum memoria much increased with fair building and use of merchandise.'

Hidden behind 19th, 20th and 21st century facades at the bottom of High Street is a row of splendid Tudor mansion houses, testimony to the wealth of 16th century Poole. Other more modest houses from this century still survive elsewhere in High Street behind the alterations carried out over the centuries.

This prosperity was partly the result of the voyage of the Italian captain John Cabot across the Atlantic and his discovery of the island of Newfoundland with its teeming fish stocks. During the following century, West Country ports like Poole began to send ships out to Newfoundland to catch cod for the lucrative salt fish trade. Individuals with a little money could invest in a small way in a ship's voyage and with shrewd judgement and good fortune, get a good return for their money. As wealth flowed into Poole, some of it was used to rebuild and embellish the town.

Early in the Tudor period, Scaplen's Court was extended again with the construction of two more ranges to the north west and north east, enclosing the courtyard completely and incorporating the separate kitchen into the main house. New doorways, fireplaces and ceilings were added (many of which survive today) and a gabled balcony was added to the north wall of the front range. As the century went on, other property owners along the street began to bring in builders and carpenters to rebuild or refurbish their medieval houses as half timbered mansions in the latest style, competing to outdo each other in splendour.

Some of this rebuilding was already complete when John Leland visited Poole in the late 1530s or early 1540s. Leland was a cleric and antiquarian who toured England describing the places he visited with the aim of making maps of them and he gave us the first description of the town since the Spanish raiders of 1405. Among other features, Leland accurately described the ferry from Hamworthy, the

Jenny Oliver

Modern facades conceal a row of Tudor mansions.

town ditch and gate, *'a fair town house of stone by the quay'* and *'a piece of town wall at one end of the quay'*. He also said that within human memory, the town was *'much increased with fair building and use of merchandise'*, reinforcing the idea of recent prosperity and development. It was suggested by the historian H. P. Smith that the *'fair town house'* was Scaplen's Court and that it was the same town house mentioned in the records as the meeting place for the Mayor and Corporation to discuss the town's business. Unfortunately it is impossible to confirm this interesting idea.

The development of High Street continued through the upheaval of the reformation in the 1530s and 1540s. The favoured style for new houses of this period consisted of a front range parallel to the street with another range running backwards at right angles to the first. The rooms at the front could be used for visitors and business and the rear wing as domestic quarters. A row of large houses, mostly in this style were built next to Scaplen's Court. In their original form they

The rear of Nos. 12-14

Part of the moulded ceiling

must have been highly impressive with stone or timber lower floors, jettied upper storeys, oak mullion windows, carved barge boards and flamboyant timber patterning picked out with dark red or black paint. Inside, the main rooms were panelled in oak or walnut and provided with fine moulded plaster ceilings.

Two of these buildings are now the King's Head (created from two adjoining properties) and the Antelope, but whether they were first built as houses or inns is not clear. The marks of the 16th century carpenters can still be seen in the roof timbers of the King's Head and the remains of an ancient spiral staircase were revealed during renovation. In the Antelope, an original stone fireplace and some ceiling beams survive and are still visible. Further down the street the large house now divided into Nos. 12 and 14 High Street had not one but two rear wings partly enclosing a small courtyard. It is the rear view of this house that gives us the best impression of how these buildings must have looked when they were built. One of the rear wings has been rebuilt in stone but the other one has retained its timber framing at first floor level and the rear wall of the front range has a long window with moulded wooden mullions and a timber-framed gable with carved barge boards overlooking the courtyard. One of the rooms on first floor was given a moulded plaster ceiling with a pattern of quatrefoils and squares ornamented with foliage and animal shapes, a double-headed eagle with a shield and the initials T.B.

It is difficult to find out who built and lived in these Tudor houses, but the initials suggest that this was the home of the merchant Thomas Byngley. His will of 1567 mentions *'my howse which I boughte of Mathewe Havyelonde lyenge in the High Streate'*, so Haviland was the previous owner, possibly even the builder of the house.

Matthew Haviland was the grandson of James, the original member of the family to set up in Poole. He was active in local affairs and travelled to London in 1563 to lobby influential contacts about the town's petition for a charter to become a county corporate. From 1566, he served as curate of St. James' church in Poole but, perhaps because of Catholic sympathies, fell foul of some of his parishioners.

Thomas Byngley was a businessman and Mayor of Poole in 1555 and 1563, with investments in trade which he described in his will as his *'goods beyond the sea'*. In the course of his business he must have known and worked with the four Poole porters (or dock workers) because he left them each 20 shillings (£1) and 1½ yards of russet cloth at 8 shillings (40p) a yard to make coats for them to carry him to his burial. He was also a property owner. Besides his dwelling house in the High Street, he owned another house occupied by William Merit and a tenement at *'Coal Corner'* (probably on the corner of High Street and New Street). He proposed that this tenement should be used for the maintenance of a free school for Poole if such a school could be founded within 5 years of his death. This may be the *'skole'* mentioned in the town accounts of 1573 when a payment of £13 6s 8d (£13.33) *'for iiij yeres at v mks per yere'* was recorded to Edward Lawghton, probably the school master. If so, it was the first school to be established in High Street and possibly in Poole.

In his High Street house, Thomas Byngley and his wife Alice brought up six children, William, Katherine, Joan, Amy, Anna and Cicely. In the rooms now occupied by offices and restaurants, we can imagine Thomas entertaining his friends and business associates and the Byngley children learning their letters with the help of horn books. The style in which the family lived is suggested by the property that Thomas left to his wife and others which included two coffers of silver, standing bowls of parcel gilt, a gilt covered cup, a beer pot of silver, silver spoons and a gold ring engraved with a death's head.

In 1563, when Byngley was mayor, one of the town's projects was the petition to Queen Elizabeth for Poole to be made a county in its own right like Southampton. To achieve this, 100 Poole residents signed up to a benevolence pledging money to help the cause, and Matthew Haviland travelled to London to make contacts and lobby for the petition. It was probably Walter Haddon, M.P. for Poole in 1559, who finally persuaded the Queen to give her consent. He wrote in a letter to Lord Cecil that *'the name of incorporation is so discredited with her that she agreed only because they had been so long suitors and to save my reputation, as she termed it, in that I had given them hope.'* Poole received its charter in 1568 along with the privileges and title of a county.

Thomas Byngley died in 1567 and in 1570 his widow Alice married leading businessman, William Green. A note in the register by the incumbent, Matthew Haviland says that they were married by another minister as William Green refused to be married or receive communion at his hands. Haviland's ministry was obviously deeply unpopular with some Poole worthies and the town procured the vicarage of

Martock for him, provided that the current incumbent should resign at the next Christmas. However Haviland then declined the living and was deprived of his position in Poole. The town accounts of 1569, mention a *'discord'* between Mathew Haviland and William Constantine, Mayor in 1565, 1566, 1567 and 1569 and that Constantine had *'obtayned his desire the removynge owte of the towne* [of] *Mr Havylond'*.

One of the Byngleys' neighbours in High Street was the shipmaster, Thomas Lambert, owner of the ship *Angel* of Poole and part-owner of the *Ann Gallant.* He also owned several properties. In the earliest census of the town's population which was drawn up in 1574, Thomas Lambert's household in High Street consisted of 13 people, himself and his wife, their three unmarried daughters, Cicely, Angel and Margaret, two maid servants and two man servants and their married daughter, Amy with her husband John Parrys, their daughter Becke and their servant. The Lamberts' two sons, William and Thomas had already left the parental home but probably worked in the family business.

Two years later when Thomas Lambert made his will, he left his house in High Street to his widow, Agnes. Each of his sons inherited a house and one of his ships, the *Angel* to William and his share of the *Ann Gallant* to Thomas. Trade was obviously good because the sons were required to pay £10 a year for 10 years from the profits of their voyages towards the maintenance of their mother and young sisters. Other legacies hint at some of the heirlooms possessed by the family. Agnes inherited 'one of the new goblets and the small silver salte', as well as the household goods that she had brought with her to the marriage. Beside their £40 dowries, Cicely, Angel and Margaret received six silver spoons each and a silver goblet or in Margaret's case, 'my best silver salte'. In these days before handy banks, the wealthy had to make their own arrangements to secure their property. Thomas requested the overseers of his will, William Dicker, John Edwards and David Tyto to put his daughters' legacies *'into a cheste with three lockes, the whiche cheste shall remayne in my dwelling house, and every one of my overseers . . . shall keepe one several key to the same cheste'.* This custom of keeping valuables in the house was to result in a brutal crime later in the century.

Other neighbours in lower High Street were John Robson and his family and the unusually named William Sifrewast. Robson is shown in the 1574 census living in High Street with his wife and five children, a man servant and a maid servant. He was a butcher by trade and was shown in a 1563 list of people required to pay Chief Rent, as owner of a slaughter house and piles or jetty. He also rented a close and a shop in Pillory Street. William Sifrewast had property in other parts of Dorset including a manor house at Moor Critchel which he left to his daughter Avice and her husband Edmund Stradlinge, and a messuage in Whitecliff, Isle of Purbeck.

An idea of how the well-to-do lived in Tudor Poole is given by an inventory, listing the contents of the house of Edward Green who died intestate in 1565.

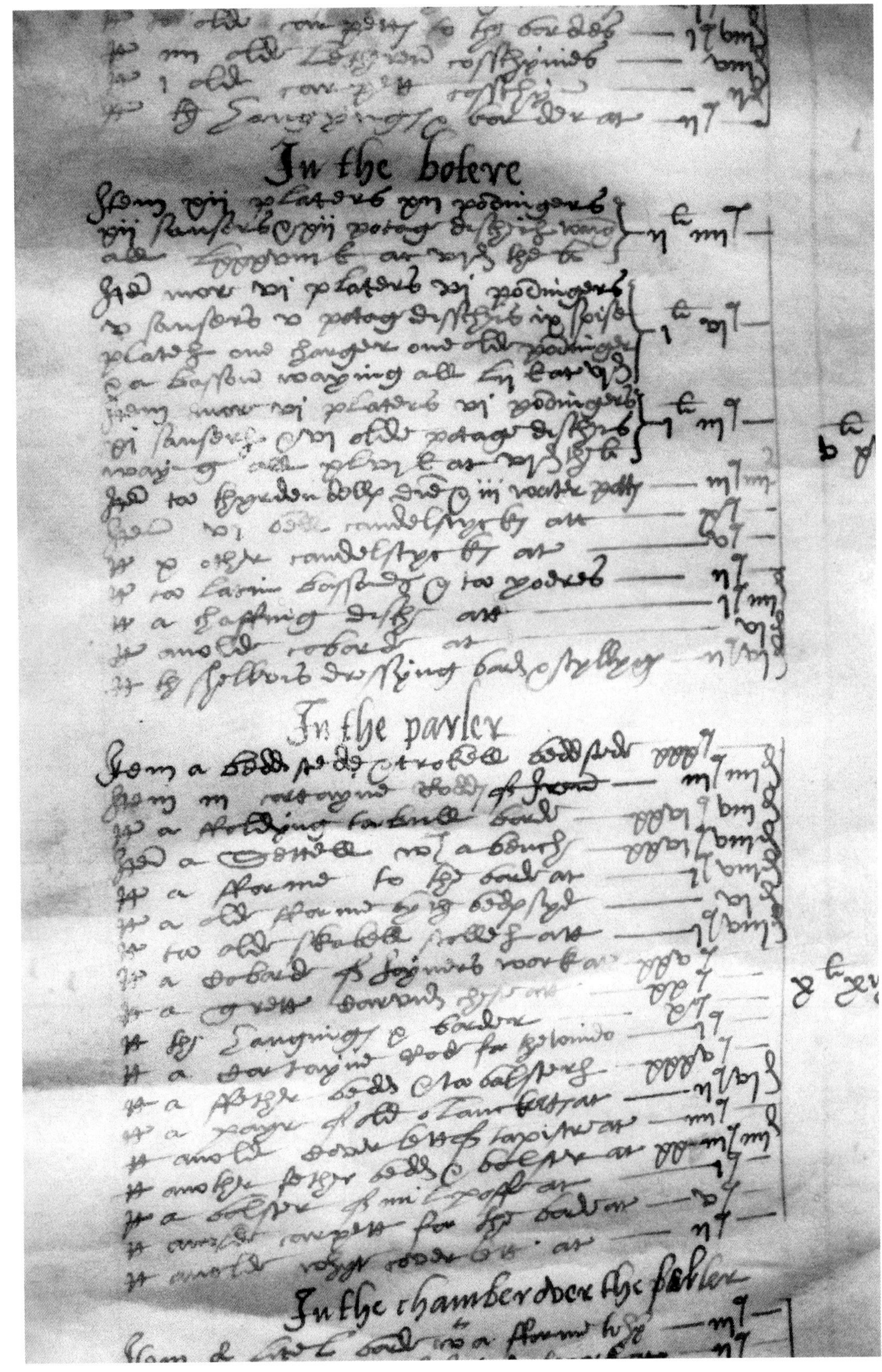
In the botere

In the parler

In the chamber over the parler

A section of Edward Green's inventory

Edward Green was probably William Green's father or at least a close relation since William was granted the administration of his estate. His substantial house of eleven or twelve rooms was obviously comfortable and well furnished.

The main living room was the great hall with its *'high board'* (or table), sideboard, forms, benches, cupboards and decorative hangings. The great fireplace was furnished with andirons, fire pan and other iron implements. Next to the hall was the buttery where plates, pottingers, saucers, and potage dishes were stored. This would also be a cool room for storing food away from the kitchen. In line with a common custom of the time, the parlour was used mainly as a bedroom and equipped with a bedstead, fully furnished with a feather bed (mattress), bolster, blankets, coverlet and hangings. Also in the room was a truckle bed, a settle with a bench, cupboards, forms and spare bedding. Another chamber next to the hall was also fitted out as a bedroom. The kitchen had a wide assortment of pots, pans and dishes of brass and pewter including dripping pans, frying pans, chaffing dishes and skillets.

On the first floor were four or five rooms, mainly furnished as bed chambers giving accommodation for quite a large household. Two chests containing mainly household linen were stored in neighbour's houses. The plate is listed separately in the inventory and consisted of gilt salts, goblets, plates, spoons and a silver cup worth in total over £40. Attached to the house was a brewhouse containing *'a ffornase of copar'*. The total value of the house contents was estimated at £95 4s 2d (£95.21), a substantial sum for the time.

Opposite the big mansions of lower High Street were a row of slightly more modest houses (now numbers 21-27), some with moulded plaster or decorative timber ceilings. Further up the street several 16th century houses remain or were demolished within the last century. One was a house known as 'The Priory', described as *'an antique building, compass-roofed'* which stood in the corn market (No. 44). Another example was the cob-built thatched cottage which used to stand on the corner of High Street and Carter's Lane. Reed thatch was probably a common roofing material for the more modest houses.

It is difficult to know how far the built-up area extended in the 16th century. In the 1574 census, three pages are headed High Street, containing a total of forty households. If we assume that this list is complete, we can reconstruct a street which was lined with fairly closely packed houses as far as the corn market but beyond this, dotted with more widely spaced houses surrounded by gardens, orchards and closes. The Chief Rent list of 1563 reinforces this picture; several people are listed as owning gardens in High Street and others 'at the town's end' which may refer to upper High Street where it ended at the town ditch.

Animals were a familiar sight in this rather rural High Street. In an account book of 1568, there is a description of how the town's herd of cows were (in

Graham Smith

An impression of the Tudor town with High Street in the foreground

modern spelling) *'driven out of the town by the cowherd... and so to the moor under Canford long refreshing themselves in the water of the said moor in the heat of the day in the summertime and there drink. After, toward evening, to be brought homeward by the said cowherd by the said moor and sides towards Longfleet, Sterte Lane and fresh waters and there to drink and so in to the town at night.'* We can imagine the slowly moving herd plodding in through the towngate in the evening and ambling down High Street to disperse to their various barns and byres for the evening milking.

On the eastern side of upper High Street was the area known as Pitwines after the Pidwine or Pintwine family, the site of Sainsbury's store today. This seems to have been the area where the town's waste was dumped by the scavengers (town officials whose job was to keep the streets clean and cart away rubbish). There are several accounts of work being done at Pitwines, as for instance in Christopher Farewell's year as mayor in 1582. Two items in the accounts read:

'Two hurdles for Bakar to stand apon workinge at the pidwines and also for caryage of two lodes of ore' [seaweed].

'Payd two laborars for fillinge and ladinge of the scavengers carts to carie the dirte or ose to fill up the greate howle in the pidwines and for drinke for the laborars'.

It sounds very much as though this end of High Street was a churned up, muddy, probably smelly area and a far from pleasant place to live. No wonder the labourers needed a drink while working there!

The road surface in High Street must have taken a lot of hard wear as carts and wagons trundled up and down to the Quay, but whether or not it was paved in the early 16th century is unclear. In 1574 the bailiff William Dicker received payment for paving and mending the High Street and by 1591 more remedial work was necessary involving loads of sand, stones and gravel including two loads *'to fill upp the two greate holes in the High Street'*. Paviours were employed to pave 13 yards in front of Mr Sydcome's house, 8 yards in front of Mr Pitt's house and 26 yards before Walter Hues' door. The total cost of the works was 27s 1d (£1.35).

At the end of the century, one of the most notable High Street residents was William Green, businessman, shipowner and Mayor of Poole in 1560, 1561, 1562, 1564 and 1571. He was involved in the petition to obtain the charter of incorporation for the town and was one of the merchants who gave his bond for £50 to Lord Mountjoy, lord of the manor of Canford, to compensate him for any loss of rights through the granting of the charter. He also produced the inventory of the former property of the Fraternity of St. George, when it was purchased by the Corporation and served twice as Poole's Member of Parliament. For several decades he was one of the leading men of affairs in the town. William died in the 1590s, leaving much of his wealth to his widow, Alice, formerly Alice Byngley. In fact she was not to survive him very long.

In 1599, a burial record in St. James' church reads: *Alice Green the wife of Willm Green was buried January 24 / Agnes Beard servant to Alyce Green was buried January 26.* These two simple entries are actually the record of a terrible crime. After William's death, his widow and her servant, Agnes, both apparently frail and getting on in years, lived alone in the Greens' High Street house, apart from a number of 'knitting girls' who were employed there during the day. Some of the property inherited by the widow including papers and bonds and *'a greate somme of money brought by one Mr Legge of Gissage'* was apparently kept in strong boxes in an upper chamber. One morning in late December 1598, something alerted neighbours that all was not well at the house. Failing to get a response they helped a small boy in at a staircase window and a grisly discovery was made. Alice Green and Agnes Beard had been battered and stabbed to death. The strong boxes had been broken open and the money and papers stolen.

The following year, a man called Robert Hill was arrested and hanged for the crime, upon what evidence we do not know. However this did not put an end to suspicion and speculation which centred on Alice's neighbour and son-in-law, John Beryman who had married Joan Byngley in 1574. A law case of the 1580s mentions a John Beryman, of Poole, chapman (a travelling salesman of ribbons, laces and other haberdashery). If this was the same man or a family connection, he had certainly come up in the world. By the 1590s he was a merchant, brewer, one time lessee of the Three Mariners Inn, former Mayor of Poole and married to the daughter of one of Poole's leading families. He was however rumoured to have been dissatisfied with the terms of William Green's will and he also rented the cellar under the Greens' house through which the murderers had probably gained entry. Although he was questioned, nothing could be proved against him. He went on to be Mayor again in 1602.

In fact the case continued to haunt the town for decades, occasionally coming back into prominence as some new information came to light. In 1610 a statement was made by Elinor, the widow of Gowin Spencer, a neighbour of the Berymans. She testified to the mayor, Roger Mawdley, that the murderers had been Robert Hill, a servant of Beryman's called Richard Parmenter, and her husband Gowin Spencer. On the night of the murder, Spencer came home with blood on his cloak and stocking and told his wife that his nose had been bleeding. Later, however, he related how the three of them had entered the house through the cellar. They first surprised Agnes, hitting her over the head with a pressing iron and then stabbing her through the temples with a bodkin. Then they found the widow Alice and killed her the same way. His share of the proceeds was forty shillings and a purse of rings and pearls. Spencer's daughter Gerrard also alleged that John Beryman knew about the crime, whether or not he instigated it and said that Beryman and his wife Joan had given her a petticoat to keep quiet about what she knew. Although this testimony was apparently damning, the Spencers were not the best of witnesses having changed their story more than once and John Beryman was acquitted. The full story of what happened that night was never revealed.

One aspect of this tragedy is to give us a vivid glimpse of life in High Street in late Tudor times through the testimonies of various witnesses. In the small community of Tudor Poole, visiting and chatting with neighbours was obviously a major pastime. The hierarchy of wealth was also very important. Poor residents like the Spencers were dependant on their well-to-do neighbours for employment and charity. After she made her damning statement about John Beryman, Gerrard Spencer relates with apparent surprise how the Berymans are no longer willing to give her food. *'On thursdaie last I was at Mr Beryman's att which tyme he was brought home bomusey [i.e. drunk] from the Fayer. . . And I could have nothing but a Pice of bread, and my mother could have nothing sines he was Aquitted as before she was wont to have of him.'* The other neighbours seem to have cold-shouldered the Spencers as well. *'Now but few pittie us or had any remorse of us, to give us any Reliffe as before that they did.'*

There was also quite a lot of violence or threats of violence in the community, particularly against women, although some are ready to give as good as they get. Besides the brutal murder itself, a statement from Marie Hill, servant to Richard Parmenter, describes a quarrel between her master and his wife Margery. According to Marie, Parmenter called his wife a *'whore'* and threw a small hatchet at her head. In response, Margery called him a murderer and shouted *'I thinke thou wilt murder me as thou hast others.'* Later Margery threatened Marie with a knife and said she would kill her if she ever disclosed what she had heard. We can only guess how much these accounts were embellished by gossip and discussion over the years as the case dragged on.

It is hard to identify the house where the murder took place. In a writ of recovery dated 1599, John Beryman and others sought to reclaim property which they had sold to Edward Man the previous year, presumably because Man had not fulfilled his side of the bargain. Beryman's property is described as *'a tenement and garden with appurtenances in High St. Poole between . . . the tenement of Henry Harwarde on the west part and a tenement late of William Bingly deceased on the east part, which tenement and garden is now occupied by Jesse Bennett.'* Assuming William Byngley's house to be what is now Nos. 12 and 14 High Street, this would mean that Beryman's house was the present No. 10 and Henry Harward lived next door in No. 8, now the Antelope Inn. One of the people arrested but finally acquitted in the murder investigation was Clement Starre who lived next door to the Greens' house *'where Mr. Harwood's kitchen now is'* and could see through the tiles of his house to where the knitting girls employed by Alice Green went to supper. This suggests that the Greens' house was No. 6, currently the King's Head. However there are too many unknown factors to be sure. The location of this brutal killing which horrified and scandalised the town, will probably never be definitely identified.

Chapter Three

17th Century

'Valiente and full resolved to fight'

The records provide us with only a few names of High Street residents in the early 1600s. Most of them were merchants, ship-owners, property owners or tradesmen, but there were one or two individuals who did not fit this pattern. An example was Sir Edmund Uvedale, son of Sir Frances Uvedale of Horton near Wimborne, who had a long and eventful military career abroad before acquiring his house in Poole. He served as a captain in the Netherlands campaign but either through dishonesty or incompetence, got into difficulties with his accounts. The Muster Master General, Thomas Digges had appointed the author and dramatist, George Whetstone as his deputy and when Whetstone questioned Uvedale over the accounts, Uvedale challenged him to a duel. Whetstone was killed and Uvedale found himself back in England in disgrace.

Uvedale's career was in the balance. Some thought that he should suffer the death penalty while his supporters wrote to Sir Francis Walsingham that *'a more honest captain, and one that keepeth his soldiers in better order, is there not in the land'*. In the end, it cost him 100 marks to reinstate himself. Back in the Netherlands, he became Lieutenant Governor to Sir Philip Sidney but by 1595 was once again in financial difficulties. In England, he tried to win the Queen's favour and sent presents to Sir Robert Cecil to no avail. Eventually the affair was patched up and Uvedale returned to the Netherlands. In 1597 he was back in England for his health, writing to Sir Robert Cecil that *'an ague which takes me every day hath brought me so weak as I am not able to attend you'*. From this date, he remained in England, being appointed surveyor general of the forces, sergeant major of the army and a knight of the shire for Dorset.

Jenny Oliver

Sir Edmund Uvedale

Sir Edmund's town house in Poole was situated on the north side of High Street near the junction with New Street, the present Nos. 30 and 32. Today the property has been much altered and very little remains of the original structure except for the roof. In his will of 1606, he left the house and lands in Poole to his wife, Lady Mary for life and then to his brother, Thomas. Uvedale's life as a soldier, very different from the experience of his neighbours in Poole, was reflected in some of his legacies which included his armour, his *'beste Spanish pike'*, and a *'gilte sword'* to his kinsman Sir Edward Southe and his *'beste graven targette'* to his cousin Thomas Stoughton.

Uvedale was buried according to his wishes in Wimborne Minster without any ceremony and his monument shows him reclining at ease in full armour, the earliest High Street resident of whom we have an image. During refurbishment of the monument, the right foot of the statue was apparently damaged and replaced with a mirror image of the existing foot, giving him two left feet.

Next door to Sir Edmund's house, on the corner of High Street and New Street, was the house of Cecily Goddard. This was probably the house at *'Colcorner'* which had been left to her by her father, John Goddard, in 1583 when she was still a child. For a single woman to own property was unusual in the 16th century and it must have made her quite a matrimonial prize especially as he also left her a legacy of £100.

Other High Street residents at the beginning of the 17th century were

Nicholas Gibbon, his wife Marie and their sons Nicholas, John and Sidrach. Nicholas Gibbon was born in Heckford, educated at Cambridge where he took his M.A. in 1592 and became a minister in Dorset. In 1601, he published one of the earliest guides to the bible entitled *'Questions and Disputations concerning the Holy Scripture wherein are contained expositions of the most difficult places'*, dealing with the first fourteen chapters of the Book of Genesis.

Nicholas Gibbon junior went up to Queen's College, Oxford in 1622, finally obtaining his M.A. in 1629 when he was appointed to the rectory of Sevenoaks in Kent. Later he continued his studies to become a Doctor of Divinity. John meanwhile, was apparently pursuing a successful career in London as a deed of 1634 suggests. In this deed, *'John Gibbon Esq. of Westminster'* took over properties occupied by his father and brothers including a house on the south side of High Street which Nicholas senior had bought from John Beryman.

The early years of the 17th century saw work being carried out at both ends of High Street. In 1604 and 1605, John Grist, Richard Dibbens and others were employed by the Corporation to carry out landscaping and drainage work at Pitwines. This involved setting up posts and rails, cutting a trench to let out the water and the carriage of load after load of earth and seaweed to consolidate the area.

The lower end of High Street was also in the process of change. In 1616, the merchants of Poole proposed a development of the Quay which would ease its chronic congestion. They issued a benevolence *'for building a new quay at Measurer's Gap and a fish market this next year if God permitts'*. The accounts show that the new quay was to be *'set forthe 8 or 9 foot without Mr Dackhams furthest wall and without his wall to make a slype to land horssses and lad horsses'*. The idea was to extend the Quay to the east, but a side effect was to enable the development of lower High Street down to the sea. By 1618 the money was raised and building work began. One immediate improvement was to the environment of the area with the *'riding of the meckson at great keye'* (clearing away of the midden or rubbish dump which must have accumulated in the gap). For this unpleasant task the workmen were provided with bread, cheese and beer.

In September 1624, Poole suffered a serious fire during which six houses were burnt. This was a danger to which towns of wood-framed houses were prone. A few years later there seems to have been another incident because there are a couple of references in the town accounts of 1628-9:

'Paid when Mr Hiley's house was burnt *6s 0d*
Given a poor man that had loss by fire rather than to begg the town *6d'*

These were not as serious as the fires that devastated Dorchester, Blandford, Wareham and other towns in the following century, but the damage may have spurred on the process of rebuilding and change.

Borough of Poole Museum Service

A 17th century cottage in the corn market, now demolished.

To spare wear and tear on the streets, an order was issued that was good news for wheelwrights. The heavy brewers' carts should *'goe without iron wheeles'* on pain of a 20s fine and in compensation, the brewers should be allowed a pair of new wheels every year out of the tax that they paid to the Corporation on every brewing. In 1631, another order decreed that every householder should *'repayre and pitch the streetes before his housing and garden from the wall or part of his house within 3 foote of the next keynell or gutter where it hath beene formerly paved'*. The rest of the street was the responsibility of the Corporation. How effective this piecemeal approach proved to be is hard to say.

In the early decades of the century, there seems to have been an increase of commercialisation in High Street including the development of several of the houses as inns. Brewing was an important and profitable trade in which many of the important merchants were engaged and some of them also owned inns. The records show that in 1620 there were four inns in Poole, run by Christopher Sugar, William Dolbery, Mistress Field and Thomas Lambert, as well as twelve licensed and six unlicensed alehouses. None of the premises is named but some of them must have been in High Street.

The Antelope Inn was acquired in the 1620s by John Melledge, a prosperous grocer in Dorchester. A later will (of Alice Melledge) mentions an Indenture of Assignment for the premises dated 6th July 1624, granted by Richard Philipps the younger of Corfe Mullen, Gentleman. John was Sheriff of Poole in 1631 but died in office. In his will he granted his house in Poole *'wherein I doe nowe lodge'* to his youngest son, Johnson. He left his wife the use of a chamber in the house *'lyinge partelie over my little parlour the staiers whereunto goe upp in my kitchin'*. There was no mention of the Antelope by name, but it may have been this house left to Johnson. Whether it was an inn by this date, we do not know, but it certainly was by the 1640s. The Melledge family was to be associated with the Antelope for several generations.

Other inns in business from the first half of the 17th century (if not earlier) were the Plume of Feathers, later incorporated into the King's Head, and the Bull Head Inn (No. 73) which has a decorative plaster ceiling in the upper room. It was also during these decades that Scaplen's Court was converted into the George Inn. This growth in the number of inns may reflect Poole's increasing importance in business and trade.

Perhaps because of the number of inns appearing in the lower part of High Street, the great Tudor mansion houses were no longer so fashionable for the town's leading citizens and some 17th century residents chose to build their houses further away from the Quay. The corn market was one popular area and old houses were demolished to make way for new, stone-built mansions. These were slightly more modest than the great mansions of a hundred years before, but still substantial. Two houses, (later Nos. 47 and 49 High Street) were built on the south east side of the corn market. Each four bays wide, they would originally have boasted panelled rooms, moulded plaster ceilings and fine staircases.

Borough of Poole Museum Service

Haviland Hiley

A couple of doors down the street was a house belonging to Haviland Hiley (Nos. 41 and 43). As his name suggests, Hiley was a descendent of the Haviland family through his mother, Elinor Haviland, great granddaughter of James de Haviland. His father was William Hiley, *'Minister of God's word'* who served as rector of St.

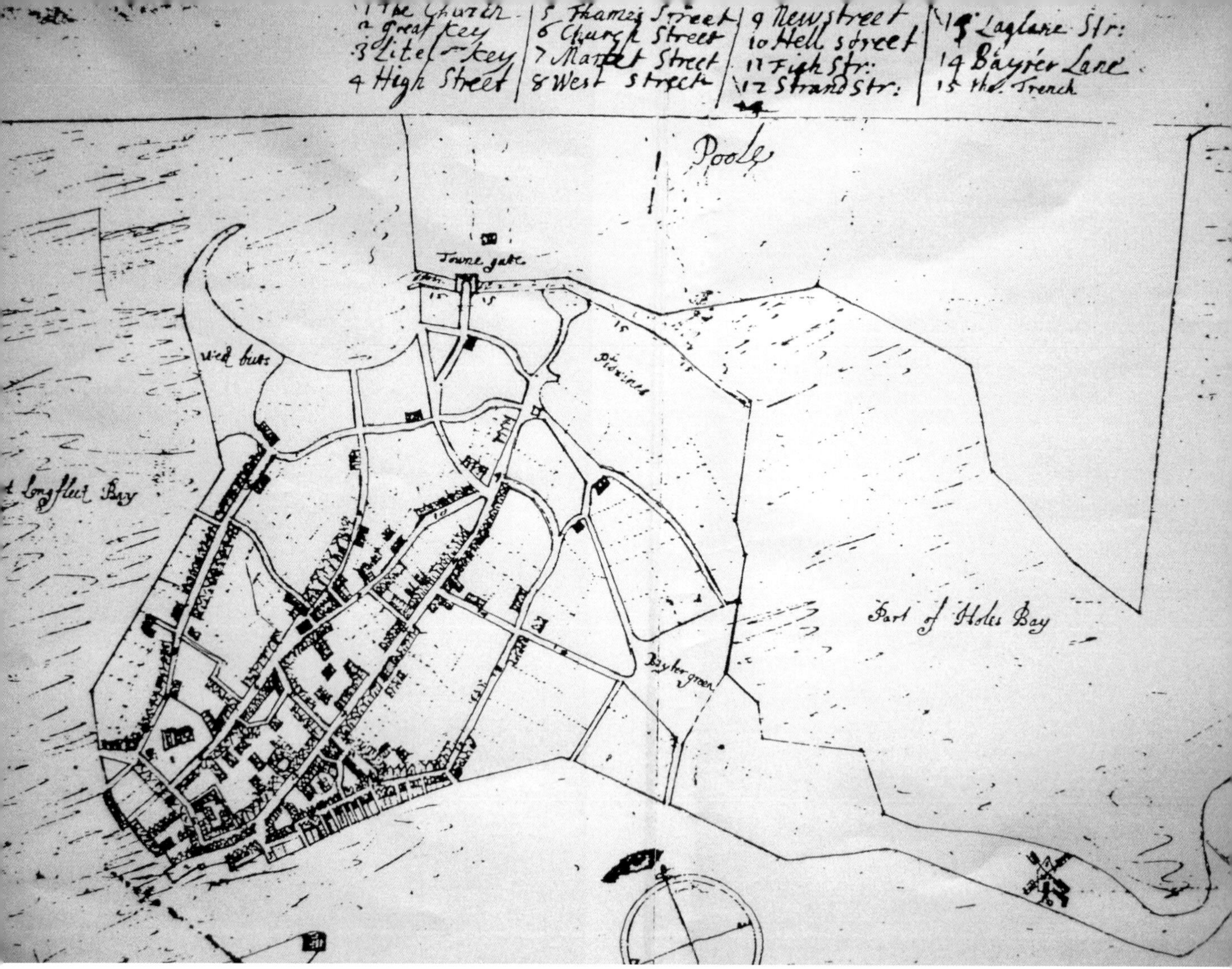

Based on an early 17th century Poole street map

James' church from 1582 until his death in 1611. William's wealth was demonstrated by the fact that he left a property to each of his five sons, besides dowries to his three daughters and ample provision for his widow. Haviland Hiley, William's fourth son, was a brewer, merchant and property owner and mayor in 1641, 1649 and 1660.

The extent of building in the early 17th century High Street is revealed in the first detailed map of Poole, dating from the 1630s. The map is surprisingly accurate for its time and shows signs of having been scientifically surveyed and measured. From it we can clearly see the new quay projecting forward at the eastern end of the great quay and the section of lower High Street running down to the sea. The lower town is quite densely built up, but in the ribbon development further up High Street, the houses all back on to open space in the form of gardens, orchards and closes. There are also several gaps in the line of building such as the area above the corner of New Street where the corn market was held. Beyond the junction with

Hell Street, Laglane Street and Towngate Lane, there are very few buildings, and High Street ends at the town ditch near Pitwines. The map gives the impression of a neat, prosperous little town with a lot of green spaces.

The next two decades were to bring a great upheaval to Poole and the whole country with the outbreak of the Civil War, a conflict that would bring opportunities to some High Street residents and disaster to others. In 1642, relations between King Charles I and Parliament finally broke down and communities and individuals had to decide their allegiances. It was not perhaps surprising that most of Poole's leaders opted to support Parliament. As a commercial port, the town tended to resist central control and it had also suffered as a result of Charles' hated 'Ship Money' tax. In religion, Poole also tended towards the puritan side. Not everyone was of one mind, however, as shown in a letter written by the Poole authorities the follow year. The letter describes a town that *'was exteamly divided by reason of feares, covetousness and falce jeloseys'*.

This was dramatically demonstrated in early 1643 when Henry Harbin, the Mayor of Poole and Johnson Melledge, inn-keeper and Collector of Customs, were arrested for suspected disloyalty to Parliament. What their offence was, we do not know, but the man who brought about their arrest was William Skutt, the Captain of the Volunteers. William was the eldest son of George Skutt, merchant, shipowner, brewer, five times mayor and one of the most important men in Poole. A list of 1628 shows that George owned four ships, the *'Desire', 'Seaflower', 'Primrose'* and *'Susannah'* and was part owner of the *'Jeane'* together with his father-in-law, Thomas Roberts. Sometime in the early 17th century he acquired an ancient property in the corn market area of High Street known as the Priory with its garden and brewhouse.

Henry Harbin and Johnson Melledge were confined on board the Parliamentary ship moored in Poole Harbour until they could be sent to London to be questioned. Once there, Harbin must have compounded or paid a fine for his freedom because by the summer he was back in Poole, still in the office of mayor and a member of the Poole committee for administering the town's affairs. As George Skutt was also on the committee, it's likely that meetings were rather tense from then on. Johnson Melledge's offence was probably more serious because his case took longer to resolve. He was stripped of his office as Collector of Customs and awaited the verdict on his delinquency which took several years to be decided. Whether he was back in Poole, in custody or elsewhere during this period, is unknown.

Meanwhile Poole was strengthening its defences and preparing to house a Parliamentary garrison of 200 to 300 soldiers. Some of these would have been local men but many would have come from outside the town, swelling the population by up to a fifth. As there was no barracks to house them, the soldiers must have been put up in the inns and billeted in people's houses including the large houses in High

Jenny Oliver

Civil War re-enactors in High Street

Street. At times the town was full to bursting point. There would also have been a large number of horses, up to 220 at one time, to house, feed and water. Unexpected evidence for this period comes from graffiti initials, dates and devices carved on an old stone mantelpiece in the George Inn. Now damaged and faded, these originally included the dates MD35 (1535), 1643, 1649, 1650 and 1653 and the names 'Arnold' and 'Agestorp' scratched by men with an idle moment to make their mark for posterity.

In the summer of 1643, most of Dorset fell to the royalists, leaving only Poole and Lyme Regis holding out for Parliament. It was a moment of reckoning for Poole. On 13th August, the town authorities met in the evening to write a hasty letter to Portsmouth asking for men and gunpowder. The leaders, including John Bingham the military Governor, George Skutt and William Skutt, now Commander in Chief of the Poole garrison, described how the town had been approached by two royalist forces demanding the town's surrender but *'our men blessed be God are valiente and full resolved to fight . . . whether we shalbe besieged or not, we are prepareing for their comeing'.* With more than a whiff of fanaticism, the letter concludes: *'God converte them, and bless you and give us hartes never to feare them that are runninge headlong into hell.'*

Fortunately for Poole, the siege never materialised and a plot to take the town by treachery in September was foiled. In 1644, with George Skutt serving as mayor, Poole was suffering increasing hardship with food shortages and the soldiers *'necessiated for want of Pay'.* In June, Parliament sent 26 dozen pairs of shoes for the use of Poole and Lyme and £500 *'for the service of Poole now in great distress'.* The same year William Constantine, Poole's M.P. and Recorder, was found in the town and arrested. Constantine (grandson of the William Constantine of Tudor times) had urged the town to yield to the royalists in 1643 and, as a punishment for his disloyalty, he was now stripped of his office as Recorder and Member of Parliament. In 1645, George Skutt became the town's Member of Parliament in his place.

Shortages continued but worse was to come in the summer of 1645 when the plague broke out in Poole. Many leading citizens, including George Skutt, William Skutt and Haviland Hiley undertook to ask local towns and individuals for help in money or kind. George Skutt managed to extract gifts of £50 from Southampton and £23 from Portsmouth as well as raising 19 bushels of meal and 40 loaves of bread. Haviland Hiley secured pledges of over £120, riding from Weymouth, to Cerne, Dorchester and many other places. This must have been a hard and dangerous task with bands of enemy troops and lawless, unpaid soldiers roaming the countryside. In his bill for expenses Hiley describes how he was *'out above 7 weeks, & lost one horse at Serne and lamed another'.*

The winter of 1645 was one of the worst Poole had endured. The town was in quarantine and High Street was unnaturally quiet. The only excitement was when the gifts arrived from local towns. Carts carrying corn, meal, loaves and cheeses trundled down from the towngate, and sheep and bullocks were driven down to the slaughter house, banishing the threat of starvation for a while. The plague claimed many lives but by mid 1646, had run its course. The war too was in its last phase, marked locally by the fall of the royalist stronghold of Corfe Castle.

Those who found themselves on the losing side had a price to pay. Nicholas Gibbon the younger had lived in Poole High Street as a boy, before becoming an academic and cleric. At the start of the Civil War he declared as a royalist and in 1647, he was sent for by the king when Charles was a prisoner in Carisbrooke Castle, to discuss issues of church government. Gibbon sent a report on the discussions to Parliament in the form of a paper but this was not destined to improve relations

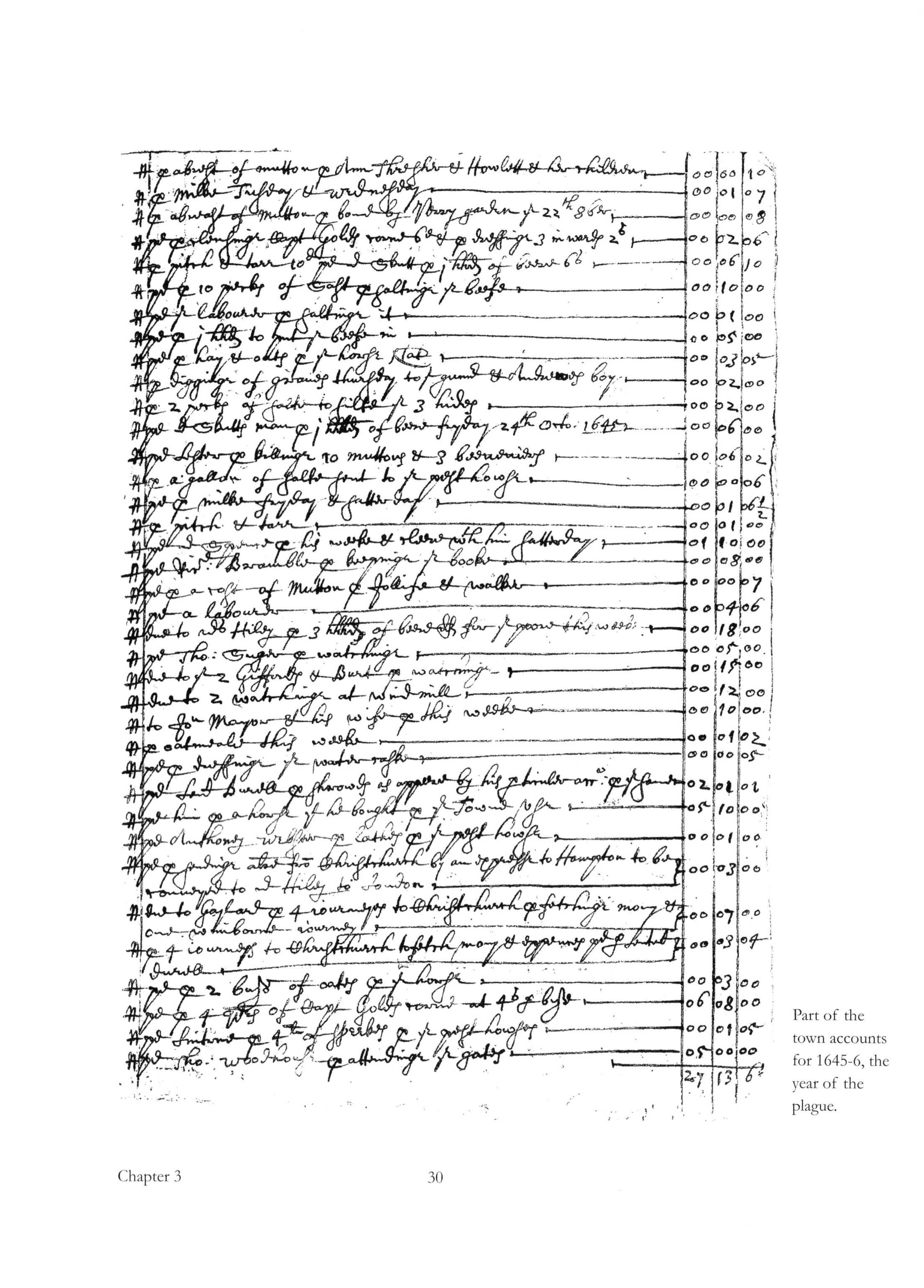

Part of the town accounts for 1645-6, the year of the plague.

between king and Parliament. Now Gibbon was turned out of his living and his property was sequestered. He then rented a little land and farmed it to support his large family until he was forced to give it up and work as a farm labourer. Brought before a Parliamentary Committee in Kent, he told them that he spent his days working and his nights in study and showed them his hands roughened with hard work. Gibbon was eventually given the rectory of Corfe Castle where he died in 1697, aged 92.

The Melledge family was also suspected of royalist sympathies. A curious incident was reported in February 1649 when silver plate worth £20 was found in a well and identified as the property of Johnson Melledge. Perhaps he had forewarning of his arrest and so crept out in secret to hide his valuables. It would be interesting to know if the well in question was close to the Antelope Inn and also who discovered the cache. The plate was sold and the value given to the mother of Melledge's children, to hold for them (suggesting that wherever he was at the time, he was not in Poole). In May 1649, six years after his arrest, Johnson Melledge was finally fined £11 8s for delinquency.

An incomplete rate book of that year provides more information about High Street residents and property owners. The disgraced M.P., William Constantine still owned a tenement there, occupied by Roger Baker. Other owners of property in the street were Mr Nicholas Gibbon (senior or junior), Johnson Melledge, Mr. William Williams, John Sutton and William Nurrey. Mrs. Man was listed as owning the Bull Head Inn, occupied by John Cock. There is also a mention of *'Mr Robert's Inne'* occupied by Mr Richard Dolbery and *'Mr Roberts Inn in High Street',* occupied by John Dibbe.

These two inns were probably the George and the Plume of Feathers respectively and Mr. Roberts was Thomas Roberts junior, brother-in-law to George Skutt. Born around 1604, Thomas went to Oriel College Oxford and graduated in 1622. In 1627, he married Melior Lovell and they had at least two sons, Thomas and John. In his father's will of 1633, Thomas junior received no specific legacies, so he may have already had the properties transferred to him, or perhaps he bought the inns himself. Unlike his father who had called himself a merchant, Thomas junior was designated a 'gentleman'.

Richard Dolbery was the eldest son of William Dolbery, merchant and part owner of the *'William'* and the *'Ark'.* William had been listed as an inn-keeper in 1620 and was Mayor of Poole in 1629. By 1635, when William made his will, Richard was presumably well established because he did not receive any legacies, although his wife Elizabeth was left a *'ring with a red stone in it'.* Richard Dolbery served as mayor in 1651 and 1661 and as keeper of one of the town's best inns, was at the centre of affairs.

112

In the name of God Amen the One and

George Skutt

89

89

Either Thomas Roberts or Richard Dolbery may have been responsible for several changes to Scaplen's Court relating to its conversion to the George Inn. The addition of a gallery reached by steps from the courtyard allowed access to individual first floor rooms or suites of rooms. The kitchen was improved with the addition of a new fireplace with the latest innovation, a water boiler. This was a specially constructed chamber beside the fireplace where a cask of water could be placed to be heated. The former service rooms in the north east range and the chamber over the kitchen were also improved with ornamental ribbed ceilings and oak mullion windows. A fireplace was added to the first floor room of the north east range to bring it up to standard as an inn chamber and surviving fragments of panelling from this period suggest a general refurbishment.

An extract from George Skutt's will

The death of George Skutt at the end of 1653 marked the end of an era. The terms of his will reveal just how well-to-do he was. His eldest son, William, was to inherit the dwelling house, in which he (William) lived, after the death of his mother, Jane. He also inherited George's *'dwelling house and brewhouse, commonly called . . the New Brewhouse together with all houses, buildings, courts, gardens, implements of brewing. . . (which said Houses and Brewhouse I bought of Thomas Phelps gent. lately deceased).'* This property was probably the house in the High Street known as the Priory. George's other five sons received either property or legacies of £450 to £500 each and his unmarried daughter, Sarah £400. His four married daughters had legacies of £100 each, to be taken out of £3000 *'public faith debts'* owing to him, and his wife received all his household goods and the stock of his farm at *'Thickfurzes'* (Heckford). Property at Gray's Inn, Middlesex was to be sold to pay his legacies to the younger children. Then there was the business which he ran with his two sons, William and George *'consisting of parts of shipping and adventures at sea'*. His share of this was to be divided between the two of them. At a time when the wage for a working man was about a shilling (5p) a day, this was real riches.

The decade after the end of the war was one of hardship and conflict throughout the country. Former enemies had to learn to live together once again. The restoration of Charles II to his father's throne meant a reversal of fortunes for some of those who had suffered losses in the war. In Poole, Johnson Melledge was back in High Street and in 1656 he and his wife Alice had a son, John who sadly died at less than a year old. Another long-term High Street resident, Nicholas Gibbon also died in 1658.

On the death of his father, William Skutt had become one of the wealthiest and most important men in Poole and by 1659, he had acquired both the George Inn and the Plume of Feathers from his uncle, Thomas Roberts. In a mortgage document of that year, the Plume of Feathers is described as *'the messuage, tenement or inn with kitchen, cellars, outhouses, stables and garden with courts and curtileges in the High Street, then or late in the occupation of Joan Dibbs, innholder'. The George is 'all that capital messuage or Inn commonly known by the name of the George with two stables, gardens, outhouses, cellars, courts, edifices and buildings then or late in the tenure of Richard Dolbery all which premises were then lately purchased and bought of Thomas Roberts gent'.*

A tax assessment of 1662, just after the king's restoration, gives us a glimpse of the mix of residents on High Street. At the top of the social scale were men like William Skutt with his *'mansion house, brewhouse etc.'*, his two inns, one occupied by Richard Dolbery and one by James Standard, a cellar on the Quay and several tenements in his property portfolio. Haviland Hiley was another major property owner with his mansion house, brewhouse and garden in High Street, the Lamb Inn and various tenements and closes. Other notable residents were Mr. James Grundy, Mr. Peter Hall senior, who served as mayor in 1655 and 1664 and Mr. Edward Taylor, mayor in 1659. Edward Taylor owned two houses opposite to each other in High Street and an inn, also in High Street, called the Black Rod.

Professional men included William Corban, listed as a 'physurgion' and Mr. Nicholas Efford, master of the 80 ton ship Concord engaged in the Newfoundland salt cod trade. Among the tradesmen were Thomas Hawkins, probably the same Hawkins who worked as a baker during the civil war period, and Edward and John Linthorne, members of a family of blacksmiths. John Lester senior was the landlord

Borough of Poole Museum Service

The room where King Charles was probably entertained to dinner

of the Bull Head Inn but his family were also butchers. The widow Rogers kept a bakehouse. Two other notable residents were Elizabeth Melledge, the landlady of the Antelope Inn and Mr. William Minty who was a mercer or cloth merchant. He was also a fervent nonconformist because after the Declaration of Indulgence in 1672 relaxed the laws against religious minorities, he applied for a licence as an independent minister *'in the malthouse of Mr. Aire'* and later lost his status as a burgess as a result of his religious affiliations. Ordinary seamen like Valentine Nicholas and Thomas Peckett also appear in the list of High Street residents. Clearly the street was home to a cross section of local society.

Three years later, on 15th September 1665, the High Street was witness to a spectacle which would have been unimaginable twenty years before. King Charles II granted the town the *'unparaleld honour'* of a visit, travelling from Salisbury where he had retired to avoid the plague in London. The reception party must have had mixed feelings as they awaited the King's arrival in their best attire, as many of them had been staunch anti-royalists in the war. However, this was a new era and everything was to be graciousness on the one side and loyal humility on the other. The King arrived, accompanied by the Duke of Monmouth, several earls, lords and local gentry, and the party was conducted down High Street to *'the house of Mr Peter*

Hiley, sett apart for that purpose' where a dinner was provided at the cost of the mayor, Peter Hall.

After the meal the visitors went for a boat trip to Brownsea in Col. William Skutt's boat, steered by Skutt and rowed by six ships' masters and the King surveyed the castle and harbour before returning to the Quay. The lower High Street was then treated to grand procession. Led by the Sheriff, William Frampton, followed by Peter Hall, Mayor and Edward Man, Senior Bailiff bearing the town's maces, the King and the royal party went on foot the short distance to William Skutt's house in the corn market *'where there was a stately banquett provyded'.* As a token of appreciation before leaving, the King appointed William Skutt as the next mayor and compliments were exchanged on all sides as the party left from the towngate.

The upper room in William Skutt's house where the banquet was probably held survived into the 20th century as part of much altered premises on the north west side of the corn market. It was a large room with an arched ceiling and windows looking out on to High Street with splayed openings showing the thickness of the ancient stone walls. The house of Peter Hiley (second son of Haviland Hiley) was on the opposite side of the corn market. This was demolished around two hundred years ago but a description remains in the form of an inventory taken in 1673. The grandest and most comfortable room on the ground floor was the parlour, furnished with a carpet and ten leather chairs, a glass-fronted cupboard, maps and a set of bookshelves. It was probably in this room that the royal party was entertained while in the kitchen nearby, the women worked to produce a meal fit for a king.

Whether the Poole Corporation would have honoured the King's choice of mayor we do not know but a few weeks after the royal visit, William Skutt died. In his brief will, he left his whole estate to his wife Elizabeth with the proviso that she should provide for his children. No sums of money or properties were mentioned except for the George Inn and the Plume of Feathers. The next few years saw the deaths of several other High Street veterans of the Civil War period. Haviland Hiley died in 1669 and his son Peter Hiley only three years later. In his will, Haviland left the vast sum of £1000 to his eldest son, William, together with parcels of land in Poole. His second son, Peter must already have been established because he received just £10. Peter's three sons each inherited a property. Peter the younger received Marsh farm in Bloxworth and John inherited the mansion house, brewhouse, malthouse, orchard and garden in Poole currently occupied by his father, Peter the elder. The youngest son, Charles inherited the Bull Head Inn in High Street. Their sister Mary received £100 and Haviland also left £20 a year to his daughter-in-law Rachel, Peter's wife, to be paid after her husband's death. He appointed his three grandsons as his executors and asked his overseers to *'take care of these poor children, my executors until they are able to take care for themselves'.*

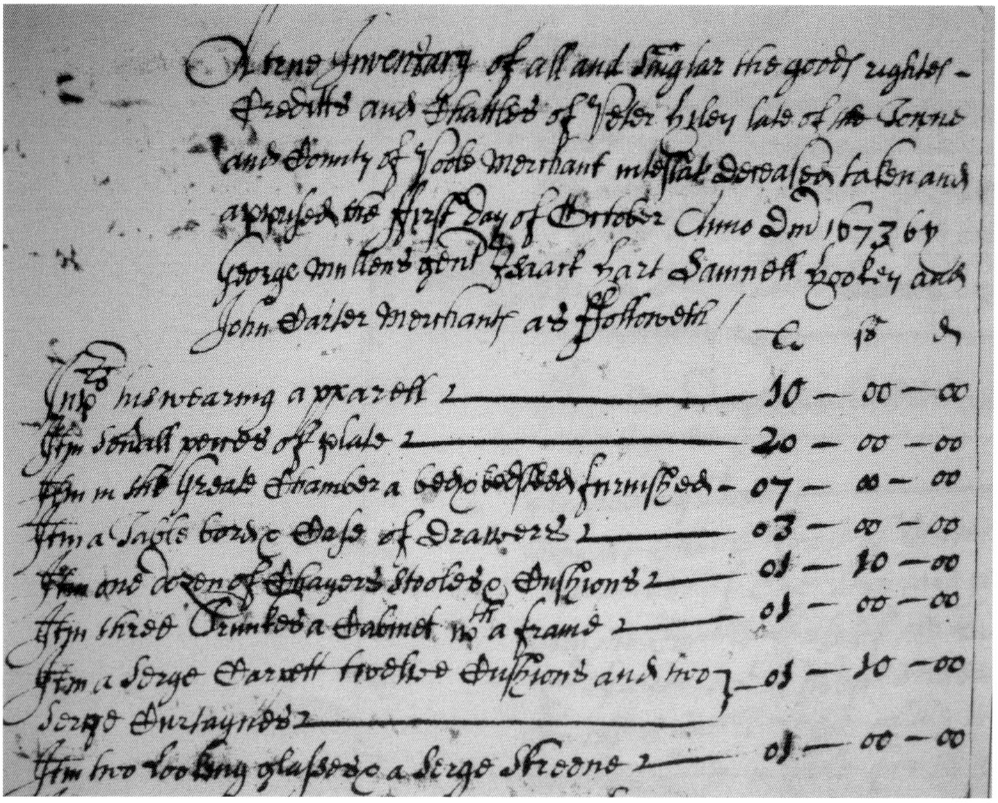
A true Inventary of all and singular the goods rights credits and chattels of Peter Hiley late of the Towne and County of Yorke merchant intestat deceased taken and apprised the first day of October Anno Dni 1673 by George Mullens gent Stuart Hart Samuell Hooley and John Tailor merchant as followeth

	L	s	d
Imprs his wearing apparell	10	00	00
Item sundrie peeces of plate	20	00	00
Item in the great chamber a bed & bedstead furnished	07	00	00
Item a table borde & case of drawers	03	00	00
Item one dozen of chayers stooles & cushions	01	10	00
Item three trunkes a cabinet wth a frame	01	00	00
Item a serge carpett twelve cushions and two serge curtaynes	01	10	00
Item two looking glasses & a serge screene	01	00	00

A section of Peter Hiley's inventory

Peter Hiley died in 1672 without making a will and an inventory was drawn up of his estate including the contents of the house in which he lived. In contrast to Edward Green's house of the previous century with its medieval features of great hall and buttery, this house was more in the modern style. It had three storeys, including the attics with four rooms on each floor. Besides the grand parlour described above in connection with the king's visit, there was the hall containing a clock, the kitchen equipped with *'pewter and brass of all sorts, two spits and a dripping pan' and a study which contained two writing desks, a chest and 'half a hundredweight of ordinary cheese'*. Apparently some rooms in the house were used to store goods for Peter Hiley's business as becomes more obvious in the description of the upper floors.

The master bedroom or *'great chamber'* was a large room, probably above the parlour. It contained a bed and bedstead *'furnished'* (with hangings, bolster, covers etc.) a table board and a chest of drawers. Also in the room were a large carpet, a dozen chairs, stools and cushions, three trunks, a cabinet with a frame, two looking glasses and a large screen. Perhaps it was in this rather cluttered-sounding room that Peter Hiley kept the plate worth £20 that the house contained. We do know that the inventory makers found *'twenty dozen of worsted stockings'*, value £20 stored there and stocking making was obviously one of his business interests.

In the chamber over the hall were *'a pair of brass andirons and four pictures'*, an old box and a joint stool and three new herring nets. The kitchen chamber contained a bed and bedstead, furnished, two old trunks, four old chairs, a little table, three small boxes, a looking glass and an open fronted cupboard. The other room on the first floor was the maid's chamber, simply furnished with a bed and covering. In addition the house contained sheets, table cloths, napkins, pillowcases and other linen worth £12.

Above the first floor were four attics or 'cocklofts'. One of these at least was furnished as a bedroom with two bedsteads and a covering but most of the space was used for storage. In the cockloft over the great chamber were six bags and a hundredweight of *'sorting nails'* and the other attics contained a dozen new herring nets, three dozen of line and four bushels of beans. At the back of the house was an inner court, surrounded by stores and outhouses. There were the malt lofts for the brewing part of the business containing an estimated fifty quarters (about 12 hundredweight) of malt worth £40, plus a shovel and scales. A dray cart, wheels and harness were kept there along with a *'press of healing stones'*. In the stable with its haylofts were two old saddle horses. Beyond the inner court was an outer yard where 'five fat pigs' were kept along with stores of wooden planks and rafters. The salt store held five quarters of salt and the new cellar *'a press of malting coals and old nails'*. There was also *'a dung boat'* and another small boat. Altogether, the impression is of a large, comfortable but slightly disordered house where domesticity and business overlapped.

Besides his household possessions, Peter Hiley owned or leased property in the town including the Lamb Inn, the Three Mariners and the Town Arms and owned *'table boards, bedsteads and other lumber'* at the Bell. He was also involved in the Newfoundland trade and other ventures as owner of the ship *Rachel* and part owner of the *Happy Returns* and the *Mayflower* and had various investments in *'train oil and corrfish'* (cod-liver oil and dried salt cod). A Mr. Cressey of London owed him £15 as the balance of an account for silk stockings. Obviously, he had a finger in lots of different pies and in this, was probably typical of many Poole merchants. Altogether, his estate was valued at £1593 15s 11d, not counting his quarter share in the ship *Elinor* which had lost her mast and sails due to some misfortune and lay unfitted in the Thames.

By the 1680s, Allen Skutt had inherited the George Inn and other Skutt property in High Street. He had served as mayor in 1677 and was appointed deputy mayor in 1684 in unusual circumstances. In a move to gain greater authority over cities and boroughs, Charles had withdrawn many of their charters and rights and Poole was one of the boroughs to suffer. John Wyndham of Salisbury was appointed mayor with Allen Skutt acting as his deputy. It was therefore Allen Skutt who presided over one of the grimmest episodes of the turbulent century. In September

1685, following the western rebellion in support of the Duke of Monmouth, punitive trials of rebels took place at the Dorchester assizes. A few days later, a grim procession of carts rumbled down High Street bringing convicted rebels to Poole for execution by hanging, drawing and quartering. Whereabouts in the town the grisly spectacle took place, we do not know. After the executions, the quarters of bodies were tarred and sent by order to smaller towns in the area to be displayed in public places as a dreadful warning. Allen's Skutt's letter to the constable of Lytchett Matravers, sending him *'two quarters of severall persons this day executed within this towne'*, still exists in the archives. One of the last acts of James II before his flight into exile in 1688 was the restoring of all the rights and privileges of the boroughs.

Towards the end of the century, many High Street residents were re-establishing their lives and fortunes after the upheaval of the Civil War and the Commonwealth. Alice, the widow of Johnson Melledge, had suffered reverses with her husband's arrest and disgrace, but she had achieved prosperity at the end of her life as owner of the town's most important inn, the Antelope. This property she left to her unmarried daughter, Alice junior, who thereby surely became one of the most eligible young women in the town. Another daughter, Mary Emerson inherited a house and shops in Church Street connected to the Antelope by a passage way *'from one street to another'*. Alice also inherited a parcel of ground where *'I now lay my ashes and soil . . . as long as she permits her sister Mary Emerson to lay her ashes there likewise'*. Alice placed a lot of stress on each sister allowing the other free enjoyment of her legacy, giving the strong impression that they did not get along too well. Shortly after inheriting the inn, Alice junior married John Allen and the Antelope was bought by Peter Hiley the younger.

The third Melledge daughter, Ann, was married to James Hollybread, mayor in 1682 and 1688. A trade token from 1666 indicates that the Hollybreads were then running the George Inn, a couple of doors away from the Antelope. Others involved in the lucrative inn-keeping trade were Alexander Lloyd and his wife Rachel who ran the King's Arms. This large inn had been built on the new stretch of High Street running down to the Quay with an attached tenement and *'the new building thereunto adjoining (vizt) the shop, the parlour, hall and buttery and the chambers overhead'*, quite a complex of buildings. After Alexander's death, his widow married Charles Daw, the landlord of the Plume of Feathers and the couple ran the King's Arms together.

Merchant John Carter, several times mayor of Poole, owned adjoining properties on High Street including a mansion house with malthouse and brewhouse and a house *'commonly called or known by the name of the White Bear'* which was occupied by his widowed daughter-in-law, Mary Carter. Then there was the White Hart, owned by Mary Pitman and the Bull Head Inn, run by John Lock. For those rising in the world, inns and taverns were an excellent investment. They were a type of business which could be (and frequently were) run by women. They were also well supported

Jenny Oliver

An old window at the rear of the former Bull Head Inn

by the corporation which held many of its meetings *'at Mr Daws', 'at Mrs Lloyds' or 'att the Bull Head'* with suitable expenses for refreshments.

Other High Street residents were becoming well-to-do through trade. One example was mariner Thomas Wadham. As master and owner of a quarter part of the *George and Thomas* of Poole, he was more than an ordinary sailor and was on the way to becoming a merchant. He also owned rights to the inn called Black Rod in the High Street, once owned by Edward Taylor. Another seaman who had definitely made the transition to merchant was Nicholas Efford. From being a sailor and sea captain he had became owner of seven eighths of the *Concord.* He also owned a plantation in Bay de Verde, Newfoundland. At his death in 1688, the appraisers valued the ship and the likely profit of its current voyage to Newfoundland at £1000 *'yf the said Shipp shall come safe home'.* With his comfortable house on High Street and his plantation in Newfoundland, his whole estate was valued at £1,944 4s 4d.

In the last years of the century, High Street and other streets were treated to major repairs and repitching at a cost of £18 2s 2d for 50 tons of stone, 78 loads of sand and 734 feet of pitching work. There was also the construction of a *'shead'* in the corn market. Perhaps used for storage it seems to have been a small stone building with iron fitments and was built at a cost of £7 7s. After the war, the defences of the town had been reduced and at some stage the town walls were demolished. The town ditch fell into disuse and either silted up or was partially filled in, perhaps using the mounds of waste which had accumulated at Pitwines in the area known as the Mount. The towngate remained as the entrance to the town, however, and High Street still came to a dead end as far as wheeled traffic was concerned. Nevertheless the possibility for development had been created.

After a tumultuous century and a period of recovery, a spirit of change was in the air. Many High Street residents were looking forward with increased confidence and prosperity to the future.

Chapter Four

The Age of Adventure

They that in ships with courage bold
O'er swelling waves their trade pursue,...' William Knapp

During the 18th century, Poole's commercial success was to allow the town to overtake Dorchester as the largest town in Dorset. In the 150 years between 1,662 and 1801, the population grew from around 1,650 to 4,761. In the early years of the century, however, the trade with Newfoundland was depressed as a result of the war with France. English settlements on the island were attacked and destroyed. In 1702, Thomas Wadham arrived in Poole on the *Hopewell* sailing from Trinity with *the news that '40 or 50 armed Frenchmen came over by land from Plascentia to Syllicove and surprised the inhabitants there, killing three or four, and took Mr. John Masters out of his bed, rifled his house, and carried him and his goods aboard a Jersey ship laden with fish in the harbour, and carried away the ship and fish, about 1,000 quintals. . . . God send better news; this proves fatal to this poore Towne, who will have great loss.'*

As a result of the danger in Newfoundland, John Masters had already brought his wife, son John and four daughters back to Poole and according to a later account, settled them in *'a low old house at the upper end of High Street'*. He then returned to Newfoundland and was later murdered there by Indians. To support the family, Mrs Masters *'set up an alehouse the sign of the Red Cow in a low mean way'*. John Masters junior was apprenticed at 13 to Captain William Taverner, member of an important Poole family of Newfoundland traders, a normal route for a young man to learn the trade. The Treaty of Utrecht of 1713 required the French to abandon their settlements in Newfoundland and opened up opportunities for English traders. In the next few years, Poole ships increasingly visited and established settlements in new areas of the island.

Poole merchants were also involved in other types of trade. Ships belonging to the White merchant family travelled to Barbados, Virginia, the Baltic, Holland and France carrying all sorts of cargo. In 1722, merchant William Barfoot sailed from Barbados carrying rum and slaves to Charleston, Carolina and a couple of years later, as master of the Eagle of Poole, he made another slave voyage from Madeira to the West Indies. In the 1750s, Barfoot ships took building materials out to tiny Bence Island in Sierra Leone where Richard Oswald ran a slave trading post and then sailed with another cargo of slaves to Carolina. Opinions on the ethics of this trade were to change in Poole by the end of the century but for now the town's merchants were keen to invest in every lucrative opportunity.

When Daniel Defoe visited the town in the 1720s as part of his tour through England and Wales, he described Poole as *'a considerable sea-port, and indeed the most considerable in all this part of England; for here I found some ships, some merchants and some trade; especially here were a good number of ships fitted out every year to the Newfoundland fishing, in which the Pool men were said to have been particularly successful for many years past.'* One effect of this growth was that High Street and other streets became much more built up. Orchards, gardens and closes were built upon, spaces were filled in and paths through to buildings behind the street front properties became fixed as lanes and alleyways. Another result was to put a massive strain on the town's infrastructure and services.

One of the first and grandest 18th century buildings to be built on High Street was the mansion house now Nos. 87-9. The chosen site was well north of the corn market in an area of the street only lightly developed at the time. Finished in 1704, the house was probably under construction on 26th November 1703 when a massive storm toppled trees and chimney pots and tore off roofs across the county. It was designed in the latest style based on symmetry and classical proportion which must have looked both splendid and unfamiliar in the early 1700s. Being set back from the street gave the house added grandeur. With three storeys plus cellars, the house was seven bays wide with a central three-bay projection and wings to the front and rear. The façade was enhanced by quoins and horizontal bands at first and second floor level, with a decorative cornice beneath the parapet. Originally there would have been one central entrance, no doubt similar to the present columned and pedimented doorway. An ornamental garden was laid out at the back, stretching through to Lagland Street.

Borough of Poole Museum Service

Rain water head, Nos. 87-9

The date of the house appears on a rain head together with the initials S W. This could refer to the Quaker merchant, Samuel White who helped

Borough of Poole Museum Service

Sir William Phippard

to found his family fortunes in the 17th century partly by supplying Government transports. Another candidate is Samuel Weston, merchant, property owner and M.P. for Poole from 1705 to 1708 who left his mansion house in High Street to his son William in his will of 1716. Evidence of the original owner is hard to find but by the middle of the 18th century, the house was home to another merchant, William Barfoot.

Another High Street property owner at the beginning of the century was William Phippard, one of Poole's M.P.s. Born in Poole in 1649, he became a successful Newfoundland merchant and secured lucrative government contracts transporting stores and troops in his ships the *Mary*, the *William and Elizabeth*, the *Dolphin* and the *William and Mary*. He was first elected to Parliament in 1698, when he was also serving as Mayor of Poole and remained an M.P., with one gap, until 1711. He was knighted by Queen Anne. In Parliament, Phippard served on trade committees and provided information on Newfoundland to the Government. In 1703, for instance, he and other Newfoundland merchants presented a 'Memorial' concerning the need for naval convoys for the Newfoundland ships. His high standing with the administration worked in his favour in 1706 when the *William and Mary* was seized at Barbados *'for illegally importing 20 reams of paper from Portugal, on the false evidence of a discharged seaman.'* On his petition, the Commissioners of Customs at Barbados were instructed that *'all proceedings against the William and Mary are to cease.'*

Sir William married Mary Smith-Asher, some 30 years his junior, around 1700. The couple had four children, William, John, Elizabeth and George. In 1711, the Phippards bought the estate of Merton Abbey in south west London. The following year, however, there were signs that Sir William was in financial difficulties when John Rolt brought an execution against him for a debt. In 1714, he was obliged to come to an agreement with his creditors whereby all his property should be sold to pay off his debts, except for his lady's and his children's clothes and household goods and his wife's personal possessions. It was an ignominious situation for a once successful man. The list of property to be sold covered premises in London, Purbeck and Poole, including a house occupied by the widow Christian Thoms in High Street. (Josiah Thoms had been master of Sir William's ship *Dolphin*). The house was probably in the vicinity of what is now Nos. 103-5 High Street. In fact the sale of his estate dragged on after Sir William's death in 1723 and that of his widow in 1725.

Although the High Street was home to some important men, it was not a very clean or even a safe place in the early 18th century. Pedestrians, particularly at night in the unlit streets had to pick their way around all sorts of hazards. Residents were frequently presented at the Quarter Sessions for making 'mixons' or dung heaps in the streets and leaving obstacles such as timber or stones lying about. In 1701 for instance, Simon Whiterow, woolcomer, James King, tailor, widow Jane Wadham and Peter Clarke, mariner, were indicted at the Quarter Sessions for *'obstructing High Street, Poole with dirt so that people could not pass with their chattels etc.'* In 1709, *'Mistres Hily, John Lester and Mestres Streat'*, were presented before the court for *'making a mixon in the Corn Market at the end of Mr Skut's manchon house'*. No doubt rats and other vermin were common. With many houses still thatched, another danger was the risk of fire and in 1709 Nicholas Gillingham was ordered to repair his chimney *'wch is very dangerous of fireing of several thatcht houses there about'*.

The authorities also were frequently in trouble for not cleaning, repairing and pitching the streets. With an inadequate system of waste disposal, the task of keeping the streets clean was never-ending. The accounts show regular payments for a man to clean the corn market, and the town crier was employed to call for the people to clean the streets near their houses. In 1715, the authorities also paid him to publicise a ban on the throwing of lentcrocks. This West Country tradition was a version of trick or treat performed on Shrove Tuesday. Children would go round the houses begging for the ingredients to make pancakes. If they were refused, they would retaliate by throwing broken crockery on the doorstep of the householder. It seems a rather killjoy action by the authorities to ban the practice.

In an effort to improve the condition of the streets, an agreement was drawn up in 1721 with Thomas Mackrell of Parkstone *'to take up, convey and carry out from each and every street which is pitched or paved with stone . . . in which any carts or carriage may conveniently be drawn, all such Soyle dung dirt or compost . . laid in the streets'*. This was to be deposited on waste land belonging to the town. To help the process, householders had to gather their waste into heaps to be collected. Judging by later court records, Thomas Mackrell and his successors were only partially successful in their task. Another hazard was dilapidated buildings. In 1703, the court presented the proprietors of *'the house cal'd by the name of the King's Head, the Sills Hanging very dangerous to all passers by & to be a publique nuisance.'* In the next sessions, William Skutt was

Andrew Hawkes Poole Photo Archive

The thatched cottage, possibly once the White Bear Inn

presented *'for not repairing the George it being dangrs for all passers by'*. It seems that the lower High Street was rather run down at this period.

Several inns were changing hands in the early years of the 18th century. Charles Daw, keeper of the King's Arms, died in 1701 and left all his right and title in the inn to his wife Rachel and after her death to his son, Charles. Merchant John Carter died in 1711. He was the owner of several adjoining properties in High Street including a mansion house with malthouse, brewhouse, outhouses and garden and two tenements going by the name of the White Bear, one of which was on a corner of High Street. From this description, and evidence from a church rate later in the century, it seems that the White Bear was on the corner of the lane still known as Carter's Lane. In fact the inn or one of John Carter's other tenements may have been the thatched cottage on the corner of the lane which survived into the 20th century. The inn was left to John Carter's three grand-daughters, Elizabeth, Frances and Mary Carter, to be run by their mother, Mary, until they came of age.

Another inn to change hands in the early part of the century was the Bull Head Inn on the death of landlord, John Lock. He did not own the inn but was able to leave his daughter Ann £200 and *'one Bedd and furniture Hung with Green Courtains in the Chamber in the Bull Head Inn in Poole called the Green Chamber'*. In 1735, Mary Franklin inherited the *'messuage or tenement called or known by the name of the White Hart near the Quay in Poole'*, occupied by John Churchill, from her grandmother, Mary Pitman. She also inherited another tenement *'house, stable, backside, garden and lands . .*

. *situate in the High Street . . near the said White Hart there'*, most of which was occupied by Mary Stone. The rents and profits of the premises were to be used for Mary's maintenance and education until she was 21.

The old George Inn was kept by the Price family who had come to Poole from London early in the century. The son of the family, Henry Price, was a brilliant classical scholar and went to Christ Church, Oxford, unusually for a provincial innkeeper's son. On leaving university, he started a career as a naval officer and later became a tide waiter in the Poole customs service, inspecting incoming ships. In 1733, he married Mary Stagg and they had four children, all born in Poole. Meanwhile he was writing poems on all sorts of subjects and translating poems from Greek, Latin and French. Some of his translations appeared in magazines in the 1730s which may have encouraged him to publish his *'Poems on Several Subjects By a Land-Waiter in the Port of Poole'* in 1741. The list of local subscribers for his book was impressive, running to 14 pages, and included most of the leading names in the town.

Later Price gave up the customs service and became a school teacher at Richard Corpe's free school in Poole. He died in 1750 at the early age of 48. Having composed epitaphs for many worthies of Poole, mostly now lost, he also wrote his own: *'Here lies the greatest of sinners, the least of the poets.'* The record of his burial in St. James' church register uniquely gives his profession: *'Henry Price. A Poet.'*

As the town accounts show, the High Street inns continued to be used for official town meetings and to entertain visiting dignitaries. Expenses in 1709-10 when William Skutt was Mayor include;

'Paid at the George with the Justices *1s 1d*

Paid att the ffeathers with the Justices *1s 6d*

Pd at the White Bear with the Justices *10d'*

The inns were also the focus for patriotic celebrations, such as the anniversary of George 1's coronation which seems to have been marked in 1715 by a gun salute, flags and beer for the porters and a procession accompanied by bottles of wine costing £1 8s 6d (£1 42p). That year there was also reason to celebrate the defeat of the Jacobite rebellion:

'Firing the guns at Rejoycing for victory over the Preston Rebels –

Paid at the bull's head at the same time *£1 16s 0d*

It was at the George that the authorities met in 1715 for *'examining of mumpers'* (or professional beggars), who were subsequently whipped at a cost of 3 shillings (15p). The Bull Head was the venue in 1722 when they *'sent for Mr Barfoot and Randall about the sugar they bought clandestanly of a stranger'* and 1s 7d (8p) was spent at the George *'when the Chimneysweeps sons was whip'd by their parents for Stealing tobacco'.*

The money coming into the town gradually began to transform its appearance.

In High Street, prosperous merchants and tradesmen built themselves fine houses in the new Georgian style, many of which still remain today. One property dating from this time is the present Nos. 90 and 92, a five-bay brick house with stone quoins and a small gable enclosing the semi-circular head of the central upper floor window. Another is Nos. 127/9, currently Bon Marché, which was built as a two-storey mansion house in the early 18th century. To furnish their elegant new houses, High Street residents started to replace their heavy carved furniture with light, elegantly turned pieces in the style of Chippendale and discard their sturdy dishes and pottingers in favour of delicate china and glassware.

More modest premises were also being developed. A couple of deeds in the archives relate to one property probably situated north of the corn market near the present site of No. 39. It consisted of a *'low room with a turfhouse and a little plot of ground in length 72 ft & in width 14 ft at the low room, 16 ft at the street & 11 ft at the turfhouse'*. The property was occupied by the widow Phippard and then by William Weston, a barber, who decided to add a shop on the street, a chamber and garret over the original room and a brewhouse. In 1729, Weston mortgaged the property to the schoolmaster, Richard Corpe for £76.

During the first half of the 18th century, a few of the High Street inns

Jenny Oliver

Nos. 90-92 High Street in modern times

reverted to being private houses. One of these was the ancient George Inn. By the middle of the century, in a reversal of the process of a century before, it was once more a residential property and home to several different households. Other inns such as the King's Head and the Plume of Feathers disappeared temporarily or permanently from the records, perhaps as a result of their dilapidated condition. The Antelope continued in business however and other inns appeared in upper High Street and the lanes leading off it.

Religious buildings were also going up on High Street in the early 1700s. From their first cautious formation in the later part of the previous century, dissenting congregations had expanded considerably. At first, meetings were held in people's houses. In 1706 John Gigger's house in High Street was registered to be used for this purpose, the proposal being signed by Gigger, Richard Bucknam, Abraham Smith and John Rose. In 1738, the minister Matthew Towgood registered his mansion house in High Street *'to be used for meeting or assembly of the Protestant Dissenters called Presbyterians'*. By 1741, the congregation were meeting in a newly erected building on the land of Richard Sutton, a High Street baker.

With all this construction going on, owners of older property such as the Tudor mansions in lower High Street were not to be outdone. Gradually, ancient stone walls were covered with brick or stucco facades and casements replaced with fashionable sash windows. Tudor doorways were removed in favour of classical porticoed entrances with skylights and door scrapers. The Antelope and its neighbouring properties were extensively remodelled with new facades and windows. Nos. 30 and 32, once Sir Edmund Uvedale's house, also received the Georgian treatment. During the century, High Street would rarely have been without scaffolding and piles of timber and bricks.

The street could be a fairly lawless place at times. In 1736, Elizabeth, wife of Robert Wills and others were indicted at the quarter sessions for *'gathering in an unlawful and riotous assembly, disturbing the peace and terrorising the local residents'* as well as *'destroying a bag or sack of wheat valued at 20s belonging to William Barfoot'*. They were fined 13s 4d (66p). The following year, Jane, the wife of Dudley Diggs, a High Street victualler, was fined 1s (5p) for assaulting Thomas Bushell, one of the sergeants at mace. The same year Mary Galton and Elizabeth Seymor *'did make an assault on . . William Barfoot then and there did beat, wound and so illy intreat so that his life was greatly despaired of'*. They received a fine of 1s each.

Violence was not confined to the poorer part of society. Others indicted for assault included merchant George Tito and gentlemen John Phippard and Thomas Wadham. In 1745, merchant William Barfoot was even accused of assaulting the minister, Richard Derby. Usually the punishments for such offences against the person were light. Theft and burglary were dealt with much more harshly and High

Street residents had a grandstand view of some of the punishments. In 1756, for instance, mariner John Wiles was found guilty of stealing a buoy rope, value 10d (4p) and condemned *'to be whipped from Cole corner in Poole, the tenth day of April instant, between the hours of twelve and one o'clock in the morning to the great quay and from thence back to Cole corner at the cart's tail'.*

In 1745 the peace of the country was threatened by another uprising on behalf of the exiled Stuarts. The danger was considered so serious that the authorities set men to work to dig out the old town ditch. A century before, the town's defences had been used against the king's forces; now the community rallied in support of the reigning monarch. An indictment of Gerard Lewis for making a seditious speech gives a flavour of public feeling at the time. For drinking a toast to a *'certain person . . . pretending to be and taking upon himself the title of King of England by the name of James III'*, he was described as being of *'impious, wicked, factious, seditious, turbulent and rebellious mind and disposition and disturber of the peace of our Sovereign Lord King George II'.* According to the traveller Dr. Pococke, the town spent £300 on the defences before the works were abandoned because of the cost. If the effort had been successful, it would have cut off High Street once again from extension northwards.

In 1746, another mansion house was being refurbished in High Street. It was to be the home of John Masters, last mentioned as a young apprentice to the Newfoundland trade in the early years of the century. In spite of his difficult childhood, Masters had prospered and become first a ship's captain and then a merchant in his own right. In the 1720s he started a salmon fishery near the St. Mary's Bay in Newfoundland. Through the 1730s he operated from St. John's shipping cargoes of fish on commission as well as for himself. In 1740, now over 50 and a wealthy man, he married Sarah, the daughter of his former master, William Taverner. The couple settled in Greenwich, while the Newfoundland end of the business was carried on by his partner, Michael Ballard.

Some of the details of John Masters' life are described in an account by Sir Peter Thompson, another merchant of Poole origins who made his fortune elsewhere and then retired to live in the town. According to Thompson, John Masters seems to have been rather a rough diamond, *'a fine figure of a man – only wanted polishing'.* He was also a hard worker and a shrewd businessman if not the most diplomatic of men. Masters was keen to obtain a seat in Parliament but lacked the necessary influence. His energetic campaigning to obtain better naval protection for the Newfoundland fleets and settlements helped him to be elected as a burgess of Poole in 1744, but failed to win him friends in high places. It was perhaps to pursue his political ambitions that Masters then decided to move to Poole permanently.

For his Poole residence, John Masters chose to remodel the old Red Cow in upper High Street which his mother had run as a tavern. The cost was £1,500

Jenny Oliver

A well-to-do Georgian interior

(instead of the £600 he had estimated). The house was on the site of what is now Nos. 109-113 High Street which in the mid 18th century was on the edge of the built up part of High Street, backing on to fields. Besides the house with its furniture, linen, china and plate, there were outhouses, a barn, stables for his horses and an ornamental pleasure garden. He also kept a chaise, carriages and a chariot.

In the parliamentary election of 1747, John Masters again attempted to win one of the Poole seats, spending £600 - £700 to win the support of the Corporation. However his forceful style had won him enemies and he again failed to win a nomination. He did become Mayor of Poole in 1748, the first Newfoundland born man to do so. Even this was not without controversy because he had not first served in the lesser civic offices as was the custom. By 1751, Masters' influence was high and he was again elected as mayor.

The town over which Masters presided as mayor in the middle of the century

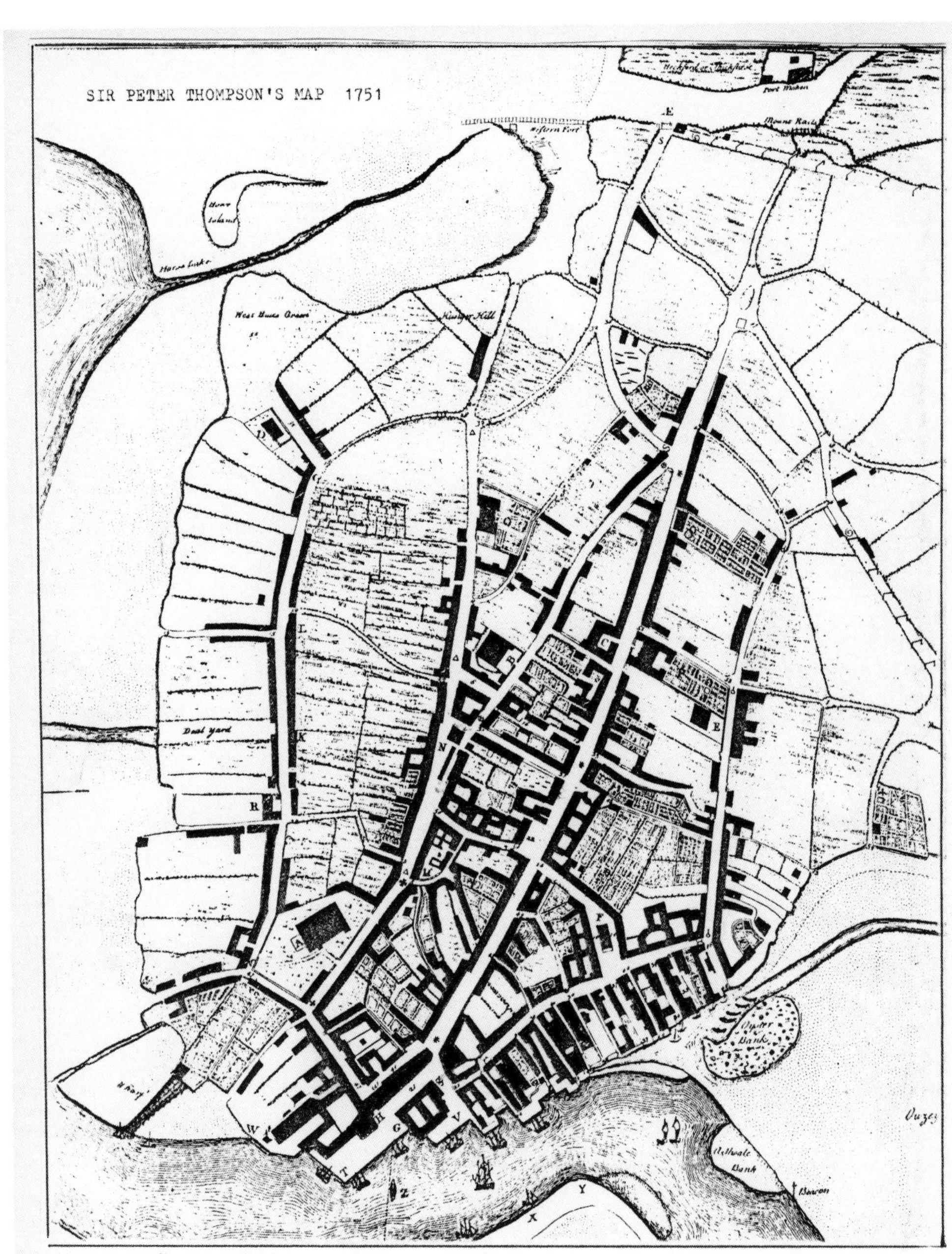

The 1751 street map

was very different from 50 years before. A 1751 rating list for poor relief, together with a map of the same year give us the best picture yet of High Street and who lived there. As the map shows, the northern end of High Street was still not a through route for wheeled traffic. A turnstile in the area of what is now Falkland Square allowed pedestrians to pass between High Street and Longfleet. Carts, wagons and carriages travelling in and out of town still had to go via Towngate Lane. South

NEW
CHURCH MELODY:
BEING A SET OF
ANTHEMS, PSALMS, HYMNS, &c.
ON VARIOUS OCCASIONS.
IN
FOUR PARTS
WITH
A great Variety of other ANTHEMS, PSALMS, HYMNS, *&c.* composed after a Method entirely new, and never printed before.

By WILLIAM KNAPP,
Author of the first Book of Psalm Tunes and Anthems on various Occasions.

WITH
An Anthem on *Psalm* cxxvii. by one of the greatest Masters in *Europe*. Together with four excellent Hymns, and an Anthem for the Nativity.

I will give thee Thanks in the great Congregation, I will praise thee among much People, Psalm xxxv. 18. *And all her Streets shall say* Alleluia. Tobit xiii. 18.

To which is added,
An Imploration to the KING of KINGS.
Wrote by King CHARLES I. during his Captivity in *Carisbrook*-Castle, in the *Isle of Wight*, *Anno Domini*, 1648.
Together with
An Anthem for the MARTYRDOM of that blessed PRINCE.

THE FIFTH EDITION.

LONDON:
Printed for R. BALDWIN, and S. CROWDER, in Pater-noster-Row; the AUTHOR at Poole; B. COLLINS, Bookseller, in Salisbury; and sold by most Booksellers in Great-Britain and Ireland. Price 3 s. 6 d.
M DCC LXIV.

Borough of Poole Museum Service

of the turnstile, a ropewalk operated right across the street and then came an area of small fields and paddocks. Mr. George Hyde and William Milner, the Collector of Customs were among those holding land here. The first buildings began near the site of what is now the old Post Office (No. 141) where the rural scene gave way to the noise, bustle, dirt and smells of High Street proper.

Following the list southwards down the eastern side of the street, one of the houses in the first block belonged to Edward Lockyer, a tailor. In 1738 he had been presented at the Quarter Sessions for *'laying a great quantity of Dirt in High Street'*, and ordered to remove it within four days. This was obviously not a permanent deterrent because in 1744 he was one of three men presented for *'laying dung and rubbish at the upper end of High Street, whereby carriages are oblig'd to break into ye footway so that passengers in a wet time are very much incommoded in walking that way'*. The next stretch of High Street was probably rather up-market because it contained the new tenement and yards of merchant John Skinner, John Master's refurbished home, the house and malt house of merchant Benjamin Linthorne and William Barfoot's grand mansion, the highest rated property in the street. Even this fashionable part of town was not without hazards however. In 1751, Barfoot was indicted at the Quarter Sessions for *'putting crosspieces to the posts before his House, the same being dangerous to Persons walking in the Night time'*.

Shortly after the Barfoot house came the Bull Head Inn, one of the most valuable inns in the street. It was run by Mrs. Dean who also held land at Pitwines. John Sherenham, plumber and glazier had his business a few doors down. Further along High Street were the tenements and bakehouse belonging to the widow Skinner. Skinner's alley led from the back of the premises through to Lagland Street at this point. Near the corner with Fish Street (now Castle Street) Aaron Durell had his ironmonger's business and Edward Saunders traded as a silversmith.

On the lower High Street were the businesses of Joseph Brassett, bookseller, Benjamin Mead, basket maker, Benjamin Bower, apothecary and William Knapp, glover maker. An advertisement shows that Joseph Brassett not only supplied books and stationery, prints, magazines, maps and charts, but also drawing instruments, musical instruments, snuff, mustard and pomatum and *'the best Silver-Plated Buckles and Spurs'*. Patent remedies in stock included *'Jesuit Drops'*, *Turlington's Balsam of Life'* and *'Daffey's Elixir'*. He also lent books out at 3d (1p) per volume per week and provided a bookbinding service.

William Knapp was better known for his secondary occupation than for his trade as a glover. In 1728, he had been appointed parish clerk at St. James' church and then devoted his time to teaching various church choirs in the villages around Poole. This work inspired him to start composing hymns aimed at country church choirs. In 1738, he published *'A Sett of New Psalm-Tunes and Anthems'* which was distributed all over the country and ran into several editions. Besides the hymns, all named after local places, later editions contained singing exercises and practical notes on how to read music. Knapp's *'New Church Melody'* was published in 1751.

In honour of his book of psalmody, Knapp's friend, Henry Price wrote a poem concluding:

'Long as the sun's enliv'ning glories shine
So long shall last this deathless work of thine
And future worlds with one consent agree
Where'er they sing of God, to mention thee.'

He could also write about his friend in a far less elevated style, perhaps as a result of being rebuked by Knapp and the sexton, George Savage for having a fit of hiccoughs in church (or so the story goes):

'From pounce and paper, ink and pen,
Save me, O Lord, I pray;
From Pope and Swift and such-like men,
And Cibber's annual lay;
From doctor's bills and lawyer's fees,
From ague, gout and trap;
And, what is ten times worse than these,
George Savage and Will Knapp.'

Near the bottom of the High Street were three inns, the Queen's Head, the St Clement and the White Hart, formerly owned by Mary Pitman. In this area, trades connected to the port predominated. James Meaden, block maker and Peter Street, sail maker had their works here as well as the shipwrights Richard Gleed and Messrs William Newnum and Richard Wills. Merchants Benjamin Skutt, William Wise, William Jolliff and others had cellars, yards and quays in the area, and mariners like Joseph Hookey, Joseph Miller and Martin Fiander lived nearby.

On the corner across the street was the King's Arms, run by John Oldmeadow, with the custom house and several tenements and cellars alongside. In January 1762, *there was a great storm and Sir Peter Thompson noted that these properties, 'all that Island of Houses between Great & Little Key'* had their lower floors full of water. The Lamb Inn listed next was probably the Lion and Lamb in what is now Salisbury Street. In 1767, Mrs Elizabeth Christian was accused of *'not raising the Chimney of her Kitchen or Washhouse it being so low that the sparks of fire issuing from thence is in the most Eminent danger of setting fire to the straw and litter on the Dung mixon of the Lion and Lamb Inn and also to the Haylofts of the said Inn'*. We can imagine a dirty, smoky little lane with more than a whiff of the farmyard about it.

At the High Street end of this lane was the George Inn, now known as the Old George, which had entered yet another phase of its long existence by being converted back into living quarters. At least three householders lived there, the widow Durell, John Harrison and John Scaplen who was a joiner and cabinet maker from Christchurch and whose name is associated with the property today. In the last half century, the old property had been thoroughly updated by the Skutt family who still owned it. The stone walls had been faced with red brick and many of the old stone mullions replaced with sash windows. The big old fireplaces were partly blocked up and plastered over or given contemporary Delft tile surrounds. Modern panelled doors, Georgian panelling and fine door surrounds were added and the property was subdivided for use by several different families.

Given his trade, John Scaplen may have enhanced and modernised his rooms. The *'best parlour'*, mentioned in his will, has been identified with the southwest room of the kitchen range which in the 18th century was separated from the kitchen by a

Borough of Poole Museum Service

A Georgian door surround, Scaplen's Court

cross passage. This room contained fine panelling and an elegant Georgian doorway which survived until the 1920s. Sash windows of the 18th century in some upper rooms may also be John Scaplen's work. Scaplen was sometimes in trouble with the authorities for leaving timber in the street near his house and elsewhere. In 1739, he was accused of breaking into the back garden of John Hayter *'using swords and staves'*, damaging the gate and the door of the necessary house and *'doing other injuries'*. What quarrel he had with John Hayter, we do not know.

Another trader who lived in the Old George or nearby was Moses Abraham, described in different documents as a silversmith, dealer, chapman or merchant. In 1758, he appeared in court to swear that he was owed £24 for goods and *'being of the Jewish profession being sworn on the Five Books of Moses'*. In the 1780s he was the target of violent anti Semitic abuse by labourer John Horner. According to the quarter sessions record, Horner assaulted him in the street, *'holding his clenched fist against him saying "Damn your Blood you Jew Son of a Bitch, I wish I had some Bacon in my Pockett, I would thrust it down your throat and choak or suffocate you, and Damn you", or words to that effect'*. We do not know the verdict of the case or what the penalty might have been.

Next door, the Plume of Feathers and the King's Head which had been so dilapidated in the early 1700s were no longer listed as inns. The Antelope however, was still in business under the management of Elizabeth Stanley, the widow of the previous landlord, Richard Stanley. Mrs. Stanley's brother in law, surgeon Alexander Campbell, also lived at or near the inn. Campbell was obviously in touch with all the latest health treatments. In 1759, 30 years before George III made sea bathing fashionable, he obtained a 21 year lease from the Corporation for a parcel of mudland on the west shore to build a bathing house. The house was duly built and survived the storm of 1762 although the rails of its bridge were all washed away. By 1763, an advertisement in the Salisbury and Winchester Journal informed the public

Jenny Oliver

18th century houses and facades, lower High Street

that *'the Bathing-House, consisting of two Dressing Rooms and Baths, is now completely fitted, and is so contrived as to admit of Bathing at any Time of the Tide. Gentlemen and Ladies may be furnished with Lodgings, by applying to Mr. Campbell, Surgeon, in Poole'*. Campbell's connection with the Antelope must have been useful here.

In 1764 when Elizabeth Stanley died, she left all her lands and tenements including the Antelope, to her nephew, David Campbell, Alexander's son. As David was a minor, Alexander was appointed his guardian and granted administration of the estate. Philip Stickland, who had been associated with the Antelope since the early 1750s, continued as landlord. As for the bathing house, it lasted some time because it was still being advertised in 1775 when it was said to be *'in compleat repair'* to welcome visitors.

A close neighbour of the Antelope was Joseph White, one of Poole's leading merchants. He lived in one of the old Tudor mansions, probably the present No. 10. The Whites were a family of successful merchants trading in Newfoundland,

Borough of Poole Museum Service

Nos. 21-7 16th century houses with Georgian facades.

Europe, the Baltic and the West Indies. Like Sir William Phippard and others, they had prospered through Government contacts to carry supplies in the French wars. As Quakers they did not take public office but still had considerable influence in the town. Joseph White owned ships and extensive lands and property in Trinity, Newfoundland and was perhaps one of the richest men in Poole in the mid 18th century. In the Seven Years' War between 1656 and 1763 he was to suffer severe reverses with the loss of 13 of his 14 ships. As was the custom with Poole merchants, none of these was apparently insured. That his business survived and prospered after such losses was a testimony of his wealth and acumen.

Further along the western side of High Street between the Quay and the corn market were the houses of Mr Courtin and George Tito, shipbuilder and mayor in 1755 and 1771. Then came Mr. Spence Young's tenement and bakehouse, Meshec Lester's butcher's shop and Richard Allen's ironmonger's business. The George Inn listed next was probably the inn called the 'George and Antelope' and later the 'New Antelope' just off High Street in Cinnamon Lane. It was run by the widow

Stanworth. Also in this area was the house of Mr. George Western, mayor in 1760, and John Pitney's barber shop.

At the north end of the corn market was old Skutt family house, the Priory, where Charles II had been entertained over 100 years before. The current owner was Benjamin Skutt a member of the Corporation and twice mayor. He was also the owner of the Old George, several cellars, a warehouse and another house near the quay. A little further up where New Orchard now crosses High Street was narrow Pluddie Lane and half a block further on, Fricker's Alley where John Fricker had his house and butcher's shop. Then came Bowling Green House, probably named after a bowling green at the back in Hill Street which also gave its name to the nearby Bowling Green Alley.

In the next block were the houses and shops of William Miller, apothecary, Samuel Bowden, tallow chandler, Captain William Phippard, William Hayward, peruke (wig) maker, and Richard Edwards, baker. Richard's father, Francis Edwards had bought some of John Carter's former tenements near the White Bear. In his will of 1744, he described his main property as a *'messuage and bakehouse with the facket [faggot] house adjoining . . . .backyard, foreyard or court, water courses, pump, well and water, cartway from the street on the north side to the facket house'*. At the rear was an enclosed garden. He also owned two other adjoining tenements fronting on to High Street. The properties were left to his wife and five children. The White Bear near the corner of Carter's Lane was now held by the merchant George Hyde who also owned a couple of John Carter's former tenements. Not far above the junction with Hill Street and Towngate Lane (now Chapel Lane), the buildings came to an end and the fields began.

It is clear that High Street in the mid 18th century was home to all classes of Poole society, gentlemen and merchants, traders and craftsmen, mariners and labourers. Many of the trades flourishing on the street are familiar today but others like those of the tallow chandler, apothecary and peruke maker, have long since died out. Not all of the traders were men. Of the nine inns listed in High Street or in the surrounding lanes, the most highly rated were the Antelope, the Bull Head and the (new) George, all run by women. The most valuable properties were the mansion houses of William Barfoot, Joseph White, John Hackman, John Masters and Mr. Courtin. Although some of these properties were quite grand, their situation was hardly quiet or exclusive as they might have been in a larger town. Here they were surrounded by shops, workshops and yards with all their accompanying traffic, noise and smells. High Street with its mix of residents and its sometimes chaotic bustle was a microcosm of the boom town that Poole was becoming.

Chapter Five

The later 18th Century

'The buildings are generally mean and low, but of late years many elegant houses have been erected.'

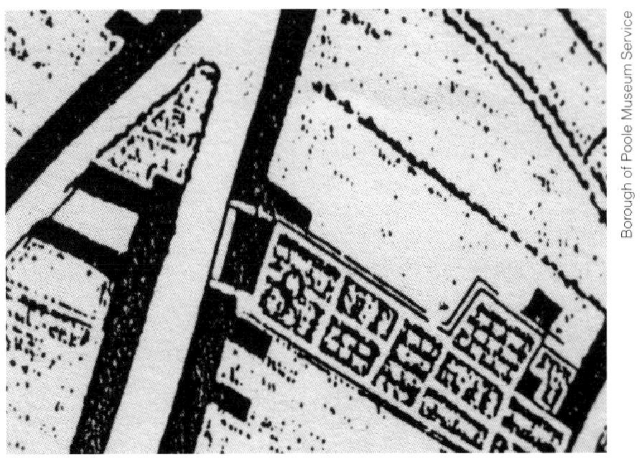

John Master's house from a map of 1770

Politics in 18th century Poole could be a riotous business. In 1753, some of the leading High Street residents were involved in an unseemly fracas in the town house. John Masters was promoting the election as mayor of Aaron Durell, one of his followers, and had the support of most of the burgesses. An opposing party wanted George Hyde as mayor and had him nominated by the Aldermen according to the usual custom. When both candidates tried to take the mayoral seat, a scuffle broke out. Masters' business partner, Michael Ballard, now living in High Street, was one of those present. Entering into the fray he apparently jumped upon the table *'with great Fire and Indignation'* seized the Sheriff, George Tito and hit him in the face, although Masters later claimed it was Tito who had first jumped on the table. Meanwhile Hyde read out the proclamation against rioters, possibly more of provocation than a calming measure in the circumstances. Eventually the shouting died down and the leaders of Poole society straightened their wigs and recovered their dignity. George Hyde's party started a lawsuit against John Masters and Aaron Durell but did not follow it up and Durell was allowed to serve out his year as mayor. In 1755, Michael Ballard acquired the White Bear and various tenements from George Hyde, the man he had opposed so violently. The same year, George Tito was elected mayor. George Hyde eventually achieved the office in 1757.

John Masters never achieved his ambition of entering Parliament but he did wield considerable power in Poole. He died in London in 1755 and was brought back to Poole to be buried. As he had no children, his main heir was George Olive, husband of his niece Sarah, who inherited his principal property and lands in Newfoundland and his ship *Littleton.* Thomas Keat, husband of another niece, inherited the brigantine *Lark* together with the salmon fishery in St Mary's Bay, Newfoundland. The High Street mansion he left to his wife Sarah and after her death to George Olive. Sarah Masters lived on in the house until she died in 1762 and the Olive family moved in. They would have had to refurnish it entirely as Sarah arranged in her will for the sale of all her household furniture to provide a legacy for Rebecca Lloyd, the niece who was her companion.

Benjamin Skutt also died in 1755. He owned a lot of property but his finances seem to have been rather finely balanced. His houses, cellars and warehouses were settled on his son Benjamin junior and he directed that the Old George should be sold to repay a mortgage of £300 to William Sherring and a debt of £120 owed to Timothy Spurrier. His house in the corn market was charged with sums of £205 and £120 by the deed of settlement on his marriage with his present wife, Margaret but *'is of much greater value'.* Margaret and their two daughters, Ann and Ursula were to inherit his house, plate, household goods and personal estate. On a personal note, he left Benjamin 'my Cocoa Nut cup set in silver whereon is Engraved my Coat of Arms' and for his daughter Mary *'my Gold Watch and Chain thereto belonging and the picture of her Mother'.* Within a few years the 'Priory' in the corn market which had belonged to the family for over 100 years, was sold to John Watkinson of Ringwood. After his death it was bought by merchant Thomas Jubber.

In 1762, following the death of Benjamin Linthorne, his house came on the market and was advertised in the *Salisbury and Winchester Journal.* The house was situated near the present No. 95, between John Masters' former house and William Barfoot's mansion. It was described as having gardens, a stable and a coach house with a malt house and warehouses adjoining. Also for sale was a post chaise, a copper furnace almost new, *'made to boil off a Hogshead'* and *'a new invented Machine to grind Apples to make Cyder, as came from the Maker, never used, and is supposed will make great Dispatch'.* The house was bought or rented by George Tito who is listed there in later rating lists. A few years later, after the death of Michael Ballard, Tito also acquired his house near the White Bear.

Although he was twice mayor and also a Justice of the Peace, George Tito seems to have been a focus for trouble. During the general election of 1765 Sir Peter

Thompson had cast what was virtually the deciding vote for the winning candidate. That afternoon he was warned that supporters of the rival candidate had been drowning their sorrows at the George Inn and intended to burn him in effigy in front of his house. To keep them away from his property, he went out to face them *'and met George Tito at the Head of the Mob near Market Lane end.'* After a brief exchange *'Tito gave me several blows in my face, others pulled my wigg'*. Some friends got Thompson into the shelter of a nearby house and the mayor and constables were sent for to quell the riot. In the scuffle *'George Milner was tumbled down and trampled on – was so much hurt that he spit blood for several days. John Skinner received an unlucky blow in his eye which swell'd so much he could not open it. He kept his bed and room sometime, indeed he carries the mark still of their barbarity. Mr. Oliver had his clothes & shirt torn from his back'*. The practice of treating supporters liberally at the local inns, combined with the lack of a secret ballet was an invitation to disorder at election times.

For most High Street inhabitants, elections would be only of passing interest, because they had no vote. They were more concerned with running their businesses and providing for their families. Most fathers would hope for sons to train who could inherit the business, but if they were not so fortunate, finding good employees was important. In 1762, Samuel Bowden advertised for *'a man who understands making Tallow Candles. Anyone that can bring a Character of his Honesty and Capacity may have employ for any time, not exceeding one Year'. Another advertisement in 1775 declared: 'Wanted immediately, a JOURNEYMAN JOBBING-SMITH, he must be a good workman. Such a one, by applying to Richard Allen, ironmonger, in Poole, may have constant work.'* The same year, another High Street tradesman, William Bestland was seeking a *'well recommended'* journeyman plumber and glazier and also an apprentice about 14 years of age.

Apprenticeships were vital because tradesmen and craftsmen took care to exclude those without the proper qualifications. In 1749, for instance, Mary, the wife of mariner William Knight was accused of practising as a baker unlawfully, not having served 7 years' apprenticeship, contrary to the Statute of Apprenticeships 1563. Parents would provide for their children's future by apprenticing them to a useful trade. An advertisement in the *Salisbury and Winchester Journal* at the end of the century shows the importance of this training. *'The Parents of a Youth about 15 years of age wish to place him as an APPRENTICE to a person in the above business* [grocery] *. . .A sober, reputable family where the morals of youth are particularly attended to . . A Dissenter will be preferred.'*

Apprenticeship records list many young people who were indentured to High Street traders. Some signed on *'in the sea-faring business'* with merchants and ship's masters. Many of the girls went to learn *'the art of housewifery'*, as servants either in private houses or inns. The masters were mainly men but there were a few women who took on apprentices such as Joan Lock, innkeeper, in 1736 and more unusually, Mary Linthorne, *'widow and blacksmith'*. In most cases these were widows carrying on

Borough of Poole Museum Service

18th century Cinnamon House with steps encroaching on the street.

the family business after the death of their husbands. Mary Linthorne was still in business in 1784 when she was listed in Bailey's British Directory as an anchorsmith. Surprisingly, Poole had a second female anchorsmith; another entry lists *'Elizabeth Allen and Sons, Anchorsmiths and Ironmongers'*.

The second half of the 18th century saw little improvement in the condition of Poole's streets as court records reveal. Either the measures that were taken were inadequate or they were overtaken by the pressures of a rapidly growing population. In 1762, the scavengers were presented at the Quarter Sessions for *'leaving large heaps of dirt in every street of the town'* and in 1769, William Hillier was in trouble for *'suffering his Piggs to run about the streets'*. There were other hazards besides avoiding piles of waste. Mr Isaac Carter was presented before the court in 1767 for not repairing his High Street house, occupied by William Godden *'being in a very ruinous & dangerous condition'*. John Scaplen and Robert Henning were accused of impeding the way with their steps and shop windows. More alarmingly, Mr John Oliver was prosecuted in 1770 *'for not paling off or covering a way into the cellar of his new dwelling house being dangerous for persons in the Night time falling therein'*.

Given the sanitary state of the town, it is not surprising that infectious diseases were common. In 1763, a notice appeared in the *Salisbury and Winchester Journal* under the names of the mayor, minister, churchwardens and overseers of the poor. They reassured the readers that the town *'is now intirely free from the Small Pox and has continued so for more than a Fortnight'*. Inoculation was the only preventative measure. This involved infecting the person with a mild form of the disease so that they could build up a resistance to it, but there was also a chance that they could develop a full blown case of the disease. In 1775, the surgeon Bussey Ford advertised in the local newspaper to invite the public to Parkstone House for inoculation. A decade later, Alexander Campbell was accused of *'taking in and Innoculating several Inmates with the smallpox within this town and county'*. These were probably inmates of the poor house, but whether the authorities objected on ethical grounds or more likely on the grounds of health and safety, is not clear. The safer system of vaccination using cowpox was not developed until the end of the century.

If the town streets were in a bad state, the roads out of town were even worse, being *'in a ruinous condition, narrow in many Places and dangerous to Travellers'*. Good land communications were vital to Poole's growing trade and a group of local businessmen and landowners applied for an Act of Parliament under the turnpike legislation, *'for repairing and widening several roads leading from a gate called Poole Gate in the Town and County of Poole'*. The trustees met in the New Inn at Wimborne and later in the Antelope at Poole and their clerk was the High Street attorney, John Oliver. The Act was passed in 1755. Poole Gate, which became the turnpike gate, was on the site of the old towngate in Towngate Lane and from here four main turnpike roads ran out of the town to Coombe Bissett on the London road, to Longham, to Christchurch and to Upton. Most of the turnpike roads used old routes but many were realigned. Today their routes are preserved in Wimborne Road, Ringwood Road, Ashley Road and Blandford Road.

Through the efforts of the trustees, the state of the roads began to improve. By 1763, coach proprietors were able to advertise a service from Poole to London in only two days. The *'New Machine, Hung on steel springs, easy and commodious to carry six Passengers'*, started from the George in Poole and travelled to Romsey, where the passengers spent the night, and on to London the following day. The cost was 25s (£1.25) for inside passengers and half price for outside passengers and children. Other coach services were soon in competition, operating from the Antelope and other inns. High Street became busier than ever with public and private coaches carrying travellers and businessmen, and carts and wagons coming to and from the port.

Andrew Hawkes Poole Photo Archive

The Royal Mail ready to leave for Poole

Of course users of the improved roads had to pay tolls. The rate was 9d (4p) for a coach and six horses or a wagon and four, 6d (21/2p) for a coach and four, 8d (3p) for 20 cows or oxen and so on. On 16th June, 1775, Samuel Western, merchant, Alderman of Poole, J.P. and a Commissioner of the turnpike, was convicted on two counts of fraudulently claiming exemptions to the payment of tolls at the Poole gate, *'a practice he has many years carried on, under various pretences, with great success, till that time.'* The penalty was 40s to £5 for each offence but *'the offender pleading his own folly'*, the justices imposed two fines of 50s (£5 in total).

A lot of the traffic was connected with the business of the port and High Street inns played an important part in this. Not only did they provide accommodation but many of them, the Antelope in particular, were venues for auctions of cargoes brought into port. In 1781, the *London Chronicle* advertised a sale at the Antelope of 37 tons of elephants' teeth and in 1788, it was 1,200 quarters of Danzig wheat, *'the entire cargo of the brig Amy'* to be sold by auction at the Bull Head Inn. Other auctions at the Antelope involved 60,000 feet of Mahogany and 10 tons of logwood from the bay of Honduras in May 1788, and 2,000 barrels of Stockholm tar in September of that year. These sales brought products from across the world into the heart of High Street and generated a great bustle of customers coming to inspect samples of the merchandise or taking away their purchases in carts and wagons.

During the second half of the century, some High Street inns like the White Bear reverted to private houses. Others such as the Old Antelope, the King's Arms and the Bull's Head (as it was now called) continued to flourish. Landlord Philip

Stickland moved from the Old to the New Antelope, his tenancy being taken over by William Whettle. In the early 1760s, John Butler converted his house in the upper High Street to an inn, under the sign of the Angel. This was probably on the site of No. 88, now the Globe Café. Later the inn became the French Horn and Trumpet and by the 1770s it was known as the London Tavern.

The 1760s and 1770s saw the death of some of the 18th century merchants who had dominated Poole affairs for decades. Joseph White died in 1771 at over 80 years of age. His estate included a large trading business with lands, property, ships, boats, goods and stores in Newfoundland. This he planned to keep intact and prosperous by creating a consortium of six men, his great nephew, John Jeffery and five of his Newfoundland agents, Peter and Thomas Street, James and Joseph Randall and William Munday. They were allowed £10,000 capital and empowered to trade for 14 years for their own benefit, before handing over to the heir, his nephew, Samuel White. The firm of Jeffery, Randall and Street, later Jeffery and Street was founded on this basis and prospered. When it was dissolved in 1789, the partners were able to repay Samuel White and divide a considerable capital sum between them.

There was also White's High Street house near the Antelope with its *'kitchen and loft above and the cooperige'* (barrel workshop), two coach houses and a tenement at the back. This was bequeathed to John Jeffery for life and after his death, to Samuel White who was the ultimate beneficiary of the bulk of the estate, believed to be worth £150,000. Joseph's servant, Martha Norman, received an unusually generous legacy of a tenement, an annuity of £12 a year, and the bed and bedstead in the garret of his house *'whereon she usually laid'*.

In 1774, when George Tito died, he left all his lands and property in trust for his grandson, George Tito Brice, to be transferred to him at the age of 24. This included several properties in High Street, in Hampshire and in Newfoundland. The complex terms of his will (and three codicils) contrast with the simple arrangements of Benjamin Mead, basket and chair maker who died in the same year. He left £20 each to his son Benjamin and daughter Mary, his household goods, furniture, stock in trade and utensils to his wife and the residue of his estate to his daughter, Mellior.

Following the death of William Barfoot in 1766 and his wife, Lydia in 1771, the High Street's most magnificent mansion was inherited by their daughter Anna, wife of Anthony Hall, a London merchant. It was probably this house that was advertised to be auctioned at the New Antelope Inn in 1775. The advertisement gives us an idea of what a gentleman's High Street residence was like and which desirable features the vendor wanted to stress:

> *'A very genteel SASHED HOUSE, fifty feet and upwards in front; consisting of a spacious hall, and an elegant stair-case out of the same; two dining-parlours, a*

Borough of Poole Museum Service

The Barfoot house with one wing intact

drawing-room, and a breakfast-room on the first floor; an anti-chamber, over the hall, three very handsome bed-chambers and dressing rooms on the second floor; four very good bed-chambers with closets on the attic storey; and large arched vaults all under the house; several convenient offices such as kitchen, servants' hall, larder and laundry, servants' bed-chambers over and cellars under, with many other conveniences fit for a gentleman's family.'

The property was described as being situated in the middle of High Street with large courtyards front and rear, a walled garden at the back, planted with 'the choicest fruit trees' and an adjoining malthouse. It was to be sold along with another newly built house opposite and a two-acre field let as a garden. In fact the Barfoot mansion was too large for most households and was divided into two in 1777, a division which still remains today.

The last decades of the 18th century were a period of upheaval and change

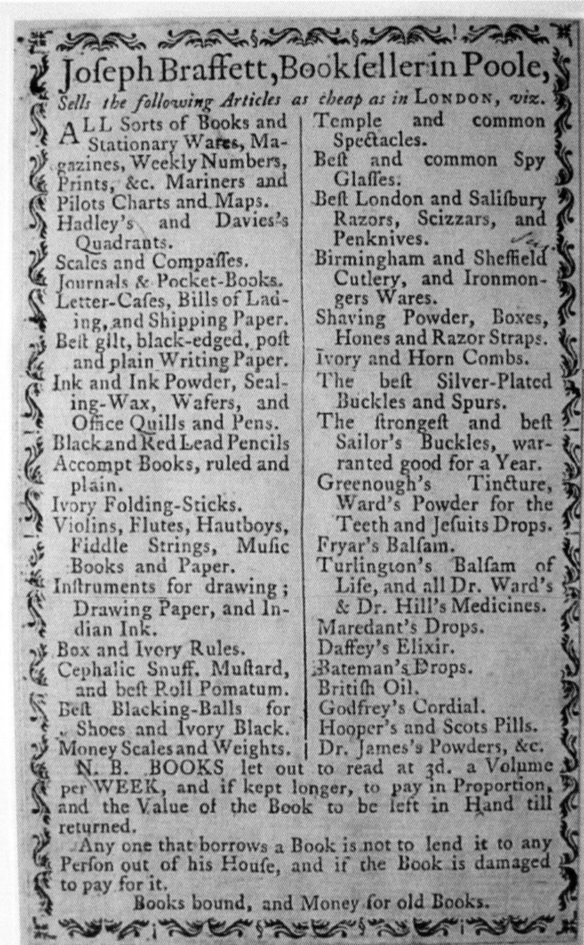

with the battle for independence of the American colonies, revolution in France and the long war against Napoleon. In wartime, large quantities of gunpowder were sometimes stored in Poole, providing a deadly hazard. In 1775, fire broke out in John Hooper's wash house which was next to a cooper's yard where piles of staves and tar were stored. Fortunately, the fire was put out before reaching the yard, but local people were quick to note that a warehouse containing a thousand weight of gunpowder was only a short distance away. The explosion of such a quantity *'would not have left one stone upon another throughout the whole town'*.

In the 1780s, High Street was no more orderly than 50 years before. Benjamin Mead junior had apparently found another source of income besides his father's basket making business. In 1787, he was brought to court for keeping a disorderly house *'in rioting and Drinking to the Disturbance of the Neighbours and others particularly Saturday nights till Sunday Mornings'*. A couple of years later, Mary, wife of John Legg was presented for keeping a disorderly house in High Street and *'breeding Riots to the great offence and disturbance of their neighbours'*. In 1788 a complaint was made against the drivers of carts *'who are wont to walk at a Considerable Distance from the Horses who gallop after them, whereby accidents happen to children and the lives of Passengers are thereby in danger'*. As High Street was not much more than 5 metres wide for most of its length, this must have been a considerable hazard.

Sanitary conditions had not improved either. On 14th April 1788, the Salisbury and Winchester Journal reported that *'putrid fevers and sore throats are very general and very fatal this spring; many people have died of these disorders, particularly at Poole; nor have the poor been the only victims. – Mr. Saunders, an eminent merchant there, and Mr. Welch, Ironmonger, have lately fallen sacrifices.'* The newspaper recommended Doctor Norris's Drops, taken with good port as preventative or cure for all ranks. No wonder patent medicines as sold by Joseph Brassett or bookseller and stationer Joseph Moore, were popular (although not cheap). In 1788, Moore was advertising Mr. Spillbury's Drops at 5s [25p] a bottle as a cure for *'Scurvy, Gout, Rheumatism, Leprosy, Nervous Complaints &c.'*. It is hard to imagine what the drops could have contained to be effective against all these complaints.

Samuel Welch's death was reported in the local press where he was said to have 'left behind him a character worthy the attention of the gentleman, and an example for the tradesman'. His ironmongery stock was sold under the terms of his will and later that year, Welch Hawkins and Co. took out an advertisement in the local press to announce that they *had acquired his stock and also 'laid in a great assortment of IRONMONGERY, CUTLERY, and PLATED GOODS from the original Manufactories; together with a great assortment of pure and unadulterated Teas.'* These were to be sold at Samuel Welch's warehouse in High Street.

It was not the only business changing hands. The same year the *'old accustomed and well known Inn, called the OLD ANTELOPE'* was advertised to let. It was described as having *'many good conveniences for the accommodation of travellers,'* and the inn's location near the busy Quay was stressed. A few weeks later, L. Marchbank put a notice in the press that he had taken over the inn and had laid in a *'large stock of Neat Wines, &c.- He assures those who please to honour him with their commands, that his best exertions will be used for their accommodation'*. The advertisement also mentioned that there was now a daily mail coach to and from London and that a *'neat post chase, with able horses and careful drivers'* was available.

In November 1788, another newspaper notice showed that local residents were aware of events in the wider world. Following the founding of the Committee for the Abolition of the Slave Trade in 1787, the article announced the setting up of a local committee to consider the issue. It was resolved that *'the said trade is impolitic, and highly inconsistent with the Principles of sound Morality, and the Christian Religion'* and that the committee would co-operate zealously with the London society for the abolition of *'so pernicious and inhuman a Traffick'*. The chairman was the Rev. William Davis, Curate of St. James' church. The members appointed to receive subscriptions were three High Street residents, mercer and draper, Thomas Young Bird, now the owner of Peter Hiley's former house, Moses Neave, a hosier and Quaker who also lived in the corn market and leading merchant John Jeffery.

This was no abstract issue in a town where several merchant families had been involved in the trade. As High Street stationer Joseph Moore remarked in his 1788

John Jeffery

History of the Town and County of Poole, several slave voyages had been made by Poole merchants in the 1750s. However, he added, *'the hand of Providence interposed, and put an end to a traffick so repugnant to the dictates of humanity, and to the principles of true religion, but not without enriching a few individuals, some of whom are gone to "that bourn from whence no travellers ever yet returned," and others who now live, enjoying we humbly hope,*

That ease industriously they sought
With minds untortur'd by a poignant thought.'

The following year, issues of liberty were again under debate with the outbreak of the French revolution. British public opinion at first welcomed the overthrow of an oppressive regime. At the very least it was likely to distract and weaken France. However the increasing anarchy in France and the publication of Thomas Paine's *The Rights of Man* in 1791 alarmed the establishment which feared the spread of dangerous radical ideas across the channel. A meeting of inhabitants was held in Poole in 1792 concerning the *'preservation of Liberty and Property against Republicans and Levellers'*. The same year Captain Charles Craufurd of the 2nd Dragoon Guards described in a letter how the regiment had burnt an effigy of Thomas Paine in all the towns where they were quartered, Dorchester, Bridport, Weymouth and Poole.

In January 1793, King Louis XVI died on the guillotine. In February, the French revolutionaries declared war on Britain. Invasion threatened and Poole, with other south coast ports, was on the front line. Large numbers of troops awaiting transport overseas were on the move. Accommodation was required in Poole for 3,000 men, an enormous number considering the town's population was still under 5,000. As there was no large building suitable for a barracks, a large number of small barracks had to be provided throughout the town, including no doubt High Street. For some this presented an opportunity; Poole businessmen like John Jeffery were able to angle for lucrative barracks contracts from the government. Having withdrawn from active participation in his trading business, Jeffery had acquired a country seat, Sans Souci at Lytchett Minster, and turned his attention to local politics. After cutting the necessary deals he was returned unopposed as M. P. for Poole in 1796. He was also to serve as Mayor in 1798.

The presence in the town of thousands of troops was a headache for the authorities. Complaints were presented at the Quarter Sessions court. A *'large Centry box'* was obstructing the pavement in High Street. The chimney of the cook room

Borough of Poole Museum Service

Col. Joseph White Orchard (John Jeffery's brother) in regimental uniform.

at Barrack No. 78 was too low and causing a nuisance and soldiers of the 90th Regiment of Foot were depositing filth in the lane leading to the King's Arms. The fact that there was no general hospital supplied for sick troops and that each regiment had its own military hospital was considered a danger to the health of the inhabitants of the town.

On 14th April 1796, James Scott, surgeon of the 37th Regiment of Foot, was walking in High Street with Mr. McLaine, the orderly officer of the day who was doing his rounds to see that the men were in their barracks. Receiving abuse from a man called Adam Simpson who was walking with two girls, McLaine got involved in a scuffle with him and received several wounds, one *'on the thigh about two inches deep and the other on the chin quite to the bone'*. The outcome might have been worse if McLaine had not been restrained by Scott from drawing his sword.

There was nevertheless a useful side to the presence of the soldiers. When an alarming fire broke out in the town in January 1799, there were plenty of hands available to put it out. The authorities put a notice in the press thanking Wallace's Fencibles, the 2nd Worcestershire Militia and the Royal Horse Artillary for their exertions. Their expression of gratitude was slightly double-edged however, concluding that *'notwithstanding any unfavourable impressions which the misconduct of a few unworthy individuals on any former occasion may have left on the public mind, any general reflections on the character of the Corps will prove equally illiberal and unmerited'*.

The soldiers, with their red jackets and white crossbelts, white breeches and black shakos with red and white plumes, must have added considerable colour to High Street. As one of the few public open spaces in the town, the upper High Street beyond the built up area was probably used for drills and parades and the name 'Parade' for this part of the street seems to date from this period. We can imagine the locals strolling out to view the thrilling and patriotic spectacle of the regiments drilling.

There were other forms of entertainment in Poole at the end of the century. In his diary, merchant Benjamin Lester mentions a regular winter card club held at the Antelope Inn. In 1784, a theatre was opened opposite the Antelope by a theatrical manager named Bowles and various companies ran seasons there over the next couple of decades. An anonymous critic of 1799 had some scathing comments on the quality of the acting. That season's manager, Mr. Lee was said to lack versatility: *'the less he sings, the more the audience will be obliged to him'*. The aging actor Mr Kent had some talents but drank and smoked too much. As for Mr. Woods, his *'elocution, grimace, and more than common effrontery'* reminded the writer of a raree show (peep show). It may not have been very subtle entertainment, but local audiences probably enjoyed it.

There were also subscription assemblies held every three weeks during the winter in the town hall. It was a chance for young ladies of the town to meet and dance with the officers, and some romances may well have begun there. In 1798 and 1799, thirty weddings between local women and soldiers of visiting regiments were celebrated at St James' church.

The war brought inflation and shortages of food and other commodities. In the late 1790s several High Street businesses closed, perhaps hastened by the harsh economic conditions. In January 1799, the premises of Elias Burt, grocer and tea dealer was advertised for sale. The property was described as *'a commodious freehold Messuage, Tenement or Dwelling-house, an old-established Grocer's Shop, Outhouses, Stables and Hereditaments . . . situate in the High-street . . . near the Quay and very eligible for any kind of business where a shew shop is material.'* The sale also included all the stock in trade, furniture and household goods of Mr. Burt.

Later that year the contents of the Antelope Inn came on the market after the failure of W. Whittel (or Whettle) and Son. The list of sale items gives a fascinating glimpse of how the inn was furnished and included *'handsome four-post and other bedsteads and furnitures, featherbeds mattresses, blankets and counterpanes, dining, card, craw and Pembroke tables, chairs, Wilton and Scotch carpets, an excellent eight-day clock, pier and swing glasses, kitchen and stove grates and a variety of kitchen and other furniture'*. All those with demands on the Whittel's estate were told to contact Mr. Durnford, Attorney at Law who had *'engaged to pay the creditors ten shillings in the pound.'*

A few Poole merchants were wealthy enough to be largely unaffected by hard times. In 1797, Samuel White died, leaving an estate estimated at £200,000. His main heirs were his nephews, Samuel Rolles, John Rolls and Samuel Vallis and his great nephew, Samuel White junior. They inherited his extensive lands and property in Newfoundland and £23,000 to be shared between them, and each received properties in Poole or Charlton Marshall. The house in lower High Street which had belonged to Joseph White was left to Samuel Rolles with its coach-house, stables and cooperage, together with two other adjoining tenements known as Wilson's and Gould's.

On the basis of his legacy, Samuel Rolles built the last of the great 18th century High Street mansion houses, now known as Beech Hurst. At the beginning

Jenny Oliver

Beech Hurst

of the century, the Barfoot mansion had been built on what was then the edge of the built up area. John Masters' house in the 1740s was sited still further up High Street. Now Samuel Rolles acquired a 'green field' site opposite the parade for his new home, a sign of how far up the street building now extended. Finished in 1798,

George Garland

Beech Hurst is a striking Georgian brick built mansion of three storeys and cellars with the Rolles coat of arms proudly displayed on the pediment. The elegant proportions of the house give an impression of simplicity which is achieved by many fine details. The pediment is supported by the three central bays which project forward slightly from the outer bays. To emphasise the importance of the main entrance, the ground floor is raised six feet above the street and the door is approached by a flight of steps and protected by a semi-circular porch with four columns. The central windows with their moulded architraves also draw the eye to the imposing entrance. The whole house is a statement of the owner's confidence, wealth and position.

Samuel Rolles was not the only wealthy merchant living on High Street at the end of the century. His brother John, another of Samuel White's heirs, lived at what was probably No. 127/9 with Joseph Garland, corn merchant and Mayor in 1797, living next door. John Master's former mansion house was occupied by Joseph's brother, George Garland who had married Amy, the daughter of leading merchant Benjamin Lester in 1779. The couple had eleven children. Garland was an exceptionally astute businessman well capable of carrying on the vast Newfoundland trading business built up by his father-in-law. He also served as Mayor in 1788 and was to become Poole's M.P. in 1801, although his Parliamentary career seems to have taken second place to his business interests. A few doors away lived Christopher Jolliff, member of another important family of Newfoundland traders. Thomas Durell occupied part of William Barfoot's former mansion and John Jeffery's brother, Joseph White Jeffery (later Orchard) lived across the street. In fact this part of High Street was home to a number of wealthy leading citizens, although their houses neighboured less exalted premises, a malthouse, a brewhouse, warehouses, the Bull's Head Inn and two alehouses, (the Rose and the Globe).

The workshops of coopers, joiners, ironmongers and shipbuilders supplied background noise to the street and the premises of brewers, bakers, butchers and tallow chandlers provided a mixture of smells. Other traders living and working on the street included Thompson and Watts, painters and colourmen, pawnbroker James Furnell, Henry Harris, a bricklayer and a female shoemaker, Elizabeth Mitchell.

At the end of the 18th century, High Street was still a place of contrasts. The Universal British Directory of 1798 described Poole as *'the most considerable port and the populous town in the county'* adding *'The buildings are generally mean and low, but of late years many elegant houses have been erected.'* The same year that the splendid Beech Hurst was completed, complaints were made at the Quarter Sessions about *'the pernicious practice of Mr Wm Burt at the lower end of High Street in heating blubber &c. and exposing rotten fish to the great annoyance of the Neighbourhood by the insufferable smell'*. Even at the upper end of High Street near the site of Samuel Rolles' new house, there was reported to be a *'dangerous pond of water, a great nuisance to the public in general'*. The town was growing fast and its services could hardly cope.

Chapter Six

The Early 19th Century

'for them be ticklish times'

The new century in Poole ushered in a turbulent time of disaffection. Hostilities with France were briefly suspended by the Treaty of Amiens in 1802, but resumed in 1803. The threat of invasion was greater than ever before and Poole, like other south coast towns, was all too aware of Napoleon's Armée d'Angleterre, 130,000 strong, gathering at Boulogne. The government's response was a levée en masse or raising of the mass population to defend the country. Lists were drawn up of all the people capable of fighting and those who would need to be evacuated. Other lists recorded those who owned weapons and tools which could be called upon in case of need for fighting or to keep local roads and bridges in good repair for the Army and spoil them for the enemy.

The Poole lists reveal an amazing number of weapons. Among the High Street residents, Richard Ledgard had twelve swords, four pistols and four firelocks as well as one pitchfork, fourteen felling axes, one pickaxe, six saws, eighteen shovels, one hoe and two chisels. Anchorsmith and ironmonger George N. Allen had 2 swords, 50 pistols, 40 firelocks and many thousands of tools in his stores. Swords and small arms seem to have been common in many households. Other lists showed the numbers of *'Aliens, Quakers and Females of all ages; distinguishing the number who, from Age, Infancy, Infirmity, or otherwise are incapable of active service or of removing themselves in case of Invasion.'* John Scriven, a High Street grocer, for instance, was listed as capable of actual service but he had two people in his household under the age of fifteen who would need evacuating.

In November 1803, 47 men from the Parish of St. James signed a document and pledged to become special constables if the enemy were to invade. These included High Street traders such as butchers Samuel Witteridge and John Lacy, printer Joseph Moore junior, and draper John Sharp. With such preparations made, Poole and other towns in the front line anxiously waited, contemplating the prospect of facing Napoleon's hardened professional troops. The threat remained for two tense years until 1805 when Nelson's victory at Trafalgar established British supremacy at sea. At least 30 Poole sailors fought at the battle.

In spite of the glory of victories like Trafalgar, Poole did not welcome the activities of the navy to impress men into the service. In 1811, for instance, the landlord of the Lion and Lamb, Robert Gillett and his wife and daughter, were in court for attacking and insulting Lieutenant John Marshall who had impressed a seaman in the tap room of the inn. After a scuffle, the two women followed Marshall out on to the street shouting abuse and a noisy mob gathered. On another occasion, Michael Ryan, a midshipman in the Imprest Service was passing the inn when Gillett appeared with a gig *'and attempted to run deponent down. On being asked why he did it, defendant said, "If you don't you like it you might kiss my arse" which he frequently repeated and used many other opprobrious and insulting expressions'.*

Every day life in High Street continued in spite of the war. In 1804, the New Antelope came up for sale. In the advertisement it was described as *'that desirable and well-accustomed INN . . . situate in the centre of the High Street, Poole . . . late the property of Mr. John Stickland deceased. There is a large and convenient yard with commodious stabling, chaise-house, &c. and also a tap house.'* After the death of the draper John Sharp in 1807, his widow Elizabeth attempted to carry on the business and in a newspaper notice she solicited the patronage of her husband's customers *'in her attempt to provide for eight small children'.* Later in the year however, all his stock in trade of linen and woollen drapery and haberdashery was put up for sale followed by his *'substantial brick dwelling house and walled garden'* in High Street, his shop and two warehouses.

Another well-established trader selling up around this time was ironmonger, George Allen, the latest of his family to follow the trade. He occupied John Jeffery's former house and shop in lower High Street, backing on to Cinnamon Lane, with several workshops and stores at the back. These had been used for many years for the different branches of his trade as white-smith, gun-smith, tin-plate-worker and brazier.'He also owned a house, store and anchorsmith's workshop on the Quay, a house and smithy at Hamworthy, land with a barn at Seldown and other land and premises at Parkstone.

At the other end of High Street, Samuel Rolles did not enjoy his splendid mansion for very long as he died in 1809. As he had no sons to inherit, his house was left to his wife Amey during her lifetime and after her death in trust to his four daughters together with the rest of his large estate. His trustees were his wife, his son in law, Thomas Manning and his nephew, Samuel White. Beech Hurst was

Borough of Poole Museum Service

Benjamin Lester Lester

occupied by Samuel's daughter, Dove and her husband Isaac Steel.

John Jeffery continued as Poole's M.P. until 1809 when he acquired the post of British Consul in Lisbon and gave up his seat. His fellow M.P. from 1808 was Mr. Benjamin Lester Lester, son of George Garland. Born Benjamin Lester Garland, he had adopted his grandfather's surname of Lester on becoming his heir. George Garland had trained all his sons in the Newfoundland trade and Benjamin was sent out to Trinity as a young man to learn the business. To his father's disappointment however, he preferred London society and politics to becoming a partner in the business. By serving as Poole's representative he was following in the footsteps of both his father and his grandfather. According to William Mate in his publication *Then and Now,* Lester Lester was a stauch Whig and had a *'character for hospitality and good fellowship'* which *'drew around him a very large circle of friends'.* On his father's death in 1825, Lester Lester inherited his house in High Street, once John Master's mansion. He remained a batchelor but in his will of 1838 he left £3,000 in trust for Jane Moore, single woman of Perry Garden and after her death for her two daughters, Eliza and Amey Anne.

In spite of the war and uncertain economic times, High Street residents continued to enjoy their diversions. By 1805 the theatre had moved from near the Antelope to a location further up the street, probably at what is now No. 96 High Street. A newspaper advertisement for the property in 1820, described *'a substantial well-built commodious Mansion House situated in the most open and airy part of the High Street . . . also a large storehouse near the Mansion House, a part of which is at present filled up and occupied as a theatre . . . and a paved courtyard leading to and fronting Hill Street . . . these premises admeasure 49 feet in front against High Street and 160 feet in depth.'*

That year Mr. James Shatford's company was able to sell out the *'very neat theatre'*, opening on a Saturday evening with two features, *John Bull* and *Love Laughs at Locksmiths*. Plays were shown every Monday, Thursday and Saturday throughout the season for 3s (15p) for a seat in a box, 2s (10p) for the gallery and 1s (5p) for the pit. The High Street theatre was also probably the venue for Mr Gyngell and Company who advertised a full evening of *'highly amusing and instructive entertainments.'* These included magic, juggling, acrobatics, trapeze and musical glasses. Poole residents could attend one of four unique, fun-filled shows. By 1829 a theatre had opened in North Street, ending the era of treading the boards on High Street for a while.

In 1814, the abdication of Napoleon apparently brought to a close the war which had been raging almost continually for over 20 years. The occasion was marked by great celebrations in Poole including a public dinner for 5,000 people in the market place and adjoining streets, followed by a firework display. However, Napoleon's escape from Elba meant that it was not until the victory at Waterloo the following year that peace truly returned. The end of the war was a harbinger of huge change. Wartime had created a false economy and extraordinary conditions when in spite of the dangers, there were big profits to be made by Poole merchants. In the new peacetime economy, foreign competition was resumed, prices and wages plummeted and the economics of the Newfoundland trade were particularly badly hit.

Many of the merchant families found themselves in financial difficulties and by choice or necessity reduced their involvement in the Newfoundland trade. Some moved away to their country estates, bought in the days of prosperity. In the depressed conditions, many discharged servicemen could not find employment. A feeling of discontent permeated throughout the town and the country and only one year after the end of the war the national debt had reached £900 million. The decline of Poole's economy was so acute that in 1829 the town's businessmen had to fight off a threatened withdrawal of the mail coach service to London.

In 1801 the population of Poole had been 4,761; by 1821 it had risen to 6,390, no doubt increased by returning servicemen and planters fleeing hard times in Newfoundland. A map of the town produced for the Canford Enclosure Award of 1822 showed considerable changes to the town since the previous map of the 1760s. High Street was now built up for almost all its length, the only open space being a couple of closes just south of what is now Lagland Street. Even the Parade at the north end of town was filled with rows of houses on both sides, and many tenements, stores and workshops had been built in gardens behind the High Street houses.

In 1830, the *Dorset County Chronicle* reported a spate of burglaries and Ledgard, Welsh and Co. of Poole Town and County Bank were one of the victims. From 1821, the bank had operated from No. 87 High Street, half of what had been William Barfoot's mansion house. The thieves who attempted robbery in 1830 removed roof slates and created a hole in the ceiling. They then descended into the

Andrew Hawkes Poole Photo Archive

The Antelope. (In the background is Poole's subscription library)

bank but were disturbed before they could steal anything. The next night saw a house on Lagland Street also being broken into, although nothing was taken and no one was caught. The newspaper noted *'we are sorry to observe that for some weeks past the streets of this town have been infested with strangers of the very lowest grades of society: principally under the pretence of selling matches, small penny tracts etc: if the public, however refuse to purchase articles of these itinerant traders, they would soon be effectually stopped.'* The strangers 'infesting' the town were probably the displaced and unemployed, an all too common sight since the end of the war fifteen years earlier.

In spite of the recession, High Street was still a busy place for traffic. The 1830s were the peak time for coaching and certainly no-one living in lower High Street could have enjoyed a peaceful lie-in. Every morning at six o'clock, with the exception of Sunday, the coach named the Age was loaded up at the Antelope with passengers, bags and horses ready to start for London. At six thirty on Tuesdays, Thursdays and Saturdays, the Wellington would depart for Bath and Bristol. On its way out of town, each coach had to navigate the narrow street and make the sharp turn into Towngate Lane. The London Tavern was another departure point for travellers. The Independent coach arrived at half past one in the afternoon every day except Sunday en route to Southampton from Weymouth, and to add to the noise and bustle, the coach travelling from Southampton to Weymouth arrived at the same time. Carriers' wagons going to London, Lymington and Southampton on Tuesdays and Fridays used the Bull's Head as their depot.

Although coach travel made the wider country accessible and allowed freedom for the public, it was an uncomfortable way to travel and not without hazard. In 1826 the Poole mail coach was robbed, the thieves getting away with the coach and three horses. The winter of 1836-7 was one of the worst for coaching. Unprecedented wild snow storms meant that coaching routes throughout the country were closed for almost a week, fourteen coaches were abandoned and only the Poole and Portsmouth routes remained open. Accidents were common. It was reported in 1817 that the Poole mail coach had been upset between Stoney Cross and Ringwood *'by the horses having taken fright and become unmanageable'*. Fortunately, no-one was injured on that occasion. In the crowded High Street, pedestrians were at risk. On the 31st December 1844, Ann Waterman was knocked down in High Street by the Emerald coach, drawn by four horses and very heavily laden. The near leading horse forced Ann to the ground and the coach ran over her legs and *'bruised'* them. *'She lived until 2nd January 1845 when she died, languishing from the bruises.'*

For years from 1818 onwards the Poole Turnpike Trustees had proposed driving High Street right through into Longfleet to make a more direct and convenient entrance to the town for wheeled traffic. In the 1830s this was finally achieved and the road was extended from the corner of Water Street (North Street) along the line of the former footpath to the junction with Towngate Street and on to the George Inn, Longfleet where the roads to Wimborne and Ringwood diverged. The ropewalk formerly operated by Richard Ledgard and Son *'across the Highway near the Turnsyle at the entrance of the Town'* had to be relocated. This extension of High Street meant that vehicles gained a straight run in and out of town and could avoid the tight turn towards the town gate. The tollhouse and gate were moved from the site of the old towngate to an area in front of the George Inn. Once again High Street became the primary route in and out of town after languishing as a dead end for almost three hundred years.

Longfleet had once been occupied only by a few scattered cottages and an old inn, the Port Mahon Castle (probably named after a British victory of 1708). In the early decades of the 19th century however, rows of cottages and villas began to spring up there for people escaping the overcrowded streets of the old town. According to Robson's 1839 *Directory of the Western Counties, 'The old town, with the exception of some meadows on the east, is covered with streets. The modern extension of the buildings lies chiefly on the side of Longfleet, and an important suburb has sprung up in this tything, containing at the present time many good houses, and their number is rapidly increasing along the Ringwood and the Wimborne Roads.'* The removal of the barrier to traffic

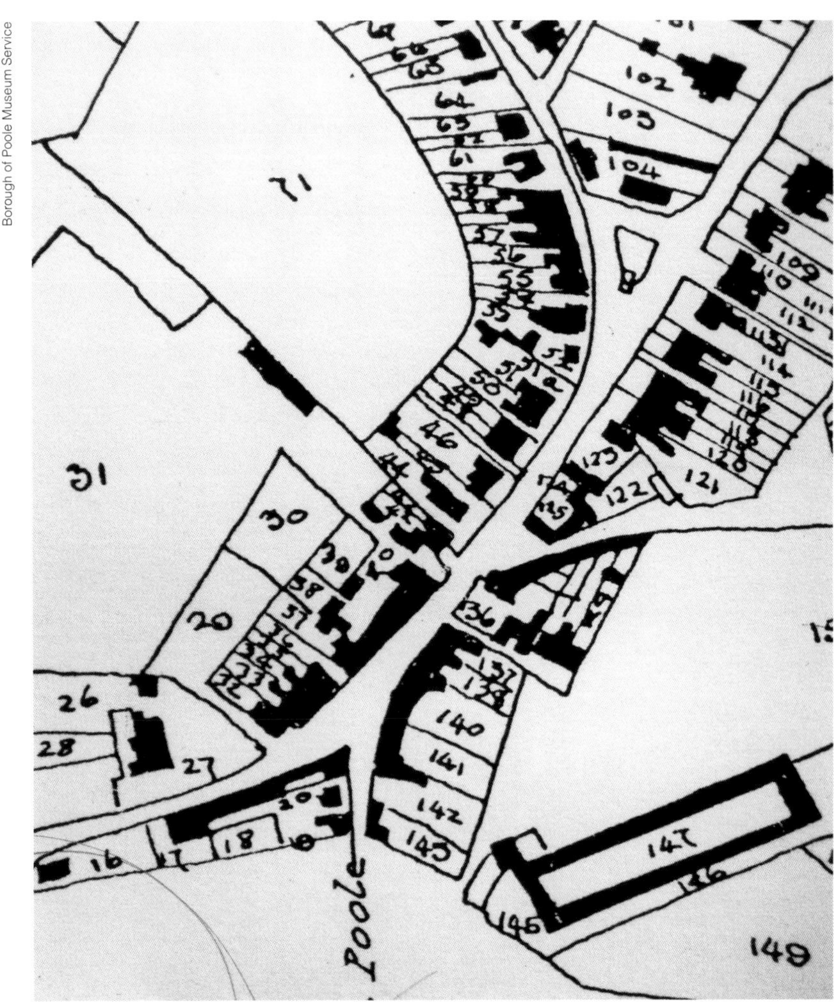

Borough of Poole Museum Service

Longfleet tithe map, 1844.

between Poole and Longfleet provided a further impetus to this development. By 1844, the tithe map showed building on both sides of the street up to and beyond the George Inn. At this date the Longfleet section of High Street was predominantly residential. Apart from Balston's rope and twine works, a solitary shop run by Peter Palmer *'baker and shoemaker'*, and a couple of carpenter's workshops, all the buildings were cottages, houses and villas.

The year 1830 was an eventful year in Poole and the rest of the country. On 15th July, shops were closed for the funeral of George IV, bells tolled and flags flew at half mast in the harbour. The accession of William IV meant a fresh election on 30th July. In Poole the current Members, the Honourable W. F. S. Ponsonby and Mr. Benjamin Lester Lester put themselves up for re-election and were returned unopposed. Events later that night showed how lively Poole elections could be even when there were no burning issues to divide the parties.

When the election closed, Ponsonby and Lester treated their supporters to a dinner at the Old Antelope Inn where many toasts were drunk and the company got very noisy. As it was a hot night, the windows were open and a crowd which had gathered outside could hear all that was going on. It was said that someone threw a glass of wine over the crowd below but for whatever reason, some people in the street began to throw stones, breaking every front window of the inn. Inside, tables were overturned, glasses and decanters broken and the M.P.'s appealed in vain for order. Some of the crowd attempted to climb in through the upstairs bay window and were at first pushed back, until those inside decided instead to grab the invaders and pitch them head first down the stairs. Fortunately, no-one was badly hurt and the hosts were able to settle the bill for repairs.

Presumably the inn was soon restored to order because the next month the Antelope housed some important guests from France. The deposed King Charles X, having fled his country, arrived at Hamworthy aboard the Royal Navy steamboat *Meteor*. The exiled King viewed the crowds with some trepidation but the *Dorset County Chronicle* recorded that he was received in a *'kindly manner'* by *'the warm-hearted inhabitants of Poole.'* The King was taken to Lulworth Castle but some members of his entourage were accommodated at the Antelope and the London Tavern. As the *Chronicle* reported with some excitement, *'the Duchess of Angouleme, with her retinue, remained at the Antelope Hotel. The houses of B. L. Lester Esq. M. P. for this town and of D. O. Lander Esq., were offered for her temporary residence here, but she was so well accommodated at the Hotel, and pleased with the attention of Mrs Claridge, that she declined their kind offers.'* In October, Charles passed through the town once again to board the Admiralty's steam packet, *Lightning* en route to Scotland where it was felt he would be safer.

At the end of 1830, an institution opened in High Street to gratify what the *Dorset Country Chronicle* called *'the literary and scientific taste which prevails in the town'*. This *'long wished for institution'* was a public library to be provided by the generosity of Poole's M.P.s. Mr Lester Lester donated the site (where the Poole Museum entrance now stands) and the Hon. Ponsonby provided the building. In November 1830, the *Dorset County Chronicle* described the design:

> *'The front of the library is to be supported on a series of arches, forming a piazza. The superstructure will be next, and the central part will have three recessed windows of good dimensions; and crowned with a low pediment. The sides are to be of white brick and finished with a blocking course. The internal arrangements are - on the ground floor, a shop, sitting and sleeping rooms for the librarian, and a commodious staircase to the library, which is a good sized room 13 feet in height, and contains five large windows. The whole length of the premises is 43 feet and the width of 24.'*

The public library was to be sustained by annual subscriptions and donations. In the event, as John Sydenham pointed out, *'the number of subscribers is not so great as*

Borough of Poole Museum Service

The subscription library later in the century with the corn store on the left and the Antelope opposite.

might have been anticipated from the extent of the population of the town and its neighbourhood. The number of books now belonging to the institution does not exceed 1700.' The disappointing number of subscribers could have stemmed from the recession, or perhaps there were too few books to tempt people to join. It seemed that the literary tastes of the people of Poole had been overestimated. However, the library continued for over 60 years until the opening of the public library service in 1886.

In the 1830s there was a resurgence of church attendance and new churches were being dedicated in several parts of the borough, often to accommodate social divisions between merchants and tradesmen. In the old town the expanding population could not comfortably fit into the new St. James' Church, built only a decade before. To ease the situation and cater for residents to the east of High Street, the Church of St Paul was opened in 1833 at the upper end of the street. St Paul's was described as a small, neat structure in the Grecian style with 700 seats, 200 of which were free. The west end of the church contained a gallery housing the organ provided by a subscription among the congregation. At the east end was a small chancel and on either side were galleries used by the Sunday School children. A tower stood at the east front of the church. The cost of the land and building the church amounted to over £4,000 and it was a testimonial to the new congregation's dedication that the sum was raised through voluntary contributions. There was also a political dimension. The new church was sponsored by the Tory faction and one of its chief opponents was the Rev. Peter Jolliffe, rector of St. James' Church, who came from a traditionally liberal family.

The consecration of the church on 17th January 1833 was reported in the *Dorset County Chronicle. 'At ten o clock the doors of the Church were opened and it was soon filled in every part with a congregation, comprising many of the most respectable families in the town.'* These included *'George Welsh Ledgard Esq., the liberal founder of the Church'.* Dr. Gray, the Bishop of Bristol, performed the consecration and dedication of the church. The Chronicle concludes: *'On leaving the Church, the Bishop, clergy, and a large party of friends, returned to the residence of G. W. Ledgard Esq., to partake of a dejeune provided for them . . . The Church which was thus auspiciously opened . . . is an elegant structure, and both in the exterior and interior exhibits evidences of superior tastes.'*

The early Parish Records from St. Paul's allow a glimpse of the congregation. Fittingly, the first child baptised at the church on 6th March 1833 was Louisa Ledgard, daughter of George Ledgard, the church's founder, and his wife Martha. The baptism records show the fathers' occupations and it seems that in the early years of the church the congregation were made up of the more affluent High Street traders such as bankers, shoemakers, tailors, butchers and bakers.

Another achievement during the 1830s was the installation of gas street-lighting, although not without the usual political squabbles. To celebrate the start of the new service on 10th March 1834, the directors of the Gas and Coke Company resolved to *'assemble at the gas works, at half-past seven o'clock and proceed from thence in procession through the town, terminating their perambulation at the Antelope Inn at 9 o'clock where the Directors will sup together.'* The shareholders were also invited. The paving of the main streets was also improved in the first decades of the century under the Highway Acts and *Robson's Directory of the Western Counties 1839* was able to report that *'the principal streets are well-paved and lighted with gas'.*

The Corporation also attempted to widen High Street to relieve the congestion. This was particularly difficult in the lower part of the street which was closely lined with old buildings. In 1832, the Corporation sold a house and two other properties in lower High Street, backing on to Cinnamon Lane, to Robert Turtle, *'saving and excepting such parts of the messuages as shall be necessary to widen the High Street, which said parts measure 675 superficial feet.'* It is not clear whether this particular work was ever carried out but some widening was achieved in upper High Street. Samuel Lewis's *Topographical Dictionary of England 1848* recorded that *'considerable improvements have been made by the corporation, who recently expended £1500 in the purchase of houses, that have been taken down in order to widen the High-street.'*

In the 1830s, political change was in the air in both parliamentary and municipal affairs. There was a strong party in Poole in favour of parliamentary reform and when the Reform Act was passed in 1832, there were enthusiastic celebrations.

Andrew Hawkes Poole Photo Archive

St Paul's Church and adjoining houses

Church bells were rung, bands paraded the streets, flags were hoisted and banners hung out from the windows of private houses. The reform extended the franchise to those whose houses were rated at more than £10, adding 412 new voters to the original burgesses and removing the long domination of the merchants, the traditional leaders of Poole society. Because of boundary changes, voters from parts of Longfleet, Parkstone and Hamworthy were also now included, bringing the franchise to 460. The introduction of the Municipal Corporations Act in 1835 meant that a new elected council took the place of the old self-elected corporation of burgesses.

The new voters included over forty High Street traders such as chemist, James Hamilton, printer and bookseller, John Sydenham and boot and shoemaker, Charles Cox. Drapers, grocers, ironmongers, builders, innkeepers and plumbers were all included in the new register and so many new voters with new interests and ideas were bound to bring changes. One of the first signs was the election of George Penney as the first Liberal Mayor in 1840.

Penney was a prominent Poole citizen and a leading reformer. He was also a Quaker, a member of the Poole Corporation from 1830 and a magistrate from 1838. Ivy House, his three-storey, detached home in High Street (now No. 151) was probably built around 1817. George and Sarah Penney married in that year and moved into the house just before the birth of their first child, George Robert, in 1818. George Penney's niece described him in a letter as *'a decided Friend, but not a very strict one. He attended the Friends' meeting all his life. He was rather tall and very handsome - a perfect gentleman & Christian, thoroughly true & honourable and very kind hearted.'* The book *Ebb Tide at Poole* shows that George Penney was not always very enamoured of Poole as he is quoted as saying *'I do not participate with thee in thy love for our 'Noble Town and County'. Tis a very poor place.'*

Sadly, the euphoria of reform soon gave way to political in-fighting which reduced the Council to near bankrupcy and more or less paralyzed public affairs in Poole for years. In the 1840s the reformer Alexander Somerville visited the town and noted its derelict and depressed state: *'Between six and seven thousand inhabitants, with empty houses for the accommodation of many more. Warehouses and workshops shut up, the unopened doors and shutters worn with weather, not with work.'* The quay was quiet and almost deserted apart from a farmer trying to sell a few bundles of straw to a local inn keeper, or else take it home and go without his beer *'for them be ticklish times'*. It was a fair assessment of the recession-hit town of those years.

In 1841, the first detailed census revealed thirty four uninhabited properties in High Street. The census provided a comprehensive overview of residents and gave a glimpse inside people's households for the first time. All components of society from paupers to landed proprietors could be found on High Street. The Parade had the largest number of people of 'independent means', although this area was no longer as exclusive as in the days of Samuel Rolles. Many working people and small traders also lived there, like labourer Herbert Reeves and tailor William Hindle with his wife Jane and their six children. Their home was one of the small shops built in the Parade in the late 18th century and not very spacious for a family of eight. With William's tailoring supplies occupying part of the limited space, the family must have lived a crowded existence.

Some of the large High Street mansions were occupied by professionals such as banker Richard Ledgard who lived and ran his business in half of William Barfoot's former mansion. He was a bachelor and his household consisted of himself, his mother Susannah and two servants. Next door lived James Kemp, member of an important family of former Newfoundland merchants. His family of four was cared for by three servants. Surgeon Thomas Salter probably lived at No. 125, a large house dating from the previous century, with his wife, four children, his assistant and two servants. Next door in No. 127/9, was a school run by Robert Oake and his wife, Caroline. Also listed were Timothy and Mary Oake, probably Richard's parents, two younger siblings, the school usher and twenty one pupils aged between ten and fifteen. As there were no live-in servants to cater to this household of 28 people, presumably all the family was involved in keeping the school functioning.

Borough of Poole Museum Service

Ivy House

The bulk of High Street inhabitants were traders: grocers, drapers, ironmongers, confectioners, bakers, hairdressers and other shopkeepers like chemist James Hamilton. He had been practicing on High Street from at least the 1820s, as trade directories show. In the 1840s his shop was at No. 101 (now probably No. 69 or 71) where he lived with his wife Elizabeth, two sons, Horatio and Julius, and one servant. In 1841 almost all High Street shopkeepers and traders still lived over their shops and businesses. Many also manufactured at least some of their own goods and the Hamilton family probably made many of their pills and medicines. Traders' premises would have to accommodate home, shop, workshop and store and must have provided very tight living quarters for large families. John Lankester's book and stationery shop at No. 82 for instance, was home to himself, his wife, six children and a servant.

High Street residents also included some living in poverty. Close neighbours of the Hamiltons were Mary Bannen, described as a pauper, Mary Shean, charwoman and Sarah Marsh, who was supporting her three children aged eight, seven and two as a laundress. Women who found themselves on their own had often to turn to trades which did not require capital or large premises and were the most likely to struggle to make ends meet.

According to John Sydenham in his 1839 *History of the Town and County of Poole,*

A busy High Street showing the old Post Office

'The town of Poole presents to the stranger a very favourable appearance. The streets are, in general, wide, well paved, and remarkably clean.' He continued: *'public improvements . . . have been effected within the last twenty years, and are in addition to that general enhancement of appearance that has naturally resulted from the increase of population, and the expansion of private spirit and speculation.'* This was probably a rather glorified version of reality.

The previous few decades had seen a great deal of change in Poole, not all of it for the better. By the 1840s, the Poole peninsula of around 170 acres was home to 6,500 people. The town had lost its identity as a prominent trading port and was still suffering hard financial times, while those who had ruled the town for so long had lost their control of affairs. High Street was no longer a desirable location for Poole's leading citizens to build mansion houses and in fact some of the existing large houses were in commercial use or transformed into multiple dwellings to deal with the boom in population. Some improvements had been made in widening, paving and lighting but High Street was still an overcrowded and dirty place by modern standards.

Chapter Seven

Victorian Times

'nothing but decadence, deterioration and disgust.'

The election of the first Liberal mayor in 1840 was a sign of a new era. Something of a 'shopocracy' was emerging, a powerful grouping of middle class shopkeepers, traders and businessmen who were mainly members of the Liberal Party. The voice of the Liberals in the town was also heard through the pages of the *Poole and Dorsetshire Herald*, established in 1846 and produced in the heart of High Street. In the early 1800s, its founder John Sydenham had come from Devon to work for his uncle, Joseph Moore, a well-established stationer, printer and bookseller on High Street. In 1805, he married Joseph's daughter, Elizabeth, and eventually became a partner in the business. When Joseph Moore died in 1819 at the age of 83, John Sydenham carried on the business with his cousin Joseph Moore junior at the same premises, (the present No. 67).

The Sydenhams had eight children of whom four died quite young. The oldest surviving son, John junior, was trained in the business which by now included journalism as Moore's acted as local correspondents for the *Salisbury and Winchester Journal.* In 1825, Moore and Sydenham became part owners of the *Dorset Chronicle* and John Sydenham junior worked on the newspaper as a journalist. In 1829 (aged 22), he became its editor.

John junior was a man of many talents, interests and activities, in spite of suffering bouts of ill health through asthma. As a journalist, he was deeply involved in the issues of the day, including parliamentary reform. He was also a keen local historian and began researching and writing a history of Poole, following in the footsteps of his grandfather Joseph Moore who had published a brief history in 1788. In 1833, John married Anna Christiana Zilwood and they had three children.

The *History of the Town and County of Poole* was published in 1839 and is still a vital source of detailed information on Poole's past.

In 1842, John Sydenham senior sold his interest in the Chronicle and in 1846 launched the *Poole and Dorsetshire Herald* with his son as editor. The first edition came out on 9th April 1846, printed on the presses in the rear of the No. 67. At last Poole had a truly local voice. Sadly, John junior died a few months later at the age of only 39. A couple of years later, the newspaper was sold to local solicitors, Martin Kemp-Welch and Henry Mooring Aldridge and then to James Tribbett a printer and publisher. William Mate, a young printer from Ringwood, became Tribbett's partner in 1853.

There was plenty for the new newspaper to report such as the battle to connect Poole to the growing railway network. By the 1840's the golden age of coaching was coming to an end and the coach no longer set out daily from the Antelope Inn with maximum bustle and importance for the long run to London. Instead by 1842, according to Pigot's Directory, the *Union* coach which left the Antelope and the London Tavern at 7.00 am. went no further than Southampton where it met the train for London, so that the passengers could complete their journey with greater comfort and speed. In 1847, the railway at last reached Poole (or rather Hamworthy) at the end of a branch from the Southampton to Dorchester Railway. This first station at lower Hamworthy served Poole and the growing town of Bournemouth for the next 25 years.

William Furmage, the landlord of the London Tavern Inn, was one of the people quick to see the opportunities of the railway. A horse-drawn omnibus service from the London Tavern met every train *'day and night'* and a daily omnibus went from the inn to and from Bournemouth. At this date, the Antelope's landlord, George Knight, could still count on trade from the Wellington coach which left the inn three days a week for Bath, but the expansion of the railway was inexorable and the days of coaching were numbered.

In 1847 the newspaper reflected on a High Street which *'though tenanted by respectable and wealthy shopkeepers, gives no idea of its large trading character and in which houses may be seen almost nodding to a sudden fall.'* Overcrowded houses were now densely packed along streets essentially no cleaner than they had been 50 years before. Although the first Public Health Act came into existence in 1848 with the aim of improving sanitary conditions, its measures were not compulsory and only towns with very high death rates were required to comply. Poole was not in this category and the authorities did not see the need to adopt the Act.

In summer 1849, Poole suffered the consequences of poor sanitation. On 18th June, St. James' parish registers recorded the burial of James Joseph Wills age 3. The next day, a Mrs Hescroff was buried at Skinner Street Congregational Church,

POOLE.

At a Vestry duly holden this seventh day of November, 1832, at the usual place, for the parish of Saint James in the Town and County of Poole, pursuant to Public Notice, for the purpose of forming a Local Board of Health in this Town, in conformity to a Letter received from the Central Board of Health, Council Office, dated 3rd inst.—

Mr. JOHN ADEY, *Churchwarden,*
IN THE CHAIR:

Proposed by Mr. GEORGE PENNEY, Seconded by Mr. GEORGE KEMP, and unanimously Resolved,

That the present state of the General Health of this Town is not of such a nature as to require a BOARD OF HEALTH to be Established, and that therefore, such an establishment is totally inexpedient.

Proposed by Mr. GEORGE HANCOCK, and Seconded by Mr. JAMES BRISTOWE,

That the above Resolutions be published in The Dorset County Chronicle, and The Salisbury and Winchester Journal; a Copy forwarded to the Lords of the Council, and the Central Board of Health, and that Copies be printed and published throughout the Town.

JOHN ADEY,
Chairman.

MOORE AND SYDENHAM, PRINTERS, POOLE.

In the 1830s, the authorities had rejected the idea of a local Board of Health

with the cause of death recorded as cholera. The *Poole and Dorset Herald* of 21st June reported the fatalities: *'Considerable alarm was excited in this town on Saturday last, by a report that the much dreaded Asiatic Cholera had made its appearance here but happily this is not the case, although there have been two fatal cases of English Cholera.'* Adopting a reassuring tone, the newspaper argued that *'both these parties were predisposed to disease and the child in particular was very much emaciated; had they been of good constitution there is no doubt that the attack would have terminated differently.'*

Even so the whisper of cholera had prompted the Mayor, Richard Ledgard, to issue handbills urging the people of Poole to *'assist in cleansing and keeping the gutters etc. in a wholesome state.'* He asked all householders to throw at least six buckets of clean water into the gutters in front of their houses between eight and nine o'clock every morning. The virtues of cleanliness and proper ventilation were also strongly recommended. On 27th June, Mary Ann Hescroff, was buried at Skinner Street Congregational Church, another victim of cholera.

As with the 'putrid fevers' of the previous century, High Street traders were not slow to see a business opportunity even in these frightening circumstances. The *Poole and Dorset Herald* for 28th June 1849 carried a large advertisement on the front page from J. B. Bloomfield probably trading from No. 48, offering the recommended anti-cholera medicines for sale. In the same newspaper correspondence from 'PUBLICOLA' debated the sanitary state of Poole which, the letter suggested, fell below standards which the public had a basic right to expect: *'What is the condition of the High Street? Is it not decidedly bad? Gutters, emptying the most solid of their varied contents into open cesspools (which may be termed 'ingenious contrivances for diffusing the most noxious gases, the breath of pestilence and the seeds of death').'* The writer castigated the Poole authorities for allowing *'this prolific evil in the principal thoroughfare, causing it to be inhaled by multitudes of people.'*

Meanwhile, cholera brought tragedy to High Street boot and shoe maker, John Weeks and his wife Louisa. On 30th June, Skinner Street Church recorded the burial of Amy Weeks, aged two and Fanny Weeks, aged four and a half, victims of cholera. Harriet Weeks (six) was buried on 2nd July and George Weeks (fifteen) on 3rd. On the 5th July, Louisa followed them to the grave and the clerk recorded the cause of death as *'Cholera (or grief?)'*. John Weeks had lost half of his family and their mother. In 1851 he was listed on the census as a widower with four surviving children, Louisa, David, John and Elizabeth aged two to fifteen. The fatal spread of cholera was probably helped by the cramped conditions of their living arrangements in lower High Street.

By 12th July 1849 the cholera had passed, due in part to the quick thinking and decisive action taken by the authorities plus a providential change in the weather. The *Poole and Dorset Herald* praised the sanitary measures taken to curb the spread of the disease: *'the drains of all kinds have been thoroughly cleaned, and copious streams of water daily poured down them.'* The epidemic had pushed cleanliness and sanitation to the forefront of public attention, but the sad fact was that dirty streets, infectious diseases and the death of children were too common at the time to be very remarkable. The struggle to introduce better sanitary conditions was to continue throughout the century.

The census returns of 1851 provided more details about High Street and its residents. In 1841 twenty residents had been listed as merchants or living on independent means. By 1851 this figure had halved and out of the ten, three were corn merchants, two ship-owners and only five residents declared that they were living on private means. In 1841 there were 363 people employed in retail in Poole; by 1861 this figure had risen to 625. A shift was occurring in Poole society. The long established industries and wealthy merchant families were moving out, dying out or going out of business and were being replaced by new trades and a fresh generation of manufacturers and traders, many of them newcomers to the town. After the severe recession of the early 1800s, some prosperity was at last returning to High Street.

One of the most important businessmen in the street in 1851 was Thomas Wanhill, described as a ship-owner, ship-builder and clay merchant employing in total 147 men and 5 boys. By 1861, he had added alderman and magistrate to his portfolio, having served as mayor in the late 1840s. Together with George Penney, he operated a fleet of coasters between Poole and London. With his brother, James Manlaws Wanhill, he was also involved in the less traditional enterprise of building racing yachts. In 1845, the 35 ton cutter *Heroine*, built by Wanhill, caused a sensation by beating *Alarm*, a 193 ton giant cutter owned by Mr. Weld of Lulworth Castle which had been the champion racing yacht in England for several years. Three Wanhill yachts, *Bacchante*, *Freak* and *Eclipse* also competed in the first America's Cup race of 1851 and *Secret*, *Diadem* and *Egeria* went on to win hundreds of trophies. The success of the Wanhill vessels depended on their fine lines, raked stern posts, reduced beam and the use of lead ballast to balance a large sail area. Their last yacht, *Thalia*, launched in 1888, is still sailing today.

Another large employer was William Pearce who had come to Poole in 1840 and set up as an ironmonger at No. 91 High Street. He also started a foundry between South Road and Green Road in a disused rope works and by 1851, was employing 40 men making agricultural implements and other ironware. He joined the leading Liberal group on the Council and later served as mayor. Like Thomas Wanhill, he represented a new breed of Poole businessmen who were finding fresh opportunities to replace those associated with the almost defunct Newfoundland trade.

More typical of the majority of High Street traders was Richard Cull Hopkins, a grocer at No. 39 High Street. His shop in the corn market, now demolished, was a substantial building with five windows across the façade. It dated from the 16th century but had been refurbished in the 18th century and given a new shop front in Victorian times. This building accommodated the Hopkins family, the shop, the stock, and by 1851 maybe some of the staff employed by Richard, three men and one boy. Philip Brannon's 1855 *Guide to Poole* describes Hopkins as *'not only a tea dealer and grocer but also a tallow chandler, selling both sperm and wax candles. On the same premises you could fill up your bag with fish sauces and pickles, cigars and fancy snuffs, and round off the day with a Guinness's Dublin porter, for which he was sole agent, to be consumed, one presumes,*

Andrew Hawkes Poole Photo Archive

Hawkes' early shopfront

off the premises.' Like many High Street traders, Hopkins was a member of the town council, serving as Sheriff in 1851. When he died in 1868, leaving an estate of up to £4,000, the *Poole and Dorset Herald* described him as *'an old and a highly respected inhabitant of Poole'*. His son Samuel V. Hopkins took over the family business.

Another High Street tradesman to prosper in the mid 19th century was master boot and shoemaker, Joseph Charles Hawkes. He established his first shop around 1847 at what is probably now No. 104 High Street, but as the business grew, he moved across the street to the current No. 99. Joseph Hawkes was an expert leather cutter and specialised in hand-made thigh- and knee-length oiled leather fishing boots, hob-nailed agricultural or navy boots and elastic sided walking boots. The business also bought in factory-made boots and shoes from Clark's, 'K' Shoes and others, to provide customers with a wide range of branded products. By 1861, Hawkes was employing 21 men, 8 women and 3 boys.

Establishing a niche market was important in the competitive Victorian High Street. A stock list from grocers Smith and Goodchild emphasises their expertise as quality tea dealers with a list of *'Genuine Teas'*, described as good, fine, full-flavoured and strong. A customer could not only browse the tea selection but could also purchase luxuries such as coffee, chocolate, candy, raisins, figs, almonds and olives besides non-food items like candles, snuff, tobacco, soap, paper, wax and gunpowder.

The attitude of shopkeepers towards their customers, at least in advertisements, was one of extreme deference. They also liked to stress their knowledge of the trade and their ability to buy in quality goods at reasonable prices. An advertisement by Brine Brothers and Company's Tea and Family Grocery Establishment at No. 94 High Street was typical. They *'beg respectfully to inform the inhabitants of Poole . . . they have now received their NEW FRUITS of this SEASON which will be found unusually fine to former years, and having been enabled to purchase from the Market, under peculiarly advantageous terms, they are enabled to offer them at prices which, for the quality, will defy competition.'* The fruits in question included French plums, muscatels, shell and Jordan almonds, Turkey figs, Valencia raisins, Normandy pippins and Spanish nuts.

Shops were open six days a week for long hours, designed to catch the trade of working people whose hours were also long. Most shopkeepers would also deliver goods to their customers, the delivery cart serving as a mobile advertisement for their establishment. Some who delivered further afield would keep a horse; hence the odd occupation of 'butcher's groom' mentioned in the census.

When an Exhibition of Works of Industry and Art was held in the Town Hall in August 1854, it was an opportunity for High Street traders to display their choicest wares. Chemist J. B. Bloomfield, secretary of the Town and County Library and Literary Institute which organised the exhibition, naturally had a stall there himself. Another exhibitor was bookseller and stationer, Richard Sydenham, John Sydenham's youngest son who displayed examples of book binding, ivory, pearl and leather goods, *'papier maché articles, ladies' reticules, inlaid with steel ornaments &c.'* Robert Jeffery had brought a number of firearms from his *'gun, rifle and pistol manufactury'* opposite the Literary Institute, and two historic brass cannon captured by Nelson at the Battle of Copenhagen were lent by corn merchant Tom Rickman. Other attractions for the visitors included a case of jewellery set up by the High Street jeweller, Henry Selfe, rich silk dresses, Honiton lace and artificial flowers from Mr S. Hussey, draper, and examples of rope work manufactured by George Penney.

Andrew Hawkes Poole Photo Archive

Art works were lent by some of Poole's leading citizens. Lady Charlotte Guest of Canford contributed items from her ceramic collection. Poole's M.P., H. D. Seymour. lent curios from his travels and Colonel Waugh of Brownsea Island

Borough of Poole Museum Service

The Poole Exhibition of Industry and Art held at the Georgian Guildhall, Poole, on 19th August, 1854.

exhibited two urns from Pompeii. There were also examples of craft from local residents like Miss Cole of High Street who displayed *'a representation of Bolton Abbey in the olden time, 6 feet by 5 feet'* in Berlin wool work. Less massive was a piece of needlework by Miss Bloomfield, depicting Michelangelo in the Vatican and a mahogany chess table painted by Mrs. Hopkins. With paintings, models, fossils, stuffed birds, and many other curiosities, there was plenty for the bonneted and top-hatted visitors of the day to admire.

To sustain them during their visit, a refreshment court had been set up in the Council Chamber, supplied by George Green the High Street confectioner and pastry cook. He promised *'ices, jellies, soda water, lemonade and other refreshments'* and that *'the Paris Chocolatiere for the preparation of this delightful beverage after the most approved principles, is in daily operation'.* The exhibition was a demonstration of the range and quality of goods available in Poole and particularly its High Street and a sign of better times returning. It may not have been such a smash hit as the Great Exhibition of 1851 which made a surplus of £186, 000, but it did make a profit – of £6 7s 6d (£6.37).

One relatively new art featured in the exhibition was that of photography. High Street photographers H. Bayley and Son stressed the novel features of this

Jenny Oliver

Morgan Salter's obelisk

new invention in their advertisements, promising *'Sittings occupying only one minute. Buildings correctly taken and favourite paintings copied. . . Parties may rely on procuring the most faithful resemblances of Parents they revere, Children they adore, and friends they esteem, in order that when Death or Distance shall separate us, these interesting pledges of affection will be invaluable'.* By 1861, *'artist photographer'*, Thomas Richards had also set up in the corn market area of High Street.

High Street was not untouched by events happening elsewhere in the world. One well-known High street resident was Dr. Thomas Salter who had married Eliza, the daughter of his teacher and later partner Thomas Bell in 1812. By 1851, the couple had at least six children and were living at or near No. 125, the house later fronting the Amity Hall. The Salters were a family of high achievers and in acknowledgment of his contributions to medical journals, the College of Surgeons made Dr. Salter an Honorary Fellow in 1844. Thomas' four sons James, Hyde, Henry and Morgan all qualified in the medical profession. In 1854, Morgan sailed out to the Crimea as surgeon on board HMS *Prince*, a store ship hired by the Royal Navy to deliver supplies to the troops. They arrived off Balaclava in November and had to anchor in the bay awaiting their turn to offload their cargo. Five days later, the Turkish coast was struck by a massive storm. Four ships were sunk, including the *Prince*, and Morgan Salter was among the 500 men drowned.

His grieving father erected an obelisk in his memory in the Poole Cemetery, perhaps the most prominent monument there. The inscription reads: *'In memory of John Morgan Salter Esq. Bachelor of Arts of the University of London. Member of the Royal College of Surgeons of England and Surgeon to Her Majesty's Troop Ship Prince from the wreck of which he perished in Balaclava Bay in the great storm of November 14 1854 aged 22 years.*

The youngest son of Thomas Salter Esq. of Poole Dorsetshire.' There is something very poignant about the listing of the achievements of this promising young man who never had a chance to fulfill his potential.

Thomas Salter did not survive his son very long. He died suddenly on 20th February 1856, aged 70, setting out after a hard day's work to visit some sick poor in the area. Feeling ill, he took refuge in a friend's house. As the *Herald* described, '*the last act of his life was to hand from its pocket, with injunctions for its especial care, a watch that had belonged to his lost child, in attempting to utter whose name he expired.'*

Early in 1860, disaster threatened the livelihood and even the lives of the family of Dr. Augustus Hamilton, son of chemist, James Hamilton. The doctor lived in central High Street with his wife Mary and two young children, Augustus junior and Emily. About six o'clock on a Sunday morning, Dr. Hamilton heard crackling and found that his house was on fire. He rushed down to call for help and meanwhile, the man servant managed to carry one of the children out of the window and over the greenhouse roof to safety. The other child and the nurse maid were rescued by ladder.

According to the *Herald*, Dr. Hamilton then *'placed a ladder in front of the house, broke in one of the drawing room windows and made for his bedroom from which he brought Mrs. Hamilton, who was greatly terrified as may well be imagined.'* The maid servant was rescued by ladder from the parapet of the roof, as the fire engines managed to subdue the fire. The emergency was so great that all the family and servants were rescued in their night clothes. The fire had begun in the doctor's surgery which was totally destroyed along with his medical library and surgical instruments. Damage was estimated at several hundred pounds but fortunately no-one was injured or killed. The dramatic fire and rescue must have terrified the neighbours who included Dr. Hamilton's brother, Horatio, now practicing as a dentist in the premises next door.

In June 1860 a prominent High Street figure ex-mayor and banker Richard Ledgard died in Swanage where he had been staying for the benefit of his health. The *Herald* reminded its readers that both he and his father had served as mayor five times. *'The office of Mayor was never in the history of Poole more respected or its dignity better supported, than when filled by these gentlemen.'* Besides being a town councillor, Ledgard had also been involved with the Poole turnpike trust and was a trustee of St Paul's Church, a superintendent of the Sunday School and the *'treasurer and the main prop of the National School in Poole, subscribing also liberally to its maintenance.'*

His death would precipitate an event with huge repercussions for Poole, which symbolised the demise of the Poole merchant class. This was the failure of the Ledgard Bank, established on High Street in 1821. The collapse was so catastrophic that the *Poole and Dorset Herald* issued a special single page edition on Monday 18th February 1861 to report a meeting of the creditors held at the London Hotel.

Andrew Hawkes Poole Photo Archive

Shows on the left the Wilts and Dorset Bank, Cole's jewellers in one of the 'two handsome shops' built by Henry Selfe and beyond, Lipton's and the Bull's Head Inn. On the right, the thatched cottage and Theophilus Miles, drapers.

According to the report *'the attendance proved so numerous that the room would not afford sufficient accommodation and Mr. Welch consequently proposed an adjournment to the Town Hall.'* The list of creditors (of whom over 200 were at the meeting) read like a roll-call of High Street traders.

The bank collapse seems to have to generated bewilderment, pity and sadness rather than anger, as the special edition emphasized. The Mayor began by stressing *'the private friendship, the public character and honourable integrity of Mr Ledgard.'* The collapse had been partly triggered by the failure of the Slades, one of the few remaining Poole - Newfoundland trading firms. The bank had debts of £92,687 and potential assets of £71,067 independent of a sum of nearly £20,000 owed to the bank by the executors of the Slades, who had suspended payment.

A civilised agreement was made to keep the Ledgards out of the bankruptcy court and a legal document was drawn up by which George Ledgard and his mother Susannah would sign over all their personal and bank property and assets to the trustees of the Wilts and Dorset Bank. The trustees agreed to pay the creditors an instalment of 10s [50p] in the pound and sell all the premises formerly belonging to the Ledgards, using the proceeds to pay off their individual debts as far as possible. High Street premises to be sold included a house and yard adjoining St Paul's Church, two houses near the Antelope Hotel occupied by William Watts and George Knight, and the parsonage of St Paul's Church. The Wilts and Dorset Bank took over the bank itself at No. 87 High Street.

In spite of such financial set-backs, shopkeepers on High Street in the 1860s were building up their prosperity and improving their standard of living. For example on 8th October 1863, the *Herald* described *'the erection of 'two handsome shops'* by the jeweller Henry Selfe who was based at No. 81 High Street. The new houses adjoined the Wilts and Dorset Bank (No. 87) and were *'erected in a neat unpretending style of architectural art.'* Selfe came from Somerset, one of the many incomers who were helping to restore the fortunes of Poole in the mid 19th century.

In 1864, the printer and stationer John Sydenham died at the age of 81, having survived his son John junior by 18 years. His youngest son, Richard continued his business of *'book and music seller, stationer, binder, printer and account book manufacturer, publisher of guides, maps and views of the district, circulating library and depot for the Christian Knowledge Society'.* The *Poole and Dorset Herald* in the meantime had established its place reporting on the tangled affairs of the town in the mid 19th century. One of its publishers, William Mate lived with his wife and seven children in lower High Street, probably at No. 12, next door to his partner, James Tribbett. This building, later known as the Herald building had its printing works at the back, accessible from Cinnamon Lane. In the census of 1861, Mate was described as a bookseller and printer employing seven men, three boys, ten apprentices and three female apprentices in his business.

Richard Sydenham believed that the *Herald* had become too bland and uncritical and he decided to publish his own monthly magazine of news, comment and criticism, the *Poole Pilot.* He promised that the *Pilot* would *'devote itself to all that is good and true and . . . will be found the determined enemy of all that is base and false.'* According to Richard Sydenham, *'Poole had been allowed to move along the dreary road to ruin, in order that members of the 'cliques' and their relations might batten on the public purse. . . rates so heavy as to deter people from inhabiting houses in the town; general decay as evidenced by the state of our shipbuilding and other trades; in fact nothing but decadence, deterioration and disgust.'*

The newspaper was launched in 1867 and ran only until 1869 but during this time it attacked many things that Sydenham saw as abuses in Poole society, stagnation, corruption and in-fighting. He saw the schemes of such leaders as Charles Waring, railway contractor and M.P. for Poole, as a way of lining the pockets of a few at the expense of local people. His vitriolic pen was employed on major issues and quite trivial ones. When in 1867 the authorities decided to block up the arches of the subscription library because undesirables were hanging around there, his response was typically extreme: *'Utility in such cases, is the plea of barbarians. The 'thieves who bought and sold' in the temple might have advanced a similar argument for their desecration. . . Is there no-one to say what the law is on the point of blocking up rights of way, one after another in every direction in and about Poole?'*

Both the *Pilot* and the *Herald* took up the vexed question of poor sanitation and the water supply. On the 1st October 1867, the Poole Pilot carried piece of

Andrew Hawkes Poole Photo Archive

Building the railway and footbridge

correspondence complaining about the smell of cabbage water and rotting dinners lingering in the streets, particularly on a Sunday. A couple of weeks later, the *Poole and Dorset Herald* carried a heartfelt plea from 'Valetudinarian', on the connection between poor drainage and deaths from consumption concluding that *'when the surface soil is dried with good sewers, consumption - the cruellest and most mysterious of all our silent morbid enemies - appears to depart.'*

A water company had been formed in 1859 to bring water through gutta percha piping to all the main streets, but the fact was that the supply was still inadequate. Not all houses had piped water and those that did were not receiving the scheduled twelve hours a day supply. In the summer, this sometimes stopped altogether. Many people still relied on public and private pumps connected to wells by lead pipes. With many cesspools next to the bigger houses, there was always a danger of water contamination.

In spite of these deficiencies, houses in the Victorian High Street could be remarkably comfortable in other respects. In 1869, the *Herald* advertised a sale of the household effects of High Street draper Miss Squibb, whose shop was probably No. 27 near the Bell and Crown Inn. The house was quite small with no live-in servant but seems to have been well-furnished. The drawing room for example *contained 'Mahogany loo table, six mahogany chairs in hair seating, mahogany couch to match, four feet mahogany chiffonier, easy chair, two coffee tables with carved stands, Brussels carpet, rug to match, chimney glass in gilt frame, prints in maple frames, muslin curtains and pole, handsome table cloth, timepiece, books, chimney ornaments, fenders and fire irons.'* The other rooms were similarly filled with furniture in mahogany and damask, carpets, rugs and druggets, mirrors, prints, glass, china and plate, giving the impression of a typically Victorian interior, rich, cosy and cluttered.

A development for which Poole people were still waiting was the arrival of the railway into Poole proper. After years of discussion and schemes which came to nothing, a branch line was finally built in 1872 from Wimborne via Broadstone to a new Poole station just to the west of High Street. Two years later, a line was built from the new station to Bournemouth West, cutting across High Street itself. The route ran along the edge of the built up area and meant the demolition of a private house which was on the site needed for the new footbridge.

The fares to Bournemouth were 10d first class, 7d second class and 4d third class (or about 4p, 3p and 11/2p in modern currency). The journey from Poole to Bournemouth took 15 minutes, as compared with around 45 minutes by horse-drawn omnibus, and the first time-table provided eight trains to Wimborne and nine to Bournemouth daily. The *Herald* expressed the hope that an early train *'not later than six o'clock in the morning'* would be provided *'for the benefit of the working class'* so that workers would no longer have to walk into Bournemouth. Obviously, the railway was going to change people's lives considerably, revolutionising local travel as well as linking with the national network.

The *Poole and Dorset Herald* reported the opening of the railway on 15th June 1874 as an eagerly anticipated event. *'On leaving the Poole Station, the High Street is crossed and the occupants of the carriages get a momentary glimpse of one of the widest, if not busiest streets of Poole'.* The railway inevitably brought noise, smuts and disturbance to the Parade, still home to some of High Street's wealthier residents. Ironically, only 40 years after the High Street entrance had been opened up to traffic, the railway created a partial barrier more or less along the same line as the old town ditch. The level crossing and cast iron footbridge for pedestrians are still there today, nearly 140 years later.

More changes to the outlook of upper High Street came from the construction of two large buildings just south of the Parade. One was the Wesleyan chapel, built in 1879 on the corner of High Street and Chapel Lane, to replace the previous chapel nearby. *Kelly's Directory of Dorsetshire* 1880 describes the new chapel as *'a handsome building in the early English style'* with a *'broad and commanding frontage with double tracery windows'.* It was designed to accommodate 950 people, a testimony to the importance of religious observance at the time. Its spire, at 90 feet high, became a landmark from different vantage points up and down the street. One of the leading supporters of the chapel was the proprietor of the *Herald*, William Mate. He had saved some stones from the foundations of the old Poole gaol in which John Wesley,

Jenny Oliver

The Wesleyan Church and the tower of Bayley's store dominate upper High Street

the grandfather of the founder of Methodism had been imprisoned in 1665. These were now incorporated into the pulpit of the new chapel as a memorial. The other building in upper High Street was the large store of Henry Bayley and Son, ironmongers and house furnishers on the corner of North Street, (now No. 134). Built in a version of a French chateau style, the building dwarfed the other small shops in the row, rivalling Beech Hurst opposite in scale if not in elegance.

Another important building, but one which was not so prominent on the street, was the meeting house built around 1882 in the back garden of Thomas Salter's former house. This was used by the Ancient Order of Oddfellows and later by the Amity Lodge of Freemasons and became known as the Amity Hall. It was a large rectangular building with tall windows and rather spartan wooden seating, a useful venue for talks, concerts and entertainments of all kinds. In 1896, in the same week as a *'Grand Evening Concert'* in aid of St. James Church choir fund, Mr. John D. Ablett brought his *'Theatrograph'* to the Amity Hall. Billed as *'Animated Photographs! Scenes in real life faithfully reproduced! The marvel of the age!! The wonder of the century!!!'*, this performance was Poole's first cinema show. In the next few years, several moving picture shows came to the Amity, often combined with live variety entertainment.

Further down the street Job Loader, general and yachting outfitter occupied No. 67, the original *Herald* headquarters and brought up his family of eight children there. His father who was a builder added the terra cotta ornamentation to the 18th century building including an elaborate balustrade, window arches and four heads representing Europe, Asia, Africa and America. Loader was a supporter of the Poole Wesleyan Sunday School and served as a Liberal councillor in the 1890s.

Many of the traders were doing well and achieving middle class respectability. Some were also becoming involved in public affairs. As in previous centuries, many of the mayors of Poole in the mid Victorian era either lived or had their businesses

Andrew Hawkes Poole Photo Archive

Lipton's, the Bull's Head and Job Loader's shop (with three lamps) on the right.

in High Street. However, instead of being merchants with interests centred on the port, they were now professionals or tradesmen. Some like the banker Richard Ledgard were connected to the merchant families of the old elite, but most were not. They included printer stationers, John Lankester and William Mate, William Pearce, ironmonger and founder, surgeon Edward Lacy, surgeon dentist, Horatio Hamilton, ironmonger Henry Farmer and solicitors John Durant and Philip Budge. Over time, their influence would change the direction of the town's interests.

The long opening hours of shops was one of the factors that made it difficult for all but the most prosperous tradesmen to participate in public affairs. A campaign for shorter hours for shop workers had been running for decades. As the *Herald* reported in 1883, quoting Mr. Sutherst of the Shop Hours Labour League, *'their hours are from 75 to 90 per week; their mealtimes are neither adequate nor regular; they have no weekly half holiday; they have no time for exercise, recreation or mental improvement and their toil, though of a comparatively light nature, is by reason of the long-standing, of the most unhealthy and exhausting description'*. It was probably as a result of greater prosperity that Poole shop workers did achieve an 'early' closing time of 5 o'clock on Wednesdays around this time.

On 22nd May 1886, the whole town was shocked by a terrible event. Alderman and deputy leader of the Poole Liberal Party, Horatio Hamilton, was shot dead as he left a committee meeting at the *Guildhall*. The Times reported:

'Yesterday at Poole, Alderman Hamilton aged 75, was shot dead by John Gerrard King, 26. The latter was recently licensed as a pilot to be stationed at Swanage. The sub-commissioners,

of whom Alderman Hamilton was one, informed King that he would be required to obtain a boat or get a mate to sail with him, otherwise his licence papers would be withdrawn. King was unable to obtain £60 for the boat, and yesterday morning, after purchasing a six-chambered revolver, went to the Guildhall. Alderman Hamilton was leaving the council meeting; King stepped up to him, and after some remark drew the revolver and fired three shots into his head and neck. Mr. Hamilton was picked up insensible, and died within the hour. King, on being charged with murder, exclaimed "Dead? Is he dead; oh my God!"'

It emerged that King had purchased the six-chambered revolver from Councillor Henry Farmer's shop at No. 91 High Street. Horatio Hamilton had worked all his life in High Street, first in his father's chemist shop and then as a dentist. In 1871, he served as Mayor of Poole and by 1881 had retired to Brampton Villas, Longfleet, although he continued his council work. The murder of this professional and community minded man caused a great deal of shock and debate in the town. His funeral at Poole Cemetery was attended by hundreds of mourners and spectators, including the Mayor, the Sheriff and many town councillors. In the short service, the Rev. A. Hood described him as *'a useful and honourable townsman – a man who gave up his life in the discharge of a public duty.'*

John King was tried and sentenced to death by hanging. After the sentence was made public the *Herald* reported: *'Public opinion hitherto has been very strong against him: now that the poor misguided young man is really condemned to death, public sympathy may perhaps take a turn, and an effort be made to secure mitigation of his punishment.'* This is exactly what happened. A petition was raised to the Home Secretary and King's sentence was eventually commuted.

A drama of a less tragic nature occurred on 1st October, 1888 when fire broke out in the back of Walter J. Bacon's ironmonger's shop in the corn market. Born in Ipswich, Walter Bacon had come to Poole around 1880 and taken over George Norton's shop in or near the old Skutt house at No. 44 High Street. The fire started in a room at the rear which was being renovated and was discovered well ablaze by Walter's son, Frank, then about 25, who slept in the room above. He quietly alerted his father and according to the *Herald, 'Mr. Bacon immediately accompanied his son to the source of the fire and some of Harden's Star Hand Grenades (a chemical substance corked up in bottles) were thrown into the room. The glass of which the bottles are manufactured was thus broken, the liquid is 'sprayed' or thrown over the blaze . . and so safe and speedy are the results that they had the effect of partially subduing the flames'.*

The police were on the scene and alerted the fire brigade from the police station *'by means of the electric call'*. Arriving quickly, the brigade decided to use their latest acquisition, the *'Patent American Spreader'* which *'sent forth a powerful and plentiful supply of water from its hydra-head'*. The fire was brought under control without spreading further, although the building was badly damaged.

The following year, the brigade was called again to Bacon's shop when neighbours saw large flames shooting up at the back of the premises. It turned out that Mr. Bacon was just testing a new device called a *'Doty'* lamp or illuminator, consisting of *'a large galvanised metal tank containing paraffin, which is forced by compressed air through a spiral of copper tubing at the top of the tank to the burner, which emits a large, intensely white flame, of great illuminating power'.* It was hoped that the Doty lamp would be used by men working at night on the landscaping of the new Poole Park. One interesting aspect of these incidents is the emphasis on new inventions and technology. In their role as gas fitters and water engineers, ironmongers tended to be in the forefront of new developments in the home and elsewhere. They did not however, make very comfortable neighbours. The managers of the National Provincial Bank which was next door to Bacon's may have had some uneasy moments, especially as their neighbour on the other side, manufacturing confectioner Thomas Parrot, also suffered a couple of fires.

Since taking over his shop from George Norton, Walter Bacon had rebuilt the premises with larger windows and glass doors. On 10th July 1897, a horse and trap plunged straight through the plate glass window, landing in a display of filters, lamps and other hardware and cutting its legs severely. Mr. Bacon was in his office nearby and rushed out to hold the horse's head while others managed to unharness it from the trap and eventually extricate it from the window. According to the *Herald, 'Blood flowed from the wounds most profusely, and the scene inside Mr. Bacon's shop had the appearance of a slaughter house more than anything else. As the animal was being led out into the street it kicked with tremendous force being evidently in considerable pain, knocking a lawn mower and other things to pieces and also smashing the glass front doors.'* The driver was unconscious but recovered after treatment by Dr. Turner. The horse, a valuable animal said to be worth £160, had to be destroyed.

Other shops had also invested in modern shop fronts and windows. Joseph Charles Hawkes had handed over control of his shop to his son, Joseph Alfred (known as Alfred) in the 1870s, although he continued to reign supreme in the leather cutting room. Alfred Hawkes modernised the shop by extending it forward and putting in a 20 foot length of windows on to High Street. Later this was extended to 60 feet of window display, with a lamp above each window to highlight the goods on view.

Draper Theophilus Miles was another trader with the latest type of shop frontage. His shop was the former post office on the corner of Carter's Lane, now No. 76. A handsome building with stone facings and classical windows, it had been opened in the late 1860s under Postmaster, Joseph Derby. In the early 1890s, a new post office was built at what is now No. 141 and Theophilus Miles took over the old premises, remodelling the lower floor with large plate glass windows. Across the street was the brand new, three-storey shop of draper Butler and Son, built in front

Andrew Hawkes Poole Photo Archive

Walter Bacon's shop and the National Provincial Bank on the left

of and incorporating half of William Barfoot's old mansion house at No. 89. With its tall, impressive façade, pilasters and finials, it embodied the confident and forward-looking spirit prevailing in High Street at the end of the century.

By the time of Queen Victoria's Diamond Jubilee in 1897, the town was ready to celebrate. In the words of the *Herald, 'the tradesmen vied with each other in their efforts to produce the best possible effect. . . Lines of streamers, of almost endless variety, were stretched across the street at irregular intervals, portraits of Her Majesty were exhibited by many of the householders in prominent positions, and there was hardly a residence from Longfleet to the Quay, but what displayed some token of royal favour.'* One of the most striking displays was at the London Hotel where all the windows were decorated with fairy lights and flags with the letters 'VR'. Bacon and Co. *('Ironmongers by appointment to the Prince of Wales')*, was advertising illuminating bucket lamps in assorted colours at 1s [5p] a dozen. The Port Mahon Castle Inn had a huge placard with the words *'For sixty years we've pulled together, and yet much longer may we pull'* and Beech Hurst, home to solicitor, Phillip Budge was *'gay with bunting and illuminations'*.

Festivities included three banquets for a total of 700 people, held over three nights at the Amity Hall. The catering was done by High Street baker and confectioner, W.G. Green, whose father had catered for the 1854 exhibition. There were also two processions, one for adults and one for children, a dinner in the park for nearly 1,000 'aged poor', all of whom had to be over 60, sports, a tea for the children, a display of fireworks and a bonfire on Constitution Hill, beside religious services at all the churches. The adult procession which wound down Market Street,

Borough of Poole Museum Service

The London Hotel decorated for the Jubilee celebrations

along Thames Street and up High Street to the park, was at least three quarters of a mile long and included the entire town council, several bands, volunteer regiments, the fire brigade and members of local societies. At the tea, 3,000 children sat on 5,000 feet of timber, lent by the Poole Baltic and Quebec Timber Co. Even the paupers in the workhouse were treated to roast beef and vegetables, beer, tobacco and snuff. All these celebrations were organised and delivered by local committees which must have involved just about every leading citizen in the town, including many High Street residents and shopkeepers. It was an example of local enterprise and patriotism typical of the period.

During the 1900s a shift had occurred, both in the town and in its principal street. Both had gone through hard times but had eventually emerged with a new prosperity. During the 18th century, most new buildings appearing in High Street had been houses. In the 19th century, most new premises were either public buildings or commercial ones (even if some still contained living quarters). Many people still lived in the street, but the number of buildings that were purely residential had dwindled to a mere handful. The era of High Street as predominantly commercial thoroughfare had arrived.

Chapter Eight

The Edwardian Era and The Great War

Through the centre of this "mighty maze and all without a plan" the High Street runs: a fairly good business thoroughfare, about a mile in length.'

Descriptions of High Street by the start of the 20th century included its Longfleet section as a matter of course. In the fifty years or so since the north end of High Street had been opened up, the suburb of Longfleet had developed considerably, with estates of new houses gradually covering former farmland. As this new community grew, the houses in High Street, Longfleet were increasingly converted into shops. By 1901, there were two grocers, a butcher, a baker, two greengrocers, a fishmonger, a dairy, an ironmonger, a confectioner, three drapers, a boot and shoe maker and a chemist, all in the short stretch between the railway crossing and the George Inn. Catering for the popular new sport of cycling was King's cycle depot. At No. 203 was Henry Burden's grocery shop and model steam bakery, advertising *'superior machine made bread'*, and next door, the shop of Caleb T. Snook, stationer, newsagent, picture-framer and sub-postmaster.

Further down the road at No. 185 with the sign of a giant key, was the shop of Thomas Joyner, tinsmith and brass worker. Joyner was skilled in several metal working trades including gas fitting and also sold antiques and curios. Besides his work, he had a wide range of interests. He was a good violinist, played in and at one time led the Poole Town Band and composed much of their music. He was also a talented painter, and an inventor of several curiosities including a pipe with a nicotine

Andrew Hawkes Poole Photo Archive

King's cycle stores, Burden's and Snook's on the right, the toll house and Longfleet Church in the distance.

trap and a racing yacht that would sail to windward without the need to tack. An indefatigable reader and correspondent of the *Herald*, he conducted a long campaign backed up by plans, drawings and oil paintings on the subject of Poole harbour and the idea of creating a new harbour entrance by cutting through the Sandbanks peninsula.

The George Inn, dating from the 1820s, stood at the northern end of High Street where the Wimborne and Ringwood roads diverged. In front of the George stood the old toll house, its gates having been removed in the 1860s. This landmark, by now nearly 50 years old, was a small single storey structure with windows set at an angle to give views of approaching traffic. At the back of the building was a weighbridge. There were also several other inns in the area. The Ansty Arms was on the corner of Towngate Street, an area known as Topp's corner from the Topp family who had run a grocery and butcher's shop there. Other inns were the Port Mahon Castle Hotel, the temperance hotel run by Frank Holmes and the Blandford Arms opposite the George. Just above the railway crossing was the leafy entrance to Balston's rope and twine works and then the White House Laundry, run by George Howard.

It was probably because of the growth of Longfleet that the authorities decided to renumber the properties in High Street. Previously the numbering had started at the boundary of the old town (near the railway crossing) and worked

Andrew Hawkes Poole Photo Archive

upwards towards the Quay. Around 1895, this was reversed. The new numbers started at the Quay and increased northwards up High Street, continuing into Longfleet without a break. Although this change was a logical one, it has made identifying properties difficult for later researchers.

In January 1901, came the death of Queen Victoria after 64 years on the throne. The mayor announced the news from the Guildhall and the bells of St. James', St. Paul's and other churches were tolled. That week's edition of the *Herald* was produced with black-edged columns. Relatively few people could probably remember the death of the last monarch and it must have seemed a strange and sobering event, although not unexpected. The coronation of Edward VII took place the following year on 9th August, having been delayed because of the King's surgery for appendicitis. Poole celebrated early with a coronation carnival on the bank holiday. As the *Herald* described *'the High Street was one blaze of colour from end to end, lines of flags spanning the streets, whilst the fronts of the houses were set off with all descriptions of banners, flags, Chinese lanterns, prismatic lamps etc.'* A long procession of decorated carriages, cycles, wheelbarrows and other vehicles wound its way up High Street to the park where sports and refreshments were laid on. Three years later there was great excitement in the town when the King's sister Princess Beatrice visited Poole to open a bazaar in January 1905.

On 6th April 1901, only months after the Queen's death, Poole's first tram left its terminus in Longfleet for County Gates via upper Parkstone. A tram service

Andrew Hawkes Poole Photo Archive

A lively crowd awaits Princess Beatrice's visit.

had been under discussion since the 1880s, but all the early schemes had foundered mainly due to opposition from Bournemouth Council. In 1899 the Board of Trade finally authorised the upper Parkstone service, as far as a depot at the Bournemouth boundary. The press declared that the opening of the service marked *'an important epoch in local history'* and showed *'the development of the district, which between Poole and Bournemouth has grown with such marvellous rapidity'*.

Because of the impossibility of crossing the railway line, the trams did not come down lower High Street. Instead, the line ran into High Street Longfleet and swung right to a terminus in Towngate Street close to the station. The complete journey time to the Bournemouth boundary was about 25 minutes and the service proved very popular and more flexible than the railway journey. In 1905 the Poole and District Electric Traction Company Ltd. which ran the service was bought out by Bournemouth Corporation and the line was extended to central Bournemouth and later Christchurch. The following year, an additional Poole to Bournemouth route was opened via lower Parkstone. A proposed circular tram service from Poole station via High Street, the Quay, East Quay Road, Baiter Street, South Street and Mount Street (now Lagland Street) was never constructed. If it had ever materialised,

Andrew Hawkes Poole Photo Archive

Saunders' shopfront and staff.

it would surely have created terrible congestion in lower High Street.

The development of shopping centres in suburbs such as Longfleet and the link provided by the trams was gradually changing the focus of the town. Some of the traders saw the value of opening branches in the outer districts. The boot and shoe maker, J. A. Hawkes and Son, for instance, had two branches in High Street, (No. 99 and No. 215) as well as other shops at Parkstone and Branksome. By 1911, Bacon's ironmongers (now Bacon and Curtis Ltd.) had a second shop at No. 180 High Street and baker confectioner Frederick Cann also had a Longfleet branch.

High Street was still the place where the town's best shops were located. One prosperous trader was Herbert Saunders, grocer and provision merchant, who lived above his shop at No. 20 High Street with his wife Amelia and four children. He sold a wide variety of produce as remembered 70 years later by his daughter, Hilda Benn. *'We had a big store with all the canisters of tea round because father mixed all his own teas. Sugar came in tall cones which had to be cut with a sugar chopper. People used to come in with their jars to buy a pound of black treacle and filled them from a barrel with a tap on it.'* The shop also sold fruit and had a ripening room for bananas above the premises they owned at No. 93 High Street. Sides of bacon half a dozen or so at a time were smoked above a pit containing sawdust. Every week, Hilda's father went to Dorchester market to get new-laid eggs and blue Dorset cheese which he sent all over the country.

Saunders made all kinds of bread in the bakery behind the shop at No. 20 and were well known for their dough cakes and hot cross buns, the 1d ones being the size of plates and the ½d ones like saucers. They also made ships' biscuits for the sailing ships which came to the Quay. These were made from a thick paste and after baking were put into sacks and left to dry out for a month, *'until every drop of moisture was drawn out of them'*. They were sold to ships a ton at a time, enough to feed the crew for six weeks if they were wind-bound on the voyage home. The shop also supplied five local landowners including Mr. Van Raalte of Brownsea Island, Lord Wimborne of Canford Manor and the Llewellins of Upton House. Everything was delivered in horse-drawn vans or by boys on bicycles for local customers.

Ernest Bristowe was the grandson of William Bristowe, a carrier operating from No. 22 High Street. In his autobiography, Ernest remembered the High Street shops at the beginning of the century. *'Items like flour, tea, sugar and dried peas were stored in drawers behind the counter, from which they were extracted with scoops to be weighed on brass scales . . .One side of the shop sold butter and margarine which was cut from large blocks and patted into pounds or half pounds with two wooden patters'*. At Christmas time, the butchers *'excelled themselves by covering the whole of their shop fronts with turkeys, geese, chickens, hares and rabbits. They hung from the eaves to the pavement, leaving just enough room to get into the shop.'*

Harry Matthews, a contemporary of Ernest Bristowe, remembered Bacon and Curtis where you could buy *'anything form a screw to a sledgehammer'* and Lipton's the grocers who would sell *'a small quantity of jam taken from a large tin with a long-handled spoon'* and *'a basin full of cracked eggs for 2d'* (1p). Fish and chips cost 1p and Harry's mother would send him out with a shilling (5p) to buy a rabbit, a large swede, a bunch of carrots and four pounds of potatoes, providing a good dinner for four people.

Shop opening hours were still very long by modern standards. The Saunders' shops were open from 8 am to 8 pm from Monday to Thursday, 9 pm on Fridays and 10 pm on Saturdays with no Wednesday early closing. Sometimes a late customer on Saturday, coming in for his rasher of bacon for Sunday breakfast, would keep them open later, but the customer was king. This meant long working hours for many. Bob Russell was a school boy in the early years of the century, but he also worked as a lather boy at a small barber's shop in the corn market. He started work at the barber's at 8 am and worked until 8.45. Then he went to school from 9 until 12 noon, back to the barber's from 12 until 1 pm, school again from 1 to 4 and back to the barber's from 5 until 8. Wednesday was early closing but Saturday was a full working day at the barber's from 8 am until 10 pm. For over 34 hours of work, on top of his school hours, he earned half a crown (12½p) a week.

The barber, Mr. Day, worked equally hard. On Saturdays *'he pulled the blinds down at 10 o'clock but he wouldn't lock the door so people could come in and he would still serve them'*. At 2d for a shave and 4d a hair-cut, he could not afford to turn custom away. No wonder shop workers valued their rare free time. Sundays were for many a day for best clothes and church going. The Saunders children had a tight Sunday programe which involved Sunday school at 10 o'clock, a church service at 11.30, Sunday school again at 2.30 and evening service at 6.30. No hot food was cooked on Sundays and the evening was spent singing hymns and in other suitable activities. For others, Sunday afternoons were a time to enjoy a leisurely stroll as Ernest Bristowe describes *'up the High Street and through the park in one's Sunday clothes, feeding the swans on the lake, or the peacocks and pheasants in the bird sanctuary'*.

Life was still a struggle for many people and competition for trade was constant. This was emphasised in 1907 when the confectioner Thomas Parrott aged 78 was found dead in his bed from inhaling coal gas. Thomas Parrott had set up in Poole at No. 38 High Street in the 1880s as a manufacturing confectioner. Although the business did well, there were also problems. Over the years the premises suffered several serious fires. In May 1886 Mr. Parrott placed a notice in the *Herald* offering a £5 reward to anyone giving information to convict the person or persons who had started a rumour that smallpox had broken out in the Parrott household, a report which could have had a highly damaging impact on the business.

In spite of such difficulties, the business prospered and the Parrotts opened a confectionery works in Perry Gardens with four boilers. Bob Russell remembered the delicious smell of boiling sugar from the works. The company was supplying confectionery across England and even to France and had several vans working continually. By the early years of the new century, however, things were not going so smoothly. It transpired from the inquest that Thomas Parrott believed he would lose his factory, and had other business worries. The verdict was that he had taken his own life while suffering from temporary insanity.

Another calamity occurred in July 1909 when fire destroyed a marine store belonging to Mr. G. Wilby, a rag, skin, bottle and iron merchant at No. 10, High Street next to the Antelope Hotel. Neighbours including Councillor Evan Gambier, inn-keeper of the King's Head, grocer Herbert Saunders and others helped Mr. White of the mews to remove his horses and carriages from the nearby stables. The building, previously Messrs Hayman's brush factory, was *'totally demolished, nothing but a heap of ruins and the bare walls remaining'*. Fortunately the fire was prevented from spreading to nearby properties.

The census of 1911 gives us a snapshot of the town's main shopping street. By now very few properties were purely residential, almost all of them being converted into shops or businesses. In the mile or so between the Quay and the

Borough of Poole Museum Service

H. J. Travers' Beehive Clothing Stores on the corner of Old Orchard

George Inn, there were just over two hundred businesses including seventeen grocers, sixteen butchers, nine drapers and nine boot and shoe makers. There were also twelve hotels or public houses and seven refreshment rooms. Practically every need was catered for by suppliers of food, clothing, household goods and professional services. The Amity Hall served as a meeting room, theatre and cinema, and the two churches offered spiritual comfort and social interaction of a different kind.

Most of the businesses were still small local family concerns, but a few chain stores like Boots the Chemist (at No. 109), the Maypole Dairy, the Home and Colonial Stores Ltd. and Lipton's were beginning to appear. Some of the larger local traders like Bacon and Curtis and Butler's drapers had adopted the latest business practices and set up as limited liability companies. Another innovation was the telephone, now advertised by one or two forward-looking businesses like the White House Laundry (telephone number 100) and ironmongers W. E. Boone & Co. (telephone number 10).

Some shop owners had moved out to the suburbs leaving an employer or lodger in residence, and over a fifth of the buildings in the street were now 'lock up' businesses with no-one living on site. This implies a shift in the relationship between shopkeeper and customer because the tradesman who locked his shop door at night and went to catch the late tram home to the suburbs would no longer be available to serve the out-of-hours shopper. The daily commute to and from work was becoming a regular feature of many people's lives. In High Street the number of unlit and empty premises after hours probably meant that the street was quieter at night than it had ever been before.

Architecturally, Poole and its High Street were still a hotchpotch of old and new, as William Mate's description in *Dorsetshire Illustrated* makes clear: *'Poole is an ancient town built in an ancient style of red brick: a cluster of tenements thrown together haphazard as it would appear, without much regard for plan. . . Through the centre of this "mighty maze and all without a plan" the High Street runs: a fairly good business thoroughfare, about a mile in length.'* High Street was at least tidier and cleaner than in the previous century although many houses still had steps protruding on to the pavement to the danger of pedestrians.

From the Wesleyan Church to the toll house, the street was paved with wooden blocks set in tar. According to Ernest Bristowe these were *'about the size of a brick and about half an inch thick, and they lasted well until work had to be done to gas and water mains, when it became difficult to replace them.'* Whenever the blocks had to be taken up they were much in demand as fuel. In April 1915 the *Herald* complained that warm weather was causing the blocks to swell and the pitch to rise into *'little lumps'*, giving cyclists a rough and sticky ride. The response of the authorities was to throw sand on to the road.

Rats were a still a problem, particularly in the High Street's corn stores. The barber's shop where Bob Russell worked was next door to the office and stores of W. H. Yeatman and Sons, corn merchants, which was *'loaded with rats'*. On early closing days the barber, Bertie Day, would sometimes amuse himself by shooting them with an air pistol borrowed from Bacon's. Another corn store, owned by Bradford and Sons, was situated opposite the King's Head and the Antelope. On one occasion Evan Gambier of the King's Head reported to the Sanitary Committee that he had seen 250 rats on the roof.

Such problems aside, people's living conditions were better than ever before, at least in the more prosperous main streets. Ernest Bristowe describes the kitchen arrangements of the time: *'Before the advent of the gas cooker, every kitchen was equipped with an iron range, consisting of an oven and hot water boiler with room for three iron saucepans on the top. . . The iron range was gradually replaced by the gas cooker, and oil lamps by gas jets and then by gas mantles'*. The Bournemouth Gas and Water Company had set up its office and showrooms in Beech Hurst, the former home of solicitor Philip E. L. Budge, and were advertising the joys of *'a warm bath without the kitchen fire.'* Another new technology was electricity. Ironmongers like Bacon and Curtis and Arthur W. Hine were offering quotations on electric light installations at the lowest prices. The first High Street shop to be lit by electricity was J. A. Hawkes, the shoemakers, who installed their own gas engine and dynamo which also powered the shoe repair machines.

In 1911, Mr James Bravery, managing director of Popular Bioscope Syndicates

BACON & CURTIS, LTD., *Ironmongers,*

BOURNEMOUTH & POOLE.

Sole Agents for the Celebrated Gold Medal **EAGLE RANGES & GRATES.**

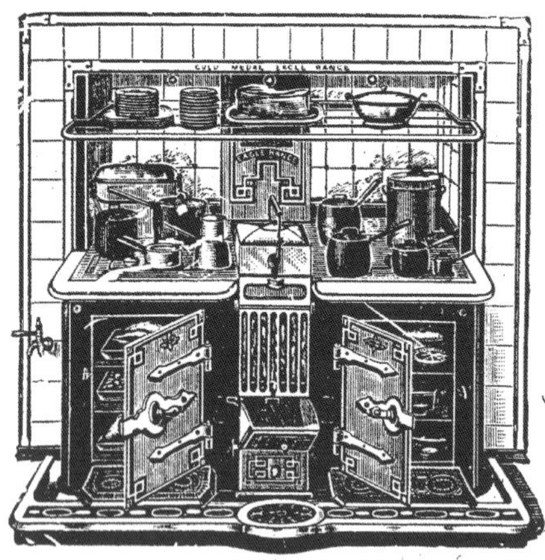

Ranges demonstrated by Practical Men.

As supplied to H.M. Government and the Crown Agents for the Colonies.

Used by all the Leading Residents and Hotel Proprietors throughout the Country.

CALL and INSPECT.

Telephone No. 11.

HEATING, VENTILATING AND ELECTRICAL ENGINEERS.

ROYAL WARRANT HOLDERS TO HIS LATE MAJESTY EDWARD VII.

The Largest and Finest Selection of ELECTRIC FITTINGS in the South of England to be seen at our Showrooms.

BEST MATERIALS. LATEST APPLIANCES. SKILLED WORKMEN.

Limited and a pioneer of local cinema entertainment, established the Poole Electric Theatre at 181 High Street opposite the Ansty Arms. At the end of the previous century the building had been a furnishing warehouse and was then transformed into the Longfleet Congregational Church with seating for 200 people before its conversion to a rather basic theatre. Inside, patrons were provided with cloth-covered bench-type seating and if the film was popular, everyone had to squeeze up. Performances were frequently interrupted by the film breaking and having to be hurriedly repaired by the operator. Nevertheless the theatre soon became a much loved venue, particularly for children. Harry Matthews remembered a trip to the Electric Theatre on Saturdays with his 2d (1p) pocket money as the highlight of his week. The matinees for children were rowdy affairs. According to Ernest Bristowe, the audience *'booed the villain and cheered the hero . . . yelled out the captions in unison . . . stood on the seats and threw peanut shells on the floor'*. Cowboys and Indians and the adventures of Pearl White were the usual fare.

Another chance to demonstrate loyalty to King, country and empire came with the coronation of George V. The day was unfortunately *'marred by rain and wind'* but as usual the traders rose to the occasion with their decorations. As the *Herald*

Andrew Hawkes Poole Photo Archive

The Poole Electric Theatre surrounded by shops. The site is now part of Falkland Square.

described, *'flags, streamers and bunting with patriotic sentiments and pictures of the King and Queen, were to be seen on all the business establishments and the few private residences in the High-street, whilst overhead the lines of flags and streamers formed a fluttering canopy. The commanding elevation of the Gas Company's office, with its handsome portico, supported by massive columns, lent itself admirably to a scheme of decoration . . . The Portmahon, White Hart and Crown Hotels also joined profusely in the colouring scheme'.*

It was an intensely patriotic period. At Lord Baden-Powell's first scout camp on Brownsea Island four years before, one day was devoted to chivalry including *'Loyalty to King and to Employers or Officers'*, and another day to patriotism which covered subjects like *'History and deeds that won the Empire'*. Ernest Bristowe's memory of learning history at school was that it *'consisted mainly of battles, particularly those which ended in victory for our side or in which our soldiers were very brave.'* He and Bob Russell both remembered as school boys parading past the Union Jack and saluting on Empire Day. With this grounding in duty, courage and derring-do, it is not surprising that when war broke out with Germany on 4th August 1914, young men flocked to join up.

Under the headline *'A Magnificent Response of Able Manhood'*, the *Herald* reported on 17th September that total recruitment in Poole was now over 1,100 men. *'In the*

Andrew Hawkes Poole Photo Archive

Poole volunteers

hour of England's need Poole has never been lacking. And it is not failing now!' Meanwhile in a nice mix of patriotism and commercial enterprise, Butler and Sons, drapers and house furnishers, were running a 'shopping week' in which 10% of all sales were to go to the Prince of Wales' National Relief Fund (£500 guaranteed). Messrs J. A. Hawkes were able to publish an *'unsolicited testimonial'* from the officer commanding the Royal Garrison Artillery, Philip Budge's son, William Hatton Budge. *'The Boots you supplied to the Territorials at our recent camp have been most satisfactory. Not a single man in the Company had wet feet once'.*

Local men soon found themselves at the front and some of their letters were regularly published in the local press. Private Horace Sartin of the Royal Army Medical Corps had worked for the pork butcher, W.L. Miller at No. 104, High Street before signing up. He wrote that *'I shall not be sorry when I get back as it is none too pleasant to be everlastingly dodging the German shells, which burst around one all day long . . . It is good of Mr. Miller to keep my place open.'* Lance-Corporal Alfred J Gambier of the 1st Herts Regiment wrote to his brother, Evan Gambier, about the mud and water in the trenches: *'To stand like that for hours wet through is terrible, and I'm afraid a lot will be laid up before we get another rest'.* News of casualties also started coming through. Hilda Benn's two brothers, Herbert and Gilbert Saunders had volunteered early in the war

Borough of Poole Museum Service

Everyone had their part to play on the home front

and in October 1914, Herbert was reported wounded at the Dardanelles but was *'making good progress'* in a London hospital. Gilbert had been invalided from the front, suffering from dysentery.

As Christmas approached, the motto in High Street was 'business as usual'. Miller's Bacon Stores were displaying the usual array of turkeys and geese and Burden and Sons, grocers, bakers and provision merchants were offering special packages: *'Soldiers' and Sailors' Comforts'* at 2s 6d (121/2p) each, containing marmalade, salmon and shrimp paste, peppermint creams, toffees, tobacco, cigarettes and antiseptic powder. Messrs C. T. Snook had a large stock of patriotic Christmas cards and calendars. All the traders stressed that they were selling their goods at pre-war prices.

As the war progressed, however, shortages inevitably pushed prices up. In spring 1915, in an effort to produce more food locally, allotments were laid out at various locations including the Ladies' Walking Field near High Street, Longfleet. The problem, with so many men in the forces, was to keep them going. Many trades and industries were also badly affected by the loss of their work force and gradually women undertook previously male jobs. Servicemen's pay and the separation allowances paid to their wives were not very generous and a Mayor's Distress Fund was set up to help those suffering hardship. Another initiative was the formation of a committee to entertain troops from local camps every week and a 'Soldiers' Home' was set up in Wimborne Road. Committees for war work abounded.

Andrew Hawkes Poole Photo Archive

Girl 'munitioneers'

Not all headline events were connected to the war. In April 1915, the *Herald* announced the sudden death of Philip E. L. Budge, solicitor, town council member and three times mayor of Poole. He had come to Poole in 1874 and set up in one of High Street's most iconic buildings, Beech Hurst, where he ran his practice and raised a family of six children. As Mayor in 1890, he had welcomed the Prince of Wales during his visit to open the town park. He had also acted as agent to several of the town's M.P.s and served as clerk to many committees including the Poole Board of Guardians and the Rural District Council. In his autobiographical book *'I Call to Mind'*, Herbert S. Carter described Philip Budge as *'an outrageously outspoken politician. . . His heart knew no malice in spite of his damning and blasting and he was extremely kind and helpful to me.'* Carter described one occasion when, after giving *'a racy and pointless speech, P.E.L. Budge sat down and, turning to his neighbour, remarked: "I'm damned if I know what I've been talking about, but anyway I made 'em laugh!"'* After retiring from his practice in 1909, he moved to Seldown while Beech Hurst was taken over as offices by the Bournemouth Gas and Water Company. At the time of Philip Budge's death all four of his sons were serving in the forces.

Every week brought more news of the death or injury of local men at the front. In May 1915, Alf Gambier was reported to be in hospital in Leicester with a head wound. In September, Mr. and Mrs. Cowles of the London Hotel heard that their son Sergeant Reginald Cowles, aged 25, had been killed in the Dardanelles, only three months after the death of his elder brother. Harry Balston, son of the late Alfred Balston J.P., rope and twine manufacturer, was also killed in Turkey. He had emigrated to Australia 25 years before but volunteered on the outbreak of war. In November, Private L. S. Knapton who had worked for the High Street grocers Giffords, died from wounds received at Kut-el-Amara near Bagdad. Bob Russell's employer Bertie Day enlisted and was killed almost immediately. In December, fish salesman, Harry Rogers of No. 55 High Street received news that his son Gunner Alfred Rogers of the Royal Garrison Artillery had been killed in France aged only 19. Every day could bring a family the news they dreaded.

Nationally the recruitment drive was not enough to keep pace with the losses. In January 1916, the Military Service Act introduced conscription for single men between the ages of 18 and 41. In May this was extended to married men. Meanwhile women were filling more and more roles on the home front. Smartly uniformed post-women were seen on High Street. The *Herald* reported on women working in engineering and on the railway as *'cleaners, porters, refreshment sellers etc.'*. One girl delivered bread for a local firm by horse and cart over a wide area. At Hawkes' shoe shop, girls replaced the errand boys who had left to join the navy. Others found work in munitions at Holton Heath. In spite of the grim circumstances, the war provided some women with more opportunities and better wages than ever before.

A few women enlisted in the services. One was Nesta Looker, the daughter of John Looker who had recently set up as a printer and stationer at No. 82 High Street. Nesta joined the Women's Royal Air Force in May 1918. At the time women were employed in a range of roles in the air force, as clerks and store-women and as skilled workers such as welders, fitters and tin-smiths. Sadly, Nesta died of appendicitis in 1919 at the age of 22.

The tragic list of local men killed or wounded continued. Lieutenant-Colonel Hubert Lionel Budge of the Royal Scots, eldest son of Philip Budge, was reported killed at the Somme in July 1916. He was 38 and left a wife and two children. In April 1917, Leslie Shave of the Dorset Regiment, whose mother had a stationers' shop at No. 156 High Street, was killed in France at the age of 20. He had been studying for the Civil Service before he enlisted with the Artists Rifles in 1915. Private George Carey of the Worcestershire Regiment, an employee of H. J. Travers, outfitters, died of wounds in hospital in September, leaving a wife of just a few months.

Not all the news was bad. Early in 1917, Douglas Sharp, the youngest son of Mr. F. A. Sharp ironmonger of No. 69 High Street was awarded the Military Medal. He had worked for some time in the Post Office before emigrating to Canada and had joined up with the 1st Canadian Division. Another local man to win the Military

Medal was Lance Corporal Arthur Stevens of the Devonshire Regiment. As a company stretcher bearer he had taken over when the senior stretcher bearer was injured, remaining at his post and attending to several wounded men over many hours.

Life in High Street continued in a fashion. The newspaper included a regular feature on what was showing at the Poole Electric Theatre and the Amity Hall. The Electric Theatre's offering for September 1917 was *'Through the Wall'*, described as a *'great Vitagraph 6-reel detective story' about a high-life criminal, 'thrilling and fascinating throughout'*. In January 1918, the Amity was advertising *the famous "Dinnie Sisters" who . . . give the most clever and daring equilibrist act we have ever seen. Sydney Parker, the blind male soprano and Frank Williams, tenor comedian, known as the Welsh Vaudeville Entertainers, present their latest songs, patter and parodies.'* In April, Councillor Gambier demonstrated how to cook *'economical dishes for ordinary families'*, at the Poole Borough Cookery School. The three dishes shown were a fish souflée from Labrador salt cod, rissoles of salt fish and stinging nettles garnished with tomato purée, providing a dinner for four at a total cost of 1s 11d (10p).

With shipping losses at sea, food shortages really began to bite, although rationing had at last been introduced. As a notice in the *Herald* from the International Stores spelt out, *'please remember that we cannot now select our supplies, but have to accept what is allotted to us'*. Herbert Carter described notices all down High Street: *"No Margarine, No Jam, No Tea, No Cheese". Butchers opened just one or two days a week and long queues of women gradually grew longer still!'* Ernest Bristowe remembered queuing *'from six o'clock in the morning until eight o'clock when the Maypole Dairy in the High Street opened, to buy half a pound of margarine.'* As a boy scout, Ernest was also involved as a messenger at the railway station meeting the hospital trains carrying the wounded from France. The Cornelia and Alderney hospitals were both extended to accommodate more casualties.

In the final months of the war, news came that another of Philip Budge's sons, Lieutenant Colonel Philip Prideaux Budge D.S.O. had been killed in the Pas-de-Calais. Arthur Reyner of the Dorset Regiment, the only son of Mrs. Reyner, tobacconist of 138, High Street, was killed in action in France aged 20. A few weeks before the armistice, High Street confectioner, George Keene and his wife heard that their second son Lance Corporal Clarence Keene of the Military Mounted Police had died of malaria in Palestine. For draper Theophilus Miles and his wife there was better news. Their son, Lance Corporal Miles of the Somerset Light Infantry, who had been wounded and taken prisoner at St Quentin, had been exchanged and was now in hospital in London. In 1918 the list of 'absent voters', recorded for the first time in the electoral register, revealed that 67 men from High Street were away serving in the forces. In November came the long awaited announcement that hostilities were at an end.

Andrew Hawkes Poole Photo Archive

The Worcestershires marching over the railway crossing.

Given the level of loss, it is not surprising that the celebrations for the end of the war were a mixture of joy and grief. The *Herald* expressed the mood: *'There are few houses in the land upon which the war has not laid some share of its sorrow and suffering, some cause for abiding grief, but in the thrilling hour of victory our first thoughts and feelings are those of heartfelt thanksgiving that the long agony of blood and tears is over'.* Families had to somehow cope with their losses and carry on. Men returning from the forces, often injured and traumatised, had to fit back into civilian life as best as they could. Some employers offered a lifeline. A notice in the press from the International Stores stated: *'All our Employees who left us to join H.M. Forces and who wish to re-enter our service are invited to communicate at once with the Staff Department'.*

The official victory celebrations came on 18th and 19th July 1919 and *'the streets were ablaze with flags and bunting . . . button-holes sported the red, white and blue, patriotic paper whips were in great demand'.* On Friday 18th 6,500 school children assembled in the park. The *Herald* made a special mention of the girls from South Road School who *'were all dressed white and carried pure white flags with the word "Peace" inscribed.'* The Mayor, Major G. A. Dolby, addressed the crowd and urged them to *'do their part for the betterment of the Empire . . . never forgetting that they belonged to a great and god-fearing nation whose honour they had to uphold'.* Next came tea, followed by sports and sideshows.

The following day brought heavy rain but the scheduled adult celebrations continued as planned. A civic procession gathered at the Guildhall and walked to the park where around 2,000 ex-servicemen and old age pensioners were given lunch (arranged by Evan Gambier and his committee). A speech was given by Captain the Hon. F.E. Guest D.S.O. M.P. He dealt with the vexed question of demobilisation and perhaps addressing the more impatient elements in the crowd, stressed the value of *'reconstruction, patience, constitutionalism and local unity'*. The *Herald* noted without comment that *'the local branch of the Association of Discharged Sailors and Soldiers did not take part in the proceedings'*. In the evening fireworks were let off in the streets and a huge bonfire was lit on Constitution Hill, which could be seen far out to sea.

Chapter Nine

The Mid 20th Century

'Most of the buildings were old, some of them very old and in very poor condition. The nearer to the Quay, the worse they became.'

The first few years after the war were a time of economic hardship, unemployment and dissatisfaction as families, some without a breadwinner, struggled to resume their lives. Aubrey Jenkins in his reminiscences *'Eighty Five Years in Poole'* described *'poor young widows struggling to bring up their families on a few shillings a week'* and *'men minus limbs, blinded, victims of gas attacks coughing their lives away'*. Jobs were in short supply. In 1921, Herbert Carter observed *'crowds of unemployed about the streets. It is said that there are 2,000 in Poole'*. Approached by a deputation of the unemployed, the Council asked the Guild of Help to organise emergency school meals for their children. It was an unhappy start to peace-time.

High Street was in a run down state. According to Aubrey Jenkins, *'Most of the buildings were old, some of them very old and in very poor condition. The nearer to the Quay, the worse they became.'* Shortly after the war the old thatched cottage at No. 78 High Street was demolished. The building was believed to date from the 16th century and may have once housed the White Bear Inn. The ancient, low building with its small windows was replaced by a substantial shop which became Poole's first *Woolworth's store. Describing themselves as a 'fancy repository' and later as the '3d and 6d stores'* F.W. Woolworth & Co. Ltd. became a much loved part of the High Street scene. Aubrey Jenkins described how Woolworth's livened up the street with its low prices and innovative sales techniques. For instance they offered *'buckets... for sixpence, much to the dismay of ironmongers. Of course only a few were on sale, but it got customers into the store and that was the idea; once in, customers were almost certain to buy something if they couldn't get a bucket.'* There was also a young woman playing the latest songs on a piano to encourage sales of sheet music.

Andrew Hawkes Poole Photo Archive

Twentieth century renovations in other old High Street buildings were bringing to light some ancient features. Just before the war, workmen had discovered what looked like a secret staircase built into a wall at the King's Head. The entrance to the staircase appeared to be through a cupboard on the right hand side. Niches in the wall led from the ground floor to the first floor with a series of steps above. An old door was also found containing a window on which was scratched *'William Milner junior November 8th Custom House 1378 Poole'*. In 1923, alterations at No. 25, the premises of hairdresser Mr. Purdue, revealed an Elizabethan window behind a wall, together with a massive bench. However it was the ancient Scaplen's Court, last mentioned in the mid 18th century divided into several dwellings, that was about to reveal the most amazing secrets.

Through the 19th century, the building had been further sub-divided into a number of tenements and workshops. Rooms were partitioned, fireplaces and doorways blocked up, walls plastered over. By 1901, there were five families (23 people) living in the building. The accommodation was basic. Mrs. Phyllis Cole who had lived there as a child, described it 40 years later as old, draughty and ugly: *'I can only remember one sink and that was out in the back garden. It was used by us and all the other tenants.'* If the weather was reasonable, all the washing had to be done out in the open but if it was too bad, bowls of water had to be carried inside.

By the 1920s, the property housed seven families and was in a very dilapidated

Andrew Hawkes Poole Photo Archive

Scaplen's Court after the storm

state. During a storm in October 1923, a chimney stack toppled over and crashed through the roof of the front range. The damage to the property meant that some of the tenements were unfit for habitation but it also revealed parts of the ancient structure which had long been hidden. In 1924, local historian and school master, Harry Peace Smith (known affectionately as H. P. or 'Gunner' Smith) was given access to the building by the owner, Mr. F. S. Allen. The owner's plan was to demolish part of the building to allow space to garage his lorries. He allowed H. P. Smith to examine the vacant parts of the building and even joined him in taking down brickwork and plaster as the search intensified.

An article written by H. P. Smith for the *Poole Observer* conveys some of the excitement of that day of discovery. *'When the partitions which had divided one room from another were removed . . . we found ourselves in a hall forty feet long and twenty four feet wide. The left hand jamb of an arched stone doorway (bricked up) was already visible, and when we had removed a brick chimney piece we found ourselves looking at a fairly well preserved Gothic doorway,*

Andrew Hawkes Poole Photo Archive

An ancient doorway rediscovered

seven feet high and three feet six inches wide.' Behind a modern mantlepiece in the upper hall and under a thick layer of plaster, was an original stone fireplace inscribed with initials and dates from the 17th century and earlier. Medieval roof timbers, carved stone window frames, 18th century panelling, cornices and carved doors were all revealed.

This was the start of a campaign to persuade the Council to preserve the building and turn it into a museum. In a speech given to the Society of Poole Men and Poole town councillors in August 1924, H. P. Smith argued that *'if you let the building come under the hammer of demolition, future generations will rise up and condemn you.'* However the owner's asking price was £1,000, money was short and while the council debated, the building deteriorated. In late 1925 a gale caused another major collapse of of the building and the cause seemed hopeless.

If no solution was in sight for Scaplen's Court, other buildings were changing the look of High Street. In 1924 the Midland Bank built a new classical style branch on the corner of High Street and Hill Street. Constructed of brick with stone dressings, it exuded traditional dependability with its classical windows and doorways and carved swags of flowers. Another change was the demolition of the George Hotel to be replaced by a new hotel on the same site. The old toll house also disappeared, its place taken by a small traffic island.

High Street was still the place for some notable shops like the superior gown

Borough of Poole Museum Service

Harry Cole in a typical pose

shop at No. 146 kept by Mrs. Prankard, the wife of the headmaster of South Road School. At No. 91 was Boone's ironmongers where, according to Aubrey Jenkins, *'you could buy tools, lamp glasses, screws, nails, candles, paraffin, in fact everything necessary for the home in those days.'* Hawkes' shoe shop had been completely modernised with a luxurious fitting room and x-ray machine installed. Further along was the shop of J. Cole jeweller, noticeable for its drum clock, and opposite was Theophilus Miles' large drapery and millinery store. Mr Miles would often stand outside his shop and greet passers-by encouraging them to enter. A little further down were the three glass balls of Tuson's pawnbrokers, run by Mr Turner, *'a dapper little man who often stood outside his shop, hands clasped behind his back ready with a pleasant greeting. Of course he did not have to invite customers in; they came because usually they had to.'*

Another tradesman well known on High Street was Harry Cole whose family had a furnishing stores and undertaking business at No. 120. He was a skilled cabinet maker and was descended from Sir William Phippard, merchant and M.P. of Poole. As a boy, Ernest Bristowe knew him as *'a genial old gentleman, known and liked by everyone. Bearded and wearing a long frock coat, he would doff his top hat to all and sundry. . . He was a great supporter of the rights of the poor and could be relied upon to raise matters that affected them whenever the Council met'.*

Tom Hockey was a fish-seller whose barrow was usually parked outside the Wesleyan Church. His voice, reputed to be the loudest in Poole, could be heard from Topp's Corner to the Post Office, advertising his 'fresh caught' mackerel and herring. Tom was a keen cinema-goer and because his eyesight was poor, liked to sit in the front row. Aubrey Jenkins recalled an incident at the Amity when *'to his annoyance his favourite seat was occupied by another who was not aware of the unwritten law about Tom's favourite seat. Tom glared at him for a few minutes then in his best costermongers voice roared "Hey, that's my seat", and promptly hauled the startled fellow out and sat in "his" seat amidst roars of laughter from those nearby.'*

Andrew Hawkes Poole Photo Archive

The Regent Theatre and shops

During the 1920s, the Council was increasing its efforts to promote Poole as a tourist resort, stressing the healthy climate and the beauties of the local scenery, *'a climate that is perpetual Spring . . . heather and bracken clad slopes, romantic chines . . . sea-girt sand dunes'* and so on. The more mundane charms of *'up to date and popular shopping centres'*, including High Street, were also promised. As well as general tourists the authorities hoped to attract artists. Augustus John had come to live at Alderney just north of the town in 1910 and Henry Lamb moved into a house in Hill Street in 1922. With their friends and visitors and several talented locals, something of an artists' colony had grown up in the area. Lamb particularly, enjoyed the atmosphere of 1920's Poole and painted a series of townscapes which convey the rather shabby, impoverished but lively town of the period.

Distinguished guests occasionally passed through the town to stay with the Van Raalte family on Brownsea Island. In September 1924, Evan Gambier of the King's Head was surprised on answering the telephone when the caller asked for Prince Nicholas. It emerged that Prince Nicholas of Rumania was in the hotel waiting for the motor boat to take him across to the island. Such exotic visitors were few however and did not have much impact on the town itself. It was the ordinary tourists that Poole hoped to attract in larger numbers.

In 1926, workers' dissatisfaction reached its climax in the general strike. The *Herald* called it *'the greatest industrial crisis in history'*. The Council concentrated on trying to manage the situation while maintaining *'a wholesome restraint of language and action'*. Food sub-committees were set up involving many High Street traders like T.S. Soul, butcher, grocer Herbert Saunders, and baker Joseph Bright. A total of 861 volunteers enlisted, some as special constables under the control of William Hatton Budge to guard the railway station and petrol depots and to patrol the town. Others volunteered to run essential services. Coal was sold in half hundredweights from door to door. The tram network shut down when all the staff withdrew their labour, but a basic service was restored on the second day by volunteers. After about 10 days, the strike was called off, the dockers being the last of the Poole workers to return to work.

In contrast, other events that year showed surprising commercial optimism. The demand for motion pictures was growing and James Bravery decided to build a larger, more functional cinema to replace the little Poole Electric Theatre. The Regent Theatre was built in High Street Longfleet on the site of two former shops and a blacksmith's forge, opposite Snook's stationers and Burden and Sons, the grocers. It was opened on December 6th 1926, by Alderman Herbert Carter, the Mayor of Poole with a gold key (supplied by James Cole the jeweller). Also present on the opening night were the Mayor of Bournemouth and Mr. G.R. Hall Caine, M.P. for East Dorset. The new theatre had seats for 1000, full stage facilities, seven dressing rooms and a splendid three-manual organ. The building's facade was covered with eye-catching white Carter's pottery tiles. For the first few years the Regent offered plays, revues and films but once the 'talkies' arrived, its programme consisted almost entirely of films.

Another eye-catching building was the rotunda next to Beech Hurst, built as a showroom by the Bournemouth Gas and Water Company. The architect's brief was *'to design a showroom which fulfilled all modern requirements as to space and lighting . . . and to make it harmonise with its old and dignified neighbour.'* The result was a building which echoed some of the classical elements of Beech Hurst with its encircling columns, while introducing modern walls of glass panes. Inside, the decoration was in keeping with that of the old house. Behind Beech Hurst, on a large area of partly reclaimed ground, the company built their Pitwines gas works with a huge boiler house and gasometer.

In 1927, the *Herald* reported the death of Thomas Joyner, musician, inventor, artist and keeper of the curio shop in High Street Longfleet. According to the paper, he *'was in his 99th year and was believed to be the oldest native of Poole'*. He had lived through the reigns of five monarchs and could remember as a tiny child hearing the guns fired in honour of the dethroned Charles X of France. Having learnt the trade of iron and brass working under his father he became a skilled craftsman, his most notable work being the weather vane on the top of the Poole Library. His death seemed like the breaking of a link with old Poole.

Borough of Poole Museum Service

Beech Hurst and the gas showroom

Another long-term Poole resident and High Street trader also died that year. Grocer and baker Herbert Hutchings had started as an apprentice to the confectioner George Green before setting up on his own account, in Market Street and Hill Street and then at 130 High Street, next to the Wesleyan Church. He brought up a family of five children and remained in business for nearly 60 years before retiring around 1925. He helped to found the Dorset Bakers' Association and was also treasurer and a trustee of Longfleet Congregational Church, being almost entirely responsible for raising the funds needed to build the new church. When he died in 1927, the Herald called him *'one of the oldest grocers in the county'*.

For a couple of years Scaplens Court had stood empty and forlorn. Then fresh discoveries in the west block encouraged the Society of Poole Men to have another attempt at preserving it. Herbert Carter described how H. P. Smith convinced them: *'He rose and in his inimitable way talked and talked, while skepticism gave gradually way to belief, and belief was reinforced by a burning zeal for preserving this unique piece of Poole History in stone.'* The sum of £430 was raised and the building was finally acquired. After repair and renovations it was opened to the public as a museum in April 1929 with H. P. Smith as Honorary Curator. The front range was still open to the sky but it had been tidied up and made secure. In the first two years, 10,000 visitors paid their sixpences to see the house and in 1931, the Poole Corporation finally took over the building for the sum of £1,600.

By the late 1920s, the tram network was in a bad state of repair. Some felt that the trams had their day and should be replaced with buses. Negotiations were begun between Poole, Bournemouth and the Hants and Dorset Motor Services Ltd and the Lower Parkstone route was closed on 5th January 1929 although the Upper Parkstone route continued to operate. A reporter for the *Echo* rode on the last tram as it *'rattled and banged over the worn out lines'*.

The motor buses which replaced the trams were comparatively silent and luxurious besides being covered against the weather. Another advantage was that they did not have to stop at the railway line. Some independent bus operators ran services to Poole Quay, bringing public transport back into lower High Street. Most Hants and Dorset services terminated next to the George Hotel or just off High Street by the public library in Mount Street, areas which became increasingly congested with buses. In 1935, the Upper Parkstone tram route finally closed, bringing more buses on to the roads. Aubrey Jenkins remembered the congestion in the old town: *'Motor traffic had by now increased enormously and the High Street was a nightmare with traffic going both ways and cars parked both sides of the road; it must have been terrible for the bus drivers.'*

A new central bus station was needed but the company's favoured site in Kingland Road clashed with plans for a 'switch road' designed to avoid the bottle neck by bridging the railway line to bring the traffic into the lower town. Eventually, with no definite plans for a road in the Council's schedule, Hants and Dorset began negotiations to buy a piece of land near the White House Laundry. Work started on a bus station in 1938.

Although times were still hard, people made the most of entertainment available. It was a great period for cinema going, especially when the 'talkies' arrived. The Amity Palace of Varieties had been managed by James Bravery's company but with the opening of the Regent, he had handed over the control to a former actor and producer, Walter West. In 1931, the Amity upgraded its facilities. The announcement read: *'This Theatre is now being equipped with the latest talking equipment and will commence all-talking programmes on Monday next July 21st with Victor McLaglen in "King, of the Khyber Rifles", the most thrilling Talkie ever heard or seen'*. The theatre was to continue until the 1950s.

Poole Carnival was a popular annual event, organised mainly by the shop assistants with the support of their employers who donated prizes. The procession was formed of walkers in fancy dress and horse-drawn floats, often advertising local businesses, with a section for the Carnival Queen and her attendants. Led by the Poole Town Band, it started from the Quay and paraded up High Street to the park where the judging took place and a fair was set up for the day with stalls and rides. The town more or less shut down for the day and everyone turned out to see the fun.

Football was another passion for many. Aubrey Jenkins described the excitement on a Saturday evening when the special yellow football edition of the

Jenny Oliver

The Longfleet Hotel with the Port Mahon Castle Hotel and the Regent beyond.

Echo came out containing all the results. *'The paper sellers came rushing down the High Street calling out "Footer Echo" with everyone scrambling to buy one. . . So there we were, all excited and arguing about the results, usually standing in the middle of the road and being honked at by the cars and buses. The 1930's Saturday evening Poole High Street where everybody knew everybody.'*

Gradually, new shops were brightening up High Street. Companies like Curry's the cycle traders and Timothy White's the chemist appeared in the 1920s. Marks and Spencer's bazaar opened in 1932 at No. 105-7. The new premises built by these firms encouraged other businesses to smarten up their shops inside and out. New facades and windows appeared like the modern Art Deco style windows of Montague Burton's shop at No. 80. In 1936, J.A. Hawkes and Son installed a brand new shop front in the latest style with an illuminated sign. The town was beginning to wake up to new methods of selling and display.

Hotels were also improving their facilities to attract the new visitors. The Longfleet Hotel at No. 180-4 advertised itself as *'Poole's most Central Modern Hotel . . . Garage 20 Cars . . . 40 Bedrooms all fitted H. & C. Running Water'*. The terms were from 31/2 guineas [£3 67p] full board in the high season. The Antelope *('The Yachting and Fishing House of Poole Harbour')* stressed its location close to the Quay and to *Florinda*, the floating club house of the Royal Motor Yacht Club. *'We cater Specially for Yachtsmen and can serve a Meal, from a Sandwich to a Full Course Dinner at any time.'*

In 1936, the London Hotel was totally rebuilt in a modern style. In the words

Andrew Hawkes Poole Photo Archive

The lounge of the rebuilt London Hotel.

of the Herald, *'The design is pleasing in its simplicity, and the only exterior decoration is in the suggestion of hops in the Purbeck stone over the entrances.'* The lounge bar was furnished in green hide and decorated with a frieze *'depicting the daily life of Poole High-street'* painted by Cecil Todd and students from the Poole Art School. Harry Cole, H.P. Smith and Scaplen's Court, the railway crossing and the buses all featured in the frieze, sections of which are now in the Poole Museum. The hotel was equipped with the latest cooking appliances by a top London supplier and furnished by Harvey Nichols and Co. Ltd.

This was also the year that the High Street butchers and provision dealers W. L. Miller and Sons Ltd. made the transition from retailers to large scale manufacturers with the opening of their new factory at Sterte by the mayor, Alderman Major M. J. Wheatley. The *Herald* gave a glowing account of the modern factory with its *'up-to-date machinery and labour-saving devices. . . its absolute cleanliness. Benches, tables, etc., are all spotlessly clean, and the smart white clad assistants fully appreciate the necessity of maintaining it in this condition.'* With their farm and piggery at Holt and their High Street shop, Miller's were now involved in the whole food production process.

By the late 1930s, war was beginning to seem inevitable. Plans to deal with air raids had begun as early as 1936 and by 1939, shelters were dug in the town. In March, recruiting meetings were held in the park and in the cinemas. The summer saw a trial black-out and a full scale civil defence exercise. By the time war was declared on 3rd September, there was almost a sense of relief that the waiting and wondering was over. A tremendous thunder storm the previous day had caused flooding throughout the town. One of the worst affected shops was Madame Ford's drapers and costumiers at No. 189-191 High Street where hundreds of yards of material and piles of garments were damaged by flood water. On the day of the declaration, High Street was closed as council workmen replaced wooden blocks washed up by the floods. Evidence of war was all around as the Herald reported: *'children and grown-ups from evacuation areas carrying their gas masks . . . A.R.P. workers dashing here and there . . . last minute touches being made to the almost completed air raid shelters, people busy perfecting their black-out arrangements'.*

A couple of weeks after the outbreak of war, the long established grocers Saunders and Sons had to close down, having run into financial problems. Bert Saunders, who had taken over the business on his father's retirement two years before, was quoted by the *Herald*: *'It was only a very small debt that led to the closing of the business and now everything has been sold up.'* The sale of effects realised *'an almost incredibly low total'*. Bert Saunders, a father of six, was left urgently looking for work, and his father Herbert was said to be said to be heart-broken about the closing of the family business in which he had worked for 62 years.

Meanwhile the newly refurbished Bon Marché *'departmental'* store (Edwin Jones & Co.) was reopening its doors at No. 89. As the Herald reported: *'The old shop has been completely rebuilt on the most modern lines and a gleaming black, white and chromium front with a wide façade of well-dressed windows presents itself to the gaze of interested shoppers.'* The ground floor was fitted with *'glass-lined show cases and chromium stands'* to display the goods, and stocked fashion, household linen, haberdashery and even gas mask carriers. Upstairs was the millinery department and the pride of the store, the restaurant which could seat 150 people and offered a *'three course lunch for 1s 6d'* [7½p]. It was Poole's first department store and a great asset to High Street but it was reopening into a very uncertain world.

The first few months of the war seemed to be a period of marking time. Traders complained about reduced bus services which they felt were affecting trade. In January 1940, rationing was introduced for bacon, ham butter and sugar, the weekly allowances for each person being 4oz of butter, 4oz of bacon and ham (31/2 oz if cooked) and 12oz of sugar. Butchers reported that they were overstocked with 'ends' of bacon (gammon and hocks) which no-one had enough coupons to buy. In May there was a drive to collect Poole's iron railings to be turned into shells.

Different branches of the services, military and civilian, were setting up their headquarters in various parts of the town. The administrative offices of the naval command were above the National Provincial Bank in High Street. The naval officer in charge was Commander Cosmo B. Hastings R.N., a veteran of the first war and the Florinda, moored at the Quay, was made naval headquarters. Meanwhile No. 4

High Street, the old subscription library and more recently the office of the 'Gondolier' pleasure boats, was renamed 'Airways House' and became the offices of the newly formed British Overseas Airways Corporation. The company had taken over Imperial Airways and relocated from Hythe to operate its flying boats from the harbour, making Poole one of the country's few international airports.

The war suddenly became very real for Poole in mid May when boats of Dutch and Belgian refugees began to arrive in the harbour, fleeing the German advance. They were accommodated on Brownsea Island for screening while the town was scoured for tents, blankets, food and other supplies. They did not have a very comfortable time because, as recalled by Mr. Lewis, a member of the Air Raid Precautions Committee, the island was overrun with rats which Brownsea's owner Mrs. Christie used to feed. She was opposed to killing any animals but in this case, the military got rid of most of them.

The British Expeditionary Force was also in retreat towards the coast of France. At the end of May, owners of small boats in Poole joined others from around the south coast to help with the evacuation of troops from the beaches of Dunkirk, St Valery, St Malo, Cherbourg and Brest. The boats from Poole included a number of pleasure boats, several of the Dutch refugee boats and the Poole inshore lifeboat, the *Thomas Kirk-Wright.* The occupation of France meant that Poole and other south coast towns were suddenly on the front line.

The next few months were spent desperately trying to improve the town's defences, seeding possible landing grounds with telegraph poles, securing the beaches, digging pits for anti-aircraft guns and putting up concrete anti-tank barriers, known as 'dragon's teeth'. It was felt that certain buildings, including the Regent Cinema with its striking white tiles, were likely targets for bombers, but trying to camouflage them might make them even more conspicuous. In July, the Local Defence Volunteers were renamed the Home Guard and 25 Lee Enfield rifles were issued to each platoon. Lt-Col Mervyn Wheatley, a retired army officer and former mayor, was appointed as the local Commanding Officer.

In the afternoon of Wednesday 21st August 1940, Poole had its first experience of bombing when a solitary Junkers 88 appeared over the town and dropped a stick of seven bombs on the old town before making its escape. Fortunately, it was early closing day. In High Street, the Fifty Shilling Tailor's at No. 84 received a direct hit. Witnesses of the raid still remember how the tailors' dummies from the window were strewn across the road, looking horrifyingly like casualties. Windows of shops opposite were blown out, including those of the brand new Bon Marché department store. The A.R.P. services were quickly on the scene clearing away debris and shoring up properties. That week the report on the raid in the *Poole and Dorset Herald* was determinedly up-beat with headlines like *'Morale was*

Bomb damage to the Fifty Shilling Tailor's with Looker's, printers and the windows of Montague Burton's in the background.

Unshaken' and 'Not as Bad as it Looked'. According to the paper, the raid proved that *'it's going to take the heck of a lot of bombs to shake the people's morale in this coast town . . . Not a tear was to be seen. People who had lived in the same house practically all their lives, though dazed and bewildered when their homes fell about their ears, soon recovered their spirits'.* The reality was probably much grimmer and more terrifying.

In the following weeks, Poole suffered a series of air attacks with incendiaries and high explosive bombs. A German invasion seemed a daily possibility and the violent drama of the Battle of Britain was taking place in the skies above. It was not until the autumn that the threat of invasion retreated for the time being. Out in the Atlantic, U-boat attacks were taking their toll of shipping convoys and food was in short supply. By 1941, the milk ration was 1/2 pint per day and the meat ration 1s 6d (7½p) per week, but even this was more than the butchers could supply. Queuing was becoming a way of life. Another trial of daily life was the black-out which applied even to buses as Aubrey Jenkins described: *'the interior lights had been tinted over with a blue substance so as not to show a light that could be seen from the air. As we sat in the bus with this ghostly blue pallor we could not help laughing at one another, it wasn't all doom and gloom.'*

To deal with the 'fire blitz', the Corporation recruited fire watchers and stirrup-pump parties for all areas of the town to deal with the continuing attacks. On 27th March 1941, in the most devastating raid to date, a bomb hit the canteen of the

Bourne Valley Gas Works as the men were gathering for lunch. The building was destroyed, 34 men were killed and 23 injured, 16 seriously. Two days after the gas works raid, Aubrey Jenkins was married to his fiancée, Gabrielle Speed. The wedding meal was held in the Bon Marché restaurant complete with ersatz wedding cake, icing sugar being impossible to get. Even this joyful occasion was tinged with apprehension. *'As I looked out of the window opposite, there were the ruins of what had been Fifty Shilling Tailors which had earlier been hit by a bomb and destroyed. It was a depressing sight and I wondered what the future would bring or if we had any future.'*

The following month, a group of ten men came to Poole and set up in the Antelope. Although few people knew of them at the time, they were part of a Small Scale Raiding Force of commandos, set up to terrorise the enemy coasts with quick, devastating raids. Their leader was Captain Gustavus March-Phillipps with Lt. Geoffrey Appleyard as second in command. They requisitioned a Brixham trawler and began to train around the harbour, visiting the town at weekends. After a few weeks they left on their first mission after a farewell lunch at the Antelope.

Most of the younger men and some of the women were of course away in the forces. David Williams, an assistant at the World's Stores was one of the many High Street employees to join up. Service with the R.A.F. took him to Singapore, Australia and Ceylon, a place he had previously only known from the packets of tea he used to sell across the counter. Victor Hawkes' son, David was serving in the Far East with a light anti-aircraft regiment. Other members of Hawkes' staff were away at the front. The Burbidge family, former fish dealers at No. 43 High Street, could boast six children engaged in war work and three in the forces, Cyril in the Royal Army Ordnance Corps, George in the navy and Alma in the WRNS.

Many of those still at home were involved in war work either paid or voluntary, as A.R.P. wardens, fire watchers, members of the Home Guard or in the W.V.S. As in the first war, women were working in many unfamiliar jobs including munitions and engineering. Post-women were to be seen once more on High Street and conductresses appeared on the buses. The Bournemouth Gas and Water Company took on women as gas fitters and the *Herald* reported that most of them found the work compared favourably with their previous jobs in domestic service, as waitresses or shop assistants. The mayor of Poole at the outbreak of war was Joseph Bright, a baker who had set up in business at No. 117 High Street in the early 1920s. He was destined to remain as mayor for an unprecedented seven years. With no elections being held, the members of the Council also found themselves serving for the duration

In the second half of 1941, Hitler's attack on Russia meant some relief from air raids. Then the attack on Pearl Harbour on 7th December brought the United States into the war. There was reason for optimism as Christmas approached but

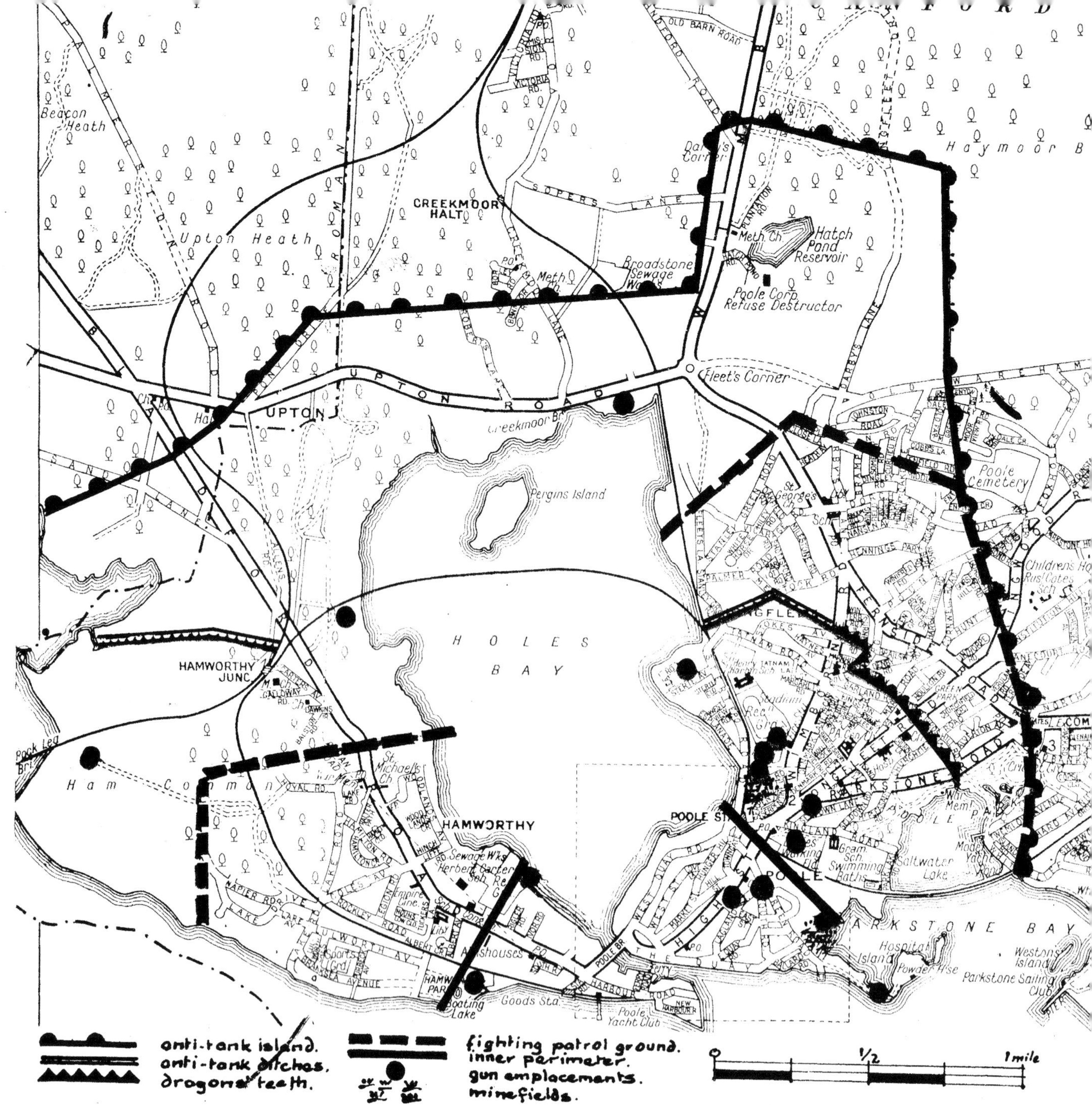

Borough of Poole Museum Service

Poole Anti-Tank Island

daily life was as difficult as ever. There were shortages of everything. Bus services were reduced. Newspapers were restricted to four pages and a ban was put on wrapping paper, posters, paper handkerchiefs and Christmas cards. Joseph Bright led another appeal for iron railings and many disappeared at this time, changing the look of the streets for ever.

In the next few months, the defence of Poole was put on a more organised footing. The harbour was already well defended so most of the plans were directed towards protecting the town from the land. The 'Poole Anti-Tank Island' was intended to *'defend the port of Poole and thereby deny the enemy its wharves, landing facilities, ship repairing installations and workshops.'* The outer area would be manned by fighting patrols whose job was to harass the enemy and defend the perimeter, consisting of a line of ditches and anti-tank 'dragon's teeth'. Reserve troops would be positioned within the perimeter to defend the inner redoubt which consisted of the old town up to the railway crossing, and lower Hamworthy. Given the topography of the town, it was not perhaps surprising that the redoubt was almost identical to the area defended during the Civil War, 300 years before.

The idea was to hold the redoubt for as long as possible to delay the enemy until relief arrived. Gun emplacements were set at strategic points including the railway station, Pitwines Gas Works, the Ladies Walking Field and outside Marks and Spencer. Road blocks consisting of *'removable girders and bent rails placed in sockets in four rows'* were planned for various streets including High Street. Casualty clearing posts and hospital facilities were identified. Water and food supplies, and alternative lighting and heating were provided. The plan was laid out in a top secret document known to very few at the time, although some of the preparations must have been obvious.

The summer of 1942 saw more air raids although their impact was reduced by decoy fires on Brownsea Island diverting the bombers from the town. Even so there were deaths and damage. On 11th June the *Herald* reported: *'In the main street of the town a grocer's shop owned by Mr. J.P. Gifford was gutted but early next morning the business was being re-started in a vacant shop a few doors away.'* The following month traders agreed on a plan to help each other with labour, salvage, storage and transport if any of their premises was damaged by bombing.

In spite of the wartime reduction in traffic, High Street was still very congested. Buses between Newtown and Upton had once travelled the length of High Street with stops at the library corner, Woolworths and the Quay but these had been diverted along North Street and West Quay Road. A plan to make this diversion permanent was rejected by shoppers. The new bus station was on hold until the end of the war but in October a *'bus roadway'* was completed, running from High Street to Kingland Road just north of the railway crossing. This was to provide a terminus for the Bournemouth service buses which would no longer need to join the queue of vehicles crossing the railway line.

Meanwhile bus services were reduced further to save fuel, clothes rations were cut again and coal was in short supply. Ernest Bristowe described how he and his family cut firewood on land he had bought at Henbury and found a ready market for it. Chocolate was added to the list of rationed food which also included tinned

Andrew Hawkes Poole Photo Archive

Fundraising outside the George Hotel

meat, fish and vegetables. People were urged to fill their baths no higher than six inches to save water and electricity. When Churchill ordered church bells to be rung for the victory at El Alamein in November, it was a rare moment of celebration. Over 2,000 people attended a thanksgiving service at St. James' church.

War Savings Weeks also provided rare breaks in the dreary wartime routine. In June 1943, a savings week with the theme 'Wings for Victory' aimed to raise £500,000 in loans for 10 Sunderland flying boats. A display of aircraft equipment and armament was on view at Butler's shop, 134 High Street and an operational Spitfire could be seen by the municipal buildings. In front of the George Hotel was built *'a novel form of indicator'* where it was promised, the Flying Training Command Band would play every morning between 11.30 and 12.30 and *'with due ceremony a German submarine will be sunk beneath the waves with every rise in Poole's wings total'*.

On Saturday a ceremonial procession with all the services and voluntary organisations represented, marched to Poole Park where 'Miss Victory' was crowned by Air Chief Marshal Mills. Shops in High Street were decorated with patriotic displays and entertainments such as sports, dancing and a rabbit show took place in the park throughout the week. The Squander Bug was also said to be at large in the borough. *'Be on the look out for this menace. A capture can increase your savings by a 15s* [75p] *certificate provided you can make the correct challenge and at the same time display a savings certificate.'* By Thursday, with three days to go, £150,000 was still needed as the *Herald* exhorted its readers. On the 1st July, Joseph Bright stood at the indicator to announce the final magnificent total of £634,282!

The following week the town was mourning the death of Councillor Harry Cole. A fierce champion of the underdog, strongly opinionated, kindly and eccentric, he was a unique character. He was a passionate debater and according to Herbert Carter *'entered with zest into a thousand contests and flayed his opponents mercilessly, yet they had seen him more than once moved to tears and speechless from generous emotion.'*

As Christmas 1943 approached, everything was still in short supply in spite of increasing success against the U-boats in the Atlantic. The reduced newspaper had little space for advertisements and few of the shops had much on offer. Henry and Co. Army and Navy Stores at No. 92 High Street was selling *'A Bevy of Bargains, all no coupons'* including ex-police trousers at 10s 6d (52p) and ex-police oilskin capes at 12s (60p). Curry's were offering to buy unused radios and the outfitters D. Bould Ltd. had a *'Sale for one week only. Coupon reductions for frozen stock and slightly soiled or imperfect goods'.*

By 1944, the build up of personnel, equipment and vessels in Poole was impossible to ignore. Everyone knew that an invasion of Europe was coming but no-one knew when or where. American troops moved into Poole, requisitioning hotels and private houses. As the *Herald* later reported, *'no colour bar was allowed to interfere with the kindly and courteous treatment invariably meted out to these comrades in arms'.* The town became a protected area and access was restricted, particularly to the Quay. Coastal Command left the area, followed by B.O.A.C., as landing craft and other vessels began to multiply in the harbour.

Poole was preparing for another War Savings Week with the theme 'Salute the Soldier' and a target of £500,000. A week before this was due to begin came the day that everyone had been waiting for. As Ernest Bristowe described: *'On 6th June 1944, we were awakened by the continuous roar of heavy bombers. We hurried out to see one of the most spectacular events of the war. The sky was full of American Flying Fortresses, Halifaxes and Albemarles, each towing a black, sinister looking glider. They flew in formation, low over the houses, heading for the English Channel'.*

According to the *Herald*, *'The news of the arrival of D-Day was greeted in Poole . . . with quiet satisfaction and confidence'.* As people waited for news, the savings week was launched by Lt-Col Wheatley and Joseph Bright with a grand parade and march past, followed by a week of entertainments, a band concert, an American evening, boxing, cricket, a rabbit show and dancing every evening in the park. At last there was something to celebrate. The exhibition at Butler's on the history of the Dorset Regiment was even able to incorporate some D-Day souvenirs. The money raised exceeded expectations, totalling £686,572.

Andrew Hawkes Poole Photo Archive

As allied forces overran German bases in France, the threat that had hung over Poole and the rest of the country for five long years was at last lifted. By 1945, people were able to contemplate the end of the war as a reality and turn their attention to mundane matters. Looking ahead, the Council resolved that as the High Street was narrow and inconvenient, they would adopt an 'improvement line' of 60 feet from the Ansty Arms to the Quay. As a first step towards this widening, Mr. R. C. Belben asked if the Council would like to buy No. 6 Grand Parade in lower High Street which had been damaged by enemy action, and negotiations were begun. Staff of B.O.A.C., which had returned to Poole in September, requested the Council to redecorate the façade of their offices at No. 4 High Street. On 21st September, the black-out was officially replaced by 'half light' and it was promised that all bus routes would be lit to some degree by the end of the week.

The end of the war finally came with Clement Attlee's announcement at midnight on 15th August that Japan had capitulated. As the *Herald* described, a moment or two after the announcement *'came the sounds of hooters and whistles and sirens; soon the streets were alive with people loudly cheering. As if by magic, processions of motor cars and motor-cycles and ordinary bicycles began to parade the main thoroughfares, followed . . . by parties of young people singing "Rule Britannia", "There'll always be an England", "Roll out the Barrel" and other patriotic and popular songs'.* Everyone made for the Quay where the celebrations continued for hours.

Chapter Ten

The Later 20th Century

'The transformation to a total pedestrian precinct is now complete and presents a true joy to shoppers.'

After the war Poole residents, traders and returning servicemen and women wanted nothing more than to resume their lives, but this was not so straightforward. Damaged shops needed to be rebuilt and businesses re-established. The Fifty Shilling Tailor's had been totally ruined and Gifford's burnt out. The London Hotel had been badly damaged and needed major renovation. People had been accommodated in whatever property was available, as the electoral roll of 1945 suggests. In High Street, twelve people were listed at No. 15, the former Red Star Coffee Tavern and fourteen people in the B.O.A.C. building at No. 4. The lodging house at No. 28 had twelve voters and elsewhere living quarters above shops and offices seem to have been brought back into use.

Bread rationing, using a complicated system of bread units, had been introduced *after* the war and was still in force. Adding to the gloom, January and February 1947 were exceptionally cold and supplies of fuel ran very low. The *Herald* reported Poole women *'shivering in the Arctic weather, shopping in poorly-lit stores and making their coal eke out as long as possible'*. With the electric current off and solid fuel hard to obtain, the Bournemouth Gas and Water Company reported gas consumption up 56% on the previous year and urged people to cut back. Most street lighting was cut off and shops were managing with a single bank of lights or just candles. *'Ironmongers and grocers report the biggest demand for candles since the war and demand for paraffin for oil lamps and stoves has far exceeded supply.'*

In 1946, a planning report for Christchurch, Bournemouth and Poole in the post war period had been produced by consultant Sir Patrick Abercrombie. For Poole he recommended the rebuilding of the old town and the construction of a

Andrew Hawkes Poole Photo Archive

A busy High Street. Bon Marché and Boone's on the right.

road to the west of High Street to take the traffic from the George Hotel area over the railway to the Quay. This would not only mean the destruction of many properties but also the by-passing of High Street which the traders feared would be disastrous for business. Professor Abercrombie also stressed the importance of preserving Poole's historic and architecturally significant buildings. The only immediate result of the report was the trial of a one way system in High Street for buses (but not for private vehicles) and the banning of parking in the narrowest part of the street.

High Street's pre-war problems had not gone away. In 1949, the question of delays at the railway crossing was again under discussion. A traffic census revealed that over 8,000 vehicles crossed the railway line in a ten hour day. The gates closed five times an hour for an average time of over three minutes, meaning that the road was actually closed for over 15 minutes in every hour. A new bus station north of the crossing was urgently needed and the bus company agreed to pay 70% of the cost.

The same year, the annual report of George Chesney, Medical Officer of Health, detailed 730 unfit houses, most of them in the old town, which had been scheduled for demolition in 1938. Of these 13 were completely derelict, 15 closed and boarded up, 12 in use for storage or other purposes and 690 still occupied. *'These houses are insanitary, unfit for habitation, and incapable of being made fit, and many of them are beyond even temporary repair.'* High Street had its share of dilapidated buildings but the worst of the run-down properties were probably in the small side streets. Some of the derelict, vandalised properties were occupied by squatters, prompting families to move out to safer areas in the suburbs.

Vera Brown's memories of the area around lower High Street were recorded by the Living Histories Project: *'There were a lot of alleyways with poor living accommodation down there; little alleyways with little tiny houses. You wouldn't walk down there as a young person . . . You didn't go beyond what was then the Bon Marché and Woolworth's. . . Was it a good thing for them to knock down and rebuild that area? Good in the main; could have been even better if more thought had been put into it.'*

Meanwhile officers of the Royal Commission on Historical Monuments were conducting the first systematic survey of Poole's historical buildings. In High Street, they identified over 70 buildings of interest, ranging in date from the 16th to the 19th century. They rediscovered the houses of Tudor and Georgian merchants behind modern shop fronts, drew layout plans of many premises and noted interesting architectural features. Ironically, that year Scaplen's Court museum was found to be structurally unsound and closed for renovation. It would be nine years before the building was opened again after major reconstruction.

Fresh enthusiasm for Poole's heritage had been raised in 1948 when Looker's published the first volume of H.P. Smith's *History of the Borough and County of the*

Town of Poole. Nevertheless, when the Commission recommended that 328 buildings should be listed as of architectural or historical interest, the Council was dismayed. Pleading the necessity of slum clearance, they appealed to the Ministry which agreed that only 131 properties should be listed and another 140 put on a secondary list of buildings which it was hoped could be preserved.

In the summer of 1951, the Festival of Britain provided a little light relief. A festival committee of local organisations provided a programme of entertainment on the understanding that there would be no cost to the ratepayer. Starting with a drumhead service in the park, there were sports and gymnastics displays, sideshows and free harbour trips for the old people. Towards the end of the festival, three trains arrived at Poole station carrying 1,200 tons of equipment, 30 monkeys, 6 lions, 20 ponies, 61 horses and 6 Burma elephants, each weighing 2 tons. Bertram Mills Circus was in town. People lined the streets to watch the circus parade through the town to the Ladies Walking Field where they were to give two shows a day.

In 1952, the publication of the County Council Development Plan brought good cheer for traders in High Street. The street was to remain the principal shopping area of the town, with no plans for development elsewhere. Statistically, it appeared that Poole was well provided with shopping facilities having around 1 shop for every 42 people, which was double the national average. However accessing High Street was still a major problem for traffic, leading the *Herald* to declare that *'Poole old town is about impregnable to traffic as an ancient walled town.'* Not only was Poole Bridge frequently raised to allow collier vessels to bring 1,000 tons of coal a day to the power station at Hamworthy, but the railway crossing gates were closed 100 times a day according to the newspaper.

That summer, Poole residents and visitors were entertained by a pageant on the town's history, performed in the park with a cast of 1,500 local people. The writers were H. P. Smith and Margaret Scott, a local novelist, and the show was the 20th pageant to be organised by a well-known pageant master, Gwen Lally. The Council allowed one end of the park to be closed off, stands for 2000 to be built and even lent some of their robes and regalia for the performance. In fact many councillors were in the cast list. In spite of bad weather the show was a great success. On the last Saturday matinée performance, the 'pageanteers' paid tribute to a particular member of the audience: *'As they entered the arena, plumed hats were doffed and farthingales swept back in a curtsey'.* The special spectator was the author, H.P. Smith, who had been recuperating from a serious operation in Poole Hospital. Afterwards, *he made a short speech concluding: "I really think I have had this afternoon one of the greatest thrills of my life – I congratulate you all. Vivat Pola! Long live Poole!"*

The coronation dominated 1953 and as the date in June approached, traders' advertisements took on a regal tone. Customers were urged to buy televisions to see

the ceremony live in their own homes, or acquire suitable outfits for the celebrations. Some shops printed loyal messages. The festivities started with the reading of a loyal address to Her Majesty by Geoffrey Bravery, the Deputy Mayor (the Mayor, Miss Llewellin, having been invited to Westminster Abbey). This was followed by a civic procession, sports, entertainments and dancing in the park. In the evening, the crowd listened attentively as the Queen's speech was relayed by a loudspeaker across the cricket ground. On Constitution Hill a beacon fire was lit by the boy scouts, part of a national chain of beacons, and then a torchlight procession wound along to the park for a final firework display.

Throughout the town there were local street parties and neighbourhood decorations. For once, the narrowness of High Street was an asset as David Hawkes, President of the Poole Chamber of Commerce, told the *Herald*. *'It enabled red, white and blue garlands to be strung across, and the result was the best decorated street in the borough. . . .The lavish decorations did not cost as much as expected. Total cost of the garlands spaced at only 40-yard intervals, was well under £200. All expenses were met by the traders themselves'.*

Sadly, one person was not there to witness the historic event. H. P. Smith died on 21st April in Poole Hospital. The *Herald* paid tribute to *'not only one of our most popular and endearing citizens, but an archaeologist and historian whose valuable life-work was dedicated exclusively to the town of his adoption.'* His achievements were remarkable, rediscovering and saving Scaplen's Court, revealing the area's Iron Age and Roman past by excavations at Hamworthy, publishing the first detailed history of Poole for

Jenny Oliver

Bright's shop (now Bennett's) retains its 1930s shopfront

a century and most of all, as a teacher inspiring a generation of young Poole people with a fascination for their town's heritage.

By the mid 1950s, some prosperity was gradually returning to the town, and trade conditions were getting back to normal. Rationing finally ended in 1954 and a buoyant employment situation meant that people had money to spend. New fashions in clothes and styles of furniture were coming into the shops and household appliances like washing machines, refrigerators and televisions were becoming available to ordinary people.

In High Street the most of the shops were still family concerns. Many of them were long established like J. A. Hawkes and Son, shoe sellers, W.H. Yeatman and Sons, corn dealers and Gifford's, grocers and provision dealers, all trading since the mid 19th century or earlier. Green's confectioners had been in business since the late 1700s. Other names familiar for decades were W. E. Boone and Co. the ironmongers who had taken over from Henry Farmer, Bacon and Curtis, Cole's the jewellers, Theophilus Miles and Sons, drapers, Caleb T. Snook, stationers, and Burden and Sons, grocers and wine and spirit merchants. Geoff Cummings remembered Bright and Son, bakers at No. 117: *'Saturday tea-times at Gran's . . . were always an occasion with a box of Bright's fancies or a lardy cake on the table and who remembers Bright's marzipan traffic lights?'*

As trade improved, shopkeepers were able to update their property, incorporating the latest display technology. In 1954 Central Tailor (Poole) Ltd., men's and boy's outfitters at No. 124 High Street was enlarged and transformed by a major refurbishment. The new façade of the shop was claimed to be the only one of its kind in the country. According to the newspaper, it possessed *'the almost magical quality that arrests the attention of even the most hard-pressed passer-by, drawing him not only to its plate glass windows but into the shop itself'*. The *'entirely new and intricate method of glazing allows two pieces of glass to be joined together without any apparent support and is a firm as concrete, a German process only recently introduced to this country'*.

The proprietor of the shop was Henry John Travers, who had moved to Poole at the beginning of the century, setting up at 52, High Street as the 'Bee Hive' clothing stores. In the 1920s, the business was relocated to No. 124 where it was still going strong, more than 30 years later, having become a private company, Central Tailor Ltd. in 1952. By 1954, H. J. Travers was 80, a remarkable age to be embarking on such a major project. The enlarged shop was reported to carry the biggest stock of any outfitters in Dorset and the *Herald* reporter found *'more pairs of trousers than he thought could ever be found in one shop – 1,500 of them'*. Besides everyday and work ware, the shop also stocked outfits for yachtsmen, H. J. Travers having been a keen sailor for over 60 years. One of his shop assistants had the summer job of acting as skipper for his yacht, *Nephaic II.*

In 1955, the long delayed bus station was built on the corner of Kingland Crescent and High Street. The modern, two-storey building with a geometric decoration of tiles was the main office of the Hants and Dorset Company as well as a station for bus passengers.

High Street seemed to be moving into more prosperous times but the underlying problems of congestion, access and development had not gone away. It had become obvious by the end of the decade that Poole's shopping facilities were not after all adequate for its population of 90,000 and that many Poole people were travelling to Bournemouth or further afield for some of their more expensive purchases. Increasing the retail space in High Street south of the railway crossing was judged difficult if not impossible. In 1957, the Corporation's solutions to these issues were incorporated into a Draft Development Plan for public consultation. The stage was set for one of the biggest upheavals in High Street's long history.

The plan included a 'traffic way' to the west of Market Street to take traffic from the George Hotel, over the railway and down to the Quay, by-passing High Street and the railway crossing. To please the conservationists, there was a 'garden precinct' in the area between the traffic way and High Street and from the Guildhall to the Quay. In this area, ancient buildings could be preserved in their setting. Most contentious of all was the idea of developing the Ladies' Walking Field as a shopping area. The Walking Field was a rather rough and frequently muddy area but it was a green open space near the centre of town, used for fairs and entertainments and held in affection by many. The idea of covering it with roads and buildings provoked furious opposition.

Under the heading *'Town will Fight 'Grab' Plan'* the *Herald* anticipated strong protest at the *'astonishing plan'* of a new shopping area on the Ladies' Walking Field. They reported that *'far-sighted townsmen are alarmed because they see in it the end of old Poole. . .They say that the level crossing gates in the High Street will form an effective barrier and that business below that point will wane and die.'* Head of the redevelopment committee, Alderman Geoffrey Bravery reassured people that nothing would be done without full consultation. Even as the debate began, the first of fifteen planned new shops was opening in Kingland Crescent.

As a first step, the Corporation employed consultants Goddard and Smith to consider the plan. Their report in 1958 largely supported the Corporation's ideas and suggested that Kingland Crescent should be extended to Kingland Road and High Street near Burden's store with shops on each side. High Street traders feared that traffic might be banned from the street altogether and tempers ran high when seven councillors with interests in the old town were barred from entering the debate or voting on the plan. They included Alderman Cole, of the High Street furnishing and undertaking business, baker Alderman Bright, the war-time mayor and Alderman Geoffrey Bravery, (nephew of James Bravery) whose company owned the Regent and several other cinemas. The Draft Plan was approved by a narrow margin and in 1960 the opening of the public consultation period launched another heated debate.

Meanwhile in 1959, Scaplen's Court at last reopened to the public after a major rebuild and in June of that year another local institution quietly closed. On 10th June, the Amity cinema advertised its programme for Sunday 14th, 'A Lawless Street', starring Randolph Scott and Angela Lansbury, followed by 'He Laughed Last'. Underneath, in small letters was the message *'This will be the last Programme at the Amity'.* Poole's first cinema and long time entertainment hall had been a big part of people's lives for nearly 80 years. Now its place was taken by a new Woolworth's store whose construction was seen as a sign that High Street was still thriving. The new building was set back to the 'improvement line' to allow for future widening, but was allowed a single storey frontage, level with the neighbouring properties. Sainsbury's was said to be *'poised to jump into the site now in preparation near the Pitwines gasworks. All of which cannot be reconciled to the prospect of a moribund High Street.'* At the time this was to be their most westerly store in England.

As part of the slum clearance programme, it was planned to demolish property on the south side of the corn market and also the old houses, Nos. 21 and 23 High Street. The Rector, the Rev. George Bevington, warned that this would

Andrew Hawkes Poole Photo Archive

The Amity shortly before closure

'finally ruin the character of the lower half of the High Street'. . . 'Do you value your High Street? Look out – or you will have lost it!' In Kingland Crescent, Poole's first supermarket, Fine Fare had opened and was the first shop in town to provide continuous piped music, (interrupted every 15 minutes for a 15 second commercial). In the run-up to Christmas 1959, High Street was reported as brighter than ever with *'1,200 coloured lights, seasonal motifs and illuminated trees'*, but under the surface, change was on its way.

While dramatic changes were planned north of the crossing, High Street was evolving and updating itself the way it always had, by gradual process. In 1962, the *Herald* reported excitedly on a shop which had been transformed in 10 days from *'Georgian building to modern pharmacy'*. The building was Leslie Miller's chemist shop at No. 102 which up to then had kept its sash windows, pillared portico and balcony with iron railings. The new shop was fitted with thermostatically controlled under floor heating and Scandinavian designed sales display units *'which make the most of every conceivable inch of space at the same time presenting ample room for shoppers to see at a*

Borough of Poole Museum Service

St Paul's in the process of demolition

glance the commodities on display'. Most dramatically, the façade of the building was transformed with the latest display windows.

Leslie Miller had been born in No. 104, High Street, the long established provisions store of W.L. Miller and Sons Ltd. After qualifying as a pharmacist, he had opened a shop at No. 142 High Street in 1935. Now he was about to open his new store at a time of change in retail when self service was just coming in. The new shop was hailed as *'Poole's first ultra-modern self-selection chemist's shop'.* During the conversion work the builders found the remains of an older bow-windowed building set back from the street with a courtyard in front. There was also a 15-foot well as one of the builders unexpectedly discovered when he removed a stone slab. This was subsequently filled with concrete.

It was the era of teddy boys, juke boxes and frothy coffee and Roger Hopkins remembers the High Street's coffee bars. The Zebra Bar, next to the George Hotel (named after nothing more exotic than the nearby zebra crossing) was *'the very image of new wave milk bar chic, boasting the latest décor of trendy Formica tables and acres of chrome trim.'* More edgy was the Ship Café close to the Ansty Arms with its jukebox set to maximum volume and *'the sweaty steam of a Gaggia coffee machine'.* Fights sometimes broke out in the Ansty or the Ship to resume later in the Regent nearby. Pepy's opposite the Kingland Crescent bus station *'seemed to attract gaggles of girls – bouffant haired and mohair coated,'* and Greco's, *'the pristine little corner café'* by the Quay was the friendliest of all. For teenagers, the Poole coffee bar scene provided excitement with an edge of danger.

The street was changing in other ways. In the decades since the war, church congregations had dwindled and in 1963, 130 years after it was opened, St Paul's Church was demolished. On March 6th, the *Herald* reported that workmen had been asked to look out for some old copies of the Herald plus other historic items which had been buried near two foundation stones laid for the extension of the church in 1880. The future of the Wesleyan Church on High Street was also in the balance. One idea was to demolish the church and free up its valuable site while the congregation used rooms on the first floor above ground floor shops. The Minister, the Rev. Frederick Hunter, explained in the *Herald* that the church, which seated 800, was very expensive to maintain and needed £1,860 for redecoration and repairs of which £1,000 had been raised. The first floor idea was only one of fourteen schemes being considered.

Meanwhile the planned precinct development was pushing slowly forward, enlivened by heated debates, objections, compulsory purchase orders and a series of public inquiries. A turning point came in 1965 when the scheme to build on the Ladies' Walking Field was approved by a majority of one vote, and an offer was accepted from Arndale Property Trust Ltd. to build a 466,000 sq. ft. covered precinct, an innovative idea in the UK at the time. It was to be designed by local architects, Lester Jones and Partners. Construction began on part of the Walking Field of the new bus station which was to be relocated from Kingland Crescent.

The development meant the demolition of a block of properties in High Street. All of the eastern side from Kingland Crescent to the George would have to go. This included the former premises of Burden's and Snook's, Thomas Joyner's old shop, the site of the Electric Theatre, the Blandford Arms and other familiar landmarks. In 1967, the first turf of the new shopping precinct was dug and construction began. The same year, the new bus station was opened and the shops in Kingland Crescent completed.

A list of businesses had shown an interest in taking up shops in the new precinct including Sainbury's and Marks and Spencer whose present shop was in High Street. A branch of Bealesons, offshoot of Beales of Bournemouth, had occupied No 187 High Street since the late 1950s. Now Beales proposed to open a department store in the new centre, reinforcing the move away from High Street. In 1968, the first store (Sainsbury's) opened in what was beginning to be called the 'Arndale Centre'. Meanwhile Hall and Woodhouse Ltd. who had owned the Blandford Arms, negotiated with the Corporation and the Arndale Company to

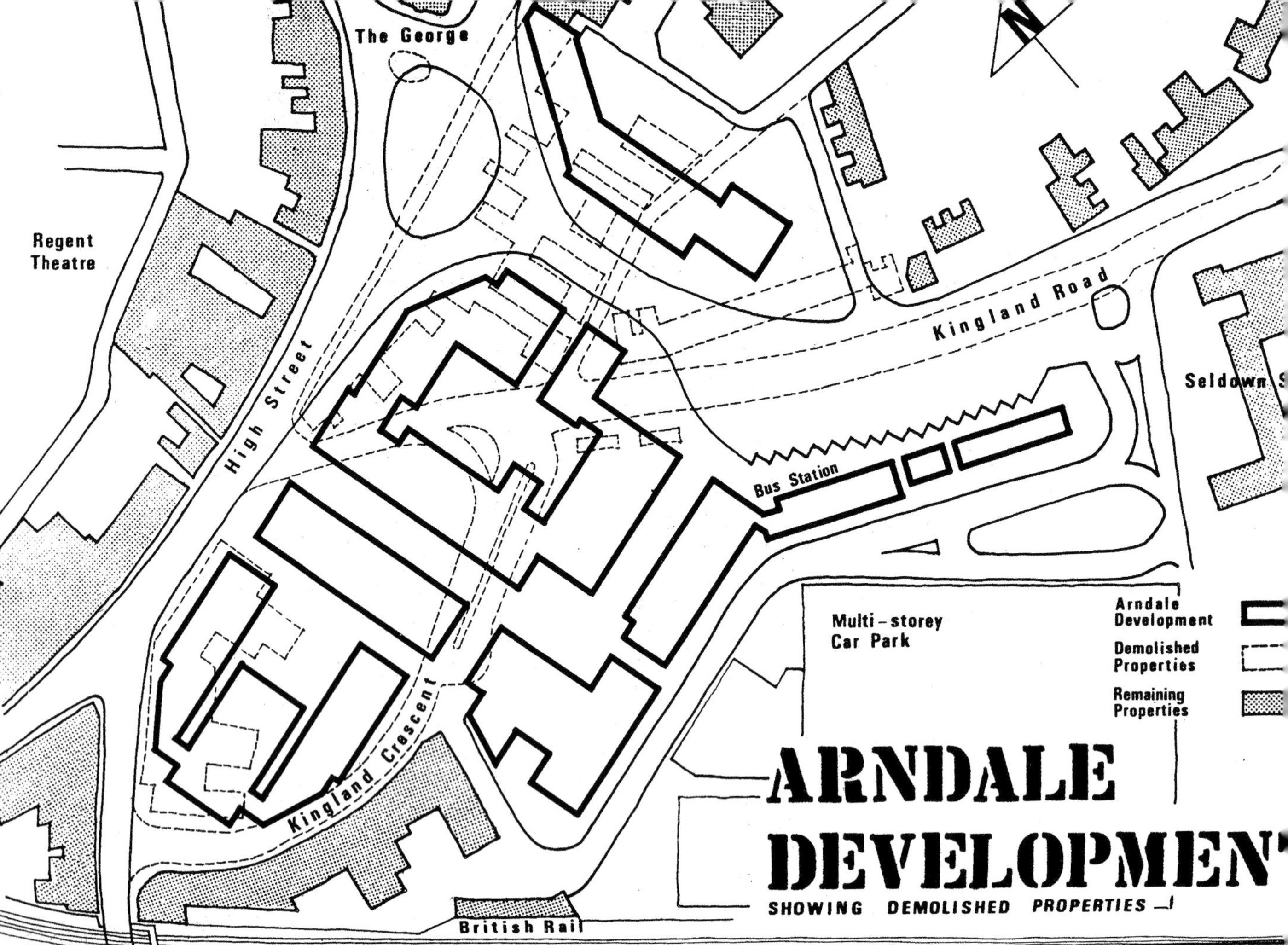

Arndale development map

lease premises for a public house in the new development. This was to be on the other side of Kingland Road from the main centre, not far from the site of the old pub. The name, inspired by the Poole coat of arms, was the Mermaid.

The Arndale Centre was opened on 1st July 1969 by the Mayor of Poole, Alderman Arthur Lloyd-Allen. In his speech, he declared that the Council had been *'quite sure that this sort of covered, air-conditioned, shopping precinct – where shoppers can come and forget the traffic and the weather – must be the sort of shopping our residents would appreciate and would be a great boon for our people.'* For High Street traders, who still had traffic and weather to contend with, this was not a welcome idea. The centre had 93 shops on two floors, accessed by stairs and escalators, a public house, restaurant, sports centre, library and bus station. It also boasted a water feature, a number of art works and three hardwood play sculptures for children, the tortoise, the serpent and the whale.

The concept of a covered centre was unusual enough at the time for the *Daily Telegraph* to devote an article to the Poole development: *'This is a lot of shops to add to a town the size of Poole, so why has the centre succeeded so quickly?'* The answer, according to the *Telegraph* was the creation of a community which offered advantages to both the retailer and shopper. *'For the customer, the community concept provides a pleasant, temperature controlled environment, clean and bright, where people can meet, sit, chat and, of course, shop.'* In comparison to this exciting, modern shopping experience, High Street's offer seemed very mundane.

One side of the new centre faced on to High Street where traditional shops, the old Port Mahon Castle Hotel and the Regent Cinema looked across at the modern block of Marks and Spencer and other Arndale stores. Within a few months of the opening, the press was talking about a second phase Arndale Centre on the opposite side of High Street and pedestrianisation of the street as far as Old Orchard. Amidst the euphoria, a few members of the Council warned that more development might persuade the chain stores to vacate High Street altogether. On September 30th 1971, the Towngate Bridge was opened by the mayor, Adrian Greenwood, allowing traffic to flow over the railway line. After 97 years, the stranglehold of the railway crossing was broken and traffic could flow freely from the Quay to the George, by-passing High Street.

One interesting side effect of slum clearance in the old town was the rare chance to explore the medieval history of the area. Amongst properties demolished in the 1960s were Nos. 39 to 57 High Street on the south east side of the corn market. In the mid 1970s, rescue excavations were carried out on this site before the building of a large office block and car park. The dig produced rich findings. The earliest evidence was from medieval ditches and pits which contained pottery from the 13th to the 15th century, showing how early this part of High Street had been occupied. Also surviving were the foundations of substantial stone buildings dating from late 15th or early 16th century, earlier than the 17th century and later buildings recorded by the Royal Commission in the 1950s. There were also several wells, 12 to 15 feet deep, which once they had been cleared out, contained water that was still pure and drinkable.

The finds from the site also gave ample evidence of occupation over 700 years. Pottery included local and imported wares from the medieval period onwards, including German Bellarmine jars, Dutch cockerel dishes and bowls from Spain and Venice dating from the 17th and 18th centuries. Also found were drinking glasses and bottles, a great number of clay pipes dating from the 1630s to the 1830s and many odd items such as a spinning top, keys, a bone whistle, a comb, fragments of shoes and the handle of a fan. It is interesting to think that a few of the objects may have come from the house where Peter Hiley entertained King Charles II in 1665.

Depression in the property market had delayed the planned second phase of the Arndale development but by late 1976, the *Herald* reported that the development

Andrew Hawkes Poole Photo Archive

The excavation in progress

was about to start and quoted Terry Hopwood, President of the Arndale Centre Traders' Association as hoping that *'the unsightly collection of rundown shops and buildings now occupying the site, would shortly be gone'*. One of these was the old Port Mahon Castle Hotel, still operating as it awaited its demise. Another was the Regent Cinema, now a bingo hall with its glory days long past. These would be replaced by a covered mall with three large stores on the north west side and five small shops opposite.

At the other end of High Street one building anticipated the demolishers' hammers. Early on Sunday 2nd April 1978, masonry began to fall from the roof of No. 15 High Street, fortunately not hitting anyone in the street below. The building, at one time the Red Star Coffee Tavern and later a lodging house, had been empty and derelict for several years with steel supports holding up part of the roof. As the building threatened to collapse, the street had to be cordoned off while demolishers were hoisted up in a skip to take down the roof and gable end. According to the

Andrew Hawkes Poole Photo Archive

No. 15 before its collapse

Bournemouth Echo, 'as bricks and beams were removed, the front of the building started to buckle'. The Council had recently granted planning permission for the building to be demolished and flats to be built, but in fact the site was not developed and is currently one of the few empty plots on the street.

Meanwhile, the bulldozers were busy demolishing landmarks of the old Longfleet High Street for the second phase of the Arndale development. New stores were built on the site and a section of upper High Street between Marks and Spencer and the George roundabout was enclosed as a covered mall. The development was opened in 1980. By agreement, this section of the shopping centre was not to be closed at night but remain open to preserve the old thoroughfare. Tesco's supermarket now occupied the site of the old Port Mahon Castle Hotel and shoppers could browse in Boot's and Littlewood's where the Regent Cinema formerly stood.

To complete the scheme, the Council now planned to develop a final area from the Arndale Centre to the railway crossing, the so-called Phase IIB, with three stores, six shops, a roof top car park and a town square. As usual, the plans provoked fierce opposition and were the subject of yet another public enquiry. In an article in *Coaster* in 1982, Ledger de la Bald quoted his mother, a Poole native, as saying that *'Poole no longer held any magic or interest for her and that the Poole she knew and loved had disappeared over the last twenty years'*. Representatives for two of the traders affected by compulsory purchase orders told the enquiry that *'as the larger multiple concerns move from the High Street, this will make an already run down shopping area less valuable for local traders. . . Already a number of traders are closing down in the High Street'*. Borough Architect and Town Planning Officer, Graham Rogers contended that High Street *'would have died a long time ago if it hadn't been for the Arndale Centre, contrary to popular belief'* and that none of the existing buildings in the area was worthy of retention. Buildings scheduled for demolition included the Ansty Arms and all the surrounding premises except for the Dolphin Hotel, once the Longfleet Hotel. Eventually, phase IIB was approved and the Council began to acquire the properties for demolition.

High Street traders may not have agreed with the way the street was described at the enquiry, but they had to accept some unpleasant truths. Since the opening of the Arndale Centre over a decade before, the focus of the town had shifted northwards. The bus station brought people to the doors of the bright, modern Arndale Centre which was able to supply most of their shopping needs. In comparison, High Street appeared old-fashioned, run down, congested and inconvenient and its trade was suffering. Having been the town's main retail artery for so long, the street would now have to accept second place and try to find a different role for itself in the future.

Ideas on the street's future character were not lacking. In 1983, Ensors estate agents proposed to create a small *'old world'* shopping arcade in the central part of High Street behind Nos. 81 (formerly J. Cole and Sons, jewellers) and 83 (Wilkins' bakery). This would include a showroom for the estate agents, two shops, a tea-room and car parking as well as first floor offices and a top floor flat. As the *Poole Advertiser* reported, Neil Gerrard, Assistant Borough Planner applauded the scheme. *'Anything which keeps that part of the street viable is to be welcomed. . . There is a need for the smaller and independent shop unit and we want to do everything we can to help. The central part of the street has to find its own level.'*

In 1984 operators of an indoor market in the former Tesco store made a planning application to turn it into an amusement arcade with prize bingo. They claimed that the market had lost stalls and was now losing money. According to their counsel, High Street was no longer a prime shopping area and never would be again. Planning expert, Michael Burroughs said that the Arndale development had caused a considerable deterioration in the standard of shopping in High Street. He expected '*more multiple traders to move out of the High Street in future years. This is not to say this area of the High Street will die as a retail area. It will be attractive to marginal retailers with new enterprises seeking low rents. The failure of businesses is likely to be high.*' John Cramond for the Council talked more positively, if cautiously about the '*gradual recovery*' and '*slow improvement*' of High Street. The same year, phase IIB opened north of the railway line with two large stores occupied by W.H. Smith and Mothercare, ten smaller shops and Falkland Square replacing Towngate Street and the Ansty Arms. The Dolphin Hotel was the only building to survive.

The long discussed idea of pedestrianising High Street from the railway crossing to Old Orchard was again on the agenda. It would relieve congestion, do away with the need for widening, and link High Street with the shopping precinct. Still, not everyone was in favour. When the policy was proposed, 54 traders signed a petition against it. It was not until 1986 that the plan was approved and work began. The scheme was to cost £250,000 and there were various problems to overcome, servicing of shops, loss of parking, road crossings and safety concerns. The plan was to provide decorative brick paving, tree planting, new street furniture including traditional street lamps, hanging baskets and a facelift for the shop fronts. There was talk of a '*continental*' High Street.

In the next few months, the transformation took place. By summer 1987, the *Bournemouth Evening Echo* was able to present a feature on the '*Poole Precinct, a new concept in shopping. . . If you haven't taken a stroll down Poole High Street just lately then it's a treat in store. The transformation to a total pedestrian precinct is now complete and presents a true joy to shoppers.*' After nearly four years of building works, the central section of High Street was free of wheeled traffic for the first time in its history. Tree planting had softened the landscape and the street itself had been opened up to allow shoppers, in the words of the *Echo*, to '*revel in its traffic-free, fume-free peace*'.

A further transformation had also taken place in Scaplens Court. After nearly 60 years open to the sky, English Heritage gave permission for the empty front area to be built upon and a floor added above to allow proper circulation around the museum. The only caveat was that the new work should be distinguished from the old. The work was carried out in a traditional style using authentic materials, to restore the house to something like its original appearance. Downstairs was a spacious entrance hall and upstairs a fine function room open to the timbered roof. The two-storey bay window which had once been a major feature of the old house was also reconstructed with modern stained glass designs relating to Poole history and the date 1986 incorporated into it. This reconstruction gave the museum staff the chance to carry out a limited excavation in part of the front range which cast light on the earliest phases of the building. The excavation revealed the chalk and stone foundations of a cross wall more or less parallel to the front wall of the building but 3 to 4 metres behind it and dating from the late 13th or early 14th century.

Repaving for pedestrianisation

Shortly after the pedestrian works were finished, an application was made to introduce 30 candy-striped market stalls into the street two days a week. It was argued that this would add interest and atmosphere and renew the vigour of High Street. All but one of the traders and most of the correspondents to the Poole Avertiser were against the idea, being keen to preserve the open aspect of the newly pedestrianised street. In the end, the Council rejected the scheme on the grounds of obstructing the street, loss of visual amenity and the objection of the traders. Thirty years on, for good or ill, the street market is well established.

By the late 1980s, after two decades of transition and upheaval, High Street was experiencing something of a revival. In the 20 years since the opening of the Arndale Centre, covered shopping centres had become much more common and consequently less exciting. In 1986, High Street had been designated a conservation area, its mixture of building styles and heights praised and its narrow alleyways (once condemned as slums) felt to give interest and character to the area. People and planners were rediscovering the attraction of traditional shopping streets and independent traders.

However the 'new' High Street was not without its problems. Like the late-night carousers of 200 years before, noisy groups of people were disturbing the residents at night with rowdy behaviour and vandalism. Sid Shaw, who had lived in

Borough of Poole Museum Service

The restored upper hall, Scaplen's Court

High Street for over 20 years, was quoted in the *Poole Advertiser*: *'People coming out of the late-night drinking and eating places make such a commotion that we can never get to sleep at the weekends before about 3.00 am. One window has been broken twice in the last three weeks.'* He estimated that there were about 30 families living over the High Street shops. The answer seemed to be a greater police presence or the installation of surveillance cameras.

A couple of months later, the Council produced a report on the disturbances. They found that there were eleven eating or take-away houses in High Street and another eleven public houses or clubs in the streets around High Street, although

Jenny Oliver

only a few of these stayed open after midnight. Officials carried out observations in High Street on two nights until the small hours and noted the rowdy revellers for themselves. The report recommended that take-away food shops should close at midnight and warned other premises about the possibility of reducing their hours if the noise continued. The result was a strong protest from the take-away shops, particularly Kentucky Fried Chicken and Hotstuff, backed by signatures of customers, which persuaded the Council to compromise at 12.30 pm.

In spite of dire forecasts, there were still many large businesses located in the street. Lloyds Bank, in business in Poole for 165 years (previously as the Wilts and Dorset Bank), had relocated in 1986 from their *'impressive Georgian building'* at the lower end of High Street (No. 87) to the former Tesco store at Nos. 101-3. This building which had housed the failing indoor market was considered ideal for a new style of informal banking service allowing customers to talk face to face with staff rather than through a glass barrier. Lloyds reported that their High Street branch had been enjoying a boom over the last four or five years. Wimpy had bought the former Newbery's furniture store (once Butler's) prompting headlines of a 'burger war' with MacDonald's a few doors away. At the end of 1987, Salisbury's opened a new fashion accessory store at No. 127-9.

Meanwhile, with the aim of restoring High Street's character and getting rid of 'flashy' shop-fronts, the Council was offering 20% improvement grants. With such a mix of architectural styles and periods it was obviously not possible to turn the clock back to the Victorian era, but Council architects had produced a design guide which they hoped would make the street more harmonious. The take-up was rather disappointing. One of the few shops to take advantage of the scheme was the long-established ironmongers, W. E. Boone who received a grant towards repairing timber work and replacing one of the pillars in front of the shop. A Pride of Place award was won by Corker's café bar at No. 1 High Street for its refurbishment under the direction of the owners, Nick and Carolyn Constandinos. The family had owned the business (once Greco's and then the Olympia Café) since 1944.

One area which the Council hoped to develop was the site of the Wesleyan Church and its neighbouring buildings near the corner of North Street. In 1990 the butcher's shop next to the church closed after over 100 years, as its lease expired. Direct Windows next door was also told that their lease would not be renewed. However the redevelopment of the site did not take place and by the following year, plans by the Trustee Savings Bank to build a new branch there were approved. The demolition of the Church had been discussed for years, but at last the value of the building and its landmark tower to the local environment had come to be appreciated. Today the building is still standing and undergoing refurbishment.

In 1993, the eccentric numbering of properties in High Street was in the news. Over the years, with the division or amalgamation of properties, all sorts of inconsistencies had arisen. There were, for instance, two properties numbered 153, Beech Hurst, occupied by Jacobs and Reeves, solicitors and the former gas showroom building, housing the Portman Building Society. The 'Grand Parade' in lower High Street, consisting of premises occupying the old corn store, had its own numbers. There was also confusion around Falkland Square and the shopping centre, by now known as the Dolphin Centre. The Council avoided the formidable prospect of wholesale renumbering and instead proposed a mixture of better signage (for instance for Grand Parade) and small scale number changes. Nos. 32 and 34 Hill Street were to become 108 and 108a High Street, Falkland Square was to be renumbered in sequence and the Dolphin Centre would have separate numbering. Shops and homes would be required to display their numbers.

The same year, another controversy arose over the activities of the Church

Jenny Oliver

The former Harvey's and Lloyd's Bank

of Scientology whose canvassers were stopping people in the street. Traders felt that they were preventing passers-by from going into the shops, while the Church said that they were there to help people and that a few individuals were running *'an anti-religious Nazi-like hate campaign'* against them. A meeting was held about the issues, to which representatives of the Church were not invited, and feelings ran high on both sides. The Council also came in for criticism when they said that there was no legislation to bar the canvassers.

The problem of disorder and vandalism had not gone away. In December 1987 it was reported that eleven of the thirty newly planted trees had been snapped by people swinging on the branches. Most of these were in lower High Street near the pubs. One solution was surveillance cameras but the council rejected this 'big brother' idea at the time in favour of requesting extra police patrols. High Street's *'mini crime wave'* continued. In November 1989, Chris Ford of the Oven Door bakery at No. 104 told the *Bournemouth Evening Echo* that his shop had been broken into four times and his windows had been smashed on 21 occasions since January. By 1994, the Council had come round to the idea of a security camera, if the traders would be willing to contribute to the cost, said to be £10,000 for each camera and set of recording equipment. The only publicly funded camera in the town at the time was in the Civic Centre car park. Eventually electronic surveillance did reach High Street.

Another recurrent theme at the end of the century was the character of High Street and what designs were suitable. This was highlighted after Harvey's furniture store was devastated by fire in the small hours of March 21st 1997. The three-storey building at No. 107 had just had a major refurbishment with new ceilings, carpets and decoration when the fire broke out. The *Bournemouth Evening Echo* reported that 16 fire crews attended from all over Dorset, residents had to be evacuated and part of the town centre was sealed off. The building was almost totally destroyed. Over the next eighteen months, Harvey's rebuilt the store at the cost of £500,000 but when the new shop front was unveiled, its design sharply divided opinion. According to the *Echo*, some saw the modern frontage with its massive arch framing a two-storey window as a *'design crime'* or an *"eyesore" and not in keeping with Poole's historic atmosphere.'* Others liked its clean, modern appearance and felt that it was bringing something fresh to the street.

Another ultra modern shop front to receive planning permission was No. 121, whose *'high quality, innovative contemporary design'* (according to the applicants) *'deals with the whole façade, giving the building a vertical emphasis not unlike that of the Harvey's building'*. The main feature was vertical stainless steel mullions with clear glass windows for the shop and translucent glass for the offices on the first floor. A couple of doors away at No. 117 was Bennett's bakery, formerly Bright's, a listed building dating from the 19th century with a rare surviving 1930s shop front and tiled entrance. Across the street was the classic bank building dating from the 1920s. As *Dorset Life* expressed it in March 1999, *Poole High Street provides more of a mixture of architectural styles in the space of a few hundred yards than most towns can provide in all their streets put together. There are some outstanding buildings and shop fronts and some frankly awful ones, but it is never dull.'*

The end of the 20th century saw a High Street as architecturally diverse and as full of contradictions and controversies as ever. In the previous 50 years it had reached a low point, lost its position as the town's principal shopping street and experienced some painful years of economic blight. It had emerged changed, traffic free, with a new atmosphere and new ideas about its future role.

Jenny Oliver

Scaplen's Court and Poole Museum's modern entrance.

Postscript

In the 21st century, traditional high streets face increasing competition from shopping centres, out of town retail parks and online selling. When the credit crunch of 2009 arrived, high streets suffered more than their share of the pain. The Local Government Minister, described them as *'underused, unloved and undervalued'* but their important role in the vitality of town centres was at last recognised. In 2011, the retail guru Mary Portas was recruited to create a vision for the future of high streets. Her report imagined them as *'destinations for socialising, culture, health, well-being, creativity and learning,'* and not just buying and selling. *'The mix will include shops but could also include housing, offices, sport, schools or other social, commercial and cultural enterprises and meeting places'*. In other words, the high street of the future could be strangely similar to that of 150 years ago.

Locally, current plans of the Borough Council and the Town Centre Partnership confirm the High Street as a secondary rather than primary retail area, but one which has a particular role to play in the town's drive to improve its provision for shoppers. The plans include *'a rejuvenated role for Poole High Street south of Lagland Street, with opportunities for independent retailers and creative industries.'* They also aim to make High Street livelier in the daytime and early evening and improve the environment with *'paving, street furniture, landscaping & lighting, incorporating public art.'* The street is still home to well over 75 households (and more when the 115 apartments in the corn market block of flats are filled). Changing the type of business use quicker and filling vacant properties have already been simplified in the planning process.

The value of High Street's long history has also been recognised. A council recent report on town centre heritage sets the street in its historic context and describes the character of its buildings and streetscape. There are for instance over 80 national and locally listed buildings of architectural or historic interest in the street, ranging from the 15th century Scaplen's Court (officially a 'Scheduled Ancient Monument') to No. 134, the Victorian shop now housing Burger King. Future development plans will hopefully treat High Street more gently and with more appreciation of its heritage than in past decades.

The Poole Town Partnership (founded by retailers, businesses, tourism and the Borough) has developed a plan to improve the town centre with the aim of creating *'the best town centre experience in Dorset'* for visitors to *'help Poole meet the challenges facing high streets across the UK'*, in the words of its Chairman Jonathan Sibbert, *'The plan is ambitious and will change and develop over time'.*

The story of Poole High Street is the story of every high street in terms of social changes and developments, but its characters, buildings and events are unique and have helped to form the identity of the town we know today. The street has been home to rich merchants and ordinary shopkeepers, slave-traders, pirates, poets and paupers. It has been a centre of both trade and industry, home to ropemakers, coopers, anchorsmiths and shipwrights, as well as butchers, bakers and grocers. Its fine mansions, from medieval times to the Georgian period, have been built on the profits of the port, and furnished with goods brought from overseas on board sailing ships. Its shops represent the retail fashions of many eras. The street has witnessed riots, celebrations, accidents, punishments, processions, bombing, murder, fire, flood and disease. People have come there to live, shop, work and worship and to be educated and entertained. High Street's story is of continual change but surprising continuity and on the evidence of the last 800 years it will survive and evolve into the future.

Jenny Oliver

Index

Abercrombie, Sir Patrick 147
Abraham, Moses 55
Accidents 80, 106
Aldridge, Henry Mooring 90
Allen, Elizabeth 62
Allen, F.S. 129
Allen, George N. 75, 76
Allen, John 38
Allen, Richard 57, 61
Amity Hall/Palace of Varieties . . . 97, 103, 107, 116, 117, 124, 131, 135, 154, 155
Angel Inn 65
Anne, Queen 43
Ansty Arms 110, 118, 1146, 156, 162, 163
Antelope Inn (new) 57, 65, 76
Antelope Inn (old) 12, 20, 25, 31, 34, 38, 48, 56, 58, 63, 64, 65, 68, 71, 79, 82, 83, 84, 90, 99, 115, 136, 141
Apprenticeship 61
Arndale Centre 158, 159, 160, 161, 162, 164
Arndale Property Trust Ltd. 157
Assemblies 71
Bacon, Frank 105
Bacon, Walter J. 105, 106, 107
Bacon and Curtis 107, 113, 114, 116, 117, 118, 152
Baker, Roger 31
Ballard, Michael 49, 59, 60
Balston, Alfred 123
Balston, Harry 123
Balston's Rope and Twine Works 81, 110
Bannen, Mary 87
Barfoot, Lydia 65
Barfoot, William . . .42, 43, 46, 48, 53, 58, 60, 65, 73
Bathing House 55, 65
Bayley, H. and Son 96, 103
Beale's 157
Bealesons 157
Beatrice, Princess 111
Bedford, John 8, 117
Beard, Agnes 18
Beehive Stores 116, 153
Beech Hurst. . . . 72, 73, 74, 103, 107, 117, 122, 133, 134, 167
Belben, R.C. 146
Bell Inn 37
Bell and Crown Inn 101
Bell, Thomas 97
Benn, Hilda 113, 120
Bennett, Jesse 20
Bennett's 169
Beryman, Joan 18
Beryman, John 18
Bestland, William 61
Bevington, Rev. George 154
Bingham, John 28
Bird, Thomas Young 68
Black Rod 33, 39
Black-out 140, 146
Blandford Arms 110, 157
Bloomfield, Miss 96
Bloomfield, J.B. 92, 95
Bombing 139, 140, 143
Bon Marché 138, 139, 141, 148
Boone, W.E. & Co. 116, 131, 148, 152, 166, 167
Boots the Chemist .116, 161
Bould, D. 145
Bournemouth Gas & Water Co. . 117, 122, 133, 141, 147
Bowden, Samuel 58, 61
Bower, Benjamin 53
Bowles, Mr. 71
Bowling Green Alley 58
Bowling Green House 58
Bradford and Sons 117
Brassett, Joseph 53, 68
Bravery, Geoffery 151, 154
Bravery, James 117, 133, 135, 154
Brice, George Tito 65
Bright, Joseph & Son 133, 141, 142, 145, 152, 154, 169
Brine Brothers 95
Bristowe, Ernest 114, 118, 124, 143
Bristowe, William 114
British Overseas Airways Corporation 139, 145, 146, 147
Brown, Vera 149
Brownsea Island 35, 119, 132, 139, 143
Bucknam, Richard 48
Budge, Hubert Lionel 123
Budge, Philip 104, 107, 117, 120, 122, 123, 124
Budge, Philip Prideaux .124
Budge, William Hatton 120, 133
Bull Head Inn . . . 25, 31, 34, 35, 38, 39, 45, 46, 53, 58, 64, 74, 80, 99, 104
Burbidge family 141
Burden, Henry and Sons . . .109, 110, 121, 133, 152, 154, 157
Burger King 171
Burglary 78
Burroughs, Michael 162
Burt, Elias 71
Bus Station 135, 143, 149, 153, 157, 162
Buses 90, 134, 135, 137, 138, 140, 143, 149, 158
Bushell, Thomas 48
Butler, John 65
Butler and Son 106, 116, 120, 144, 145, 167
Byngley, Alice 13
Byngley, Thomas 13, 20
Byngley, William 13, 20
Campbell, Alexander 55, 56, 63
Campbell, David 56

Cane Way, Thomas .4
Cann, Frederick .113
Carey, George .123
Carnival .135
Carter family .45
Carter, Herbert S. .122, 127, 133, 134, 145
Carter, Isaac .62
Carter, John .38, 45, 58
Carter, Mary .38
Carter's Lane .16, 45, 58, 106
Castle Street .53
Central Tailor Ltd. .153
Chapel Lane .5, 58, 102
Charles I, King .27, 29, 34, 35
Charles II, King .33, 34, 37, 58, 159
Charles X, King of France .82, 133
Chesney, George .149
Cholera .91, 92
Christian, Elizabeth .54
Christie, Mrs. .139
Church of Scientology .168
Churchill, John .54
Cinema .103, 116, 117, 133, 135, 154
Cinnamon House .62, 100
Cinnamon Lane .57, 76, 143
Civil War .27, 28, 29, 31
Circus .150
Claridge, Mrs. .82
Clarke, Peter .44
Coaches .63, 64, 68, 90
Cock, John .31
Cole Corner .13, 22, 49
Cole, Alderman .154
Cole, Harry .131, 137, 145
Cole, James .99, 131, 133, 152, 162
Cole, Miss .96
Cole, Phyllis .128
Colyns, Henry .4
Conservation area .164
Constandinos family .167
Constantine, William (16th c.) .14
Constantine, William (17th c.) .29, 31
Corban, William .33
Corker's .167
Corn market 7, 16. 24, 25, 27, 35, 40, 42, 44, 47, 57, 58, 60, 93, 97, 105, 114, 154, 159, 172
Coronations .111, 118, 150
Corpe, Richard .46, 47
Courtin, Mr. .57, 58
Cowles, Reginald .123
Cows .16
Cox, Charles .85
Cramond, John .163
Cummings, Geoff .152
Curry's .136, 145
D-Day .145
Davis, Rev. William .68
Daw, Charles jun. .45
Daw, Charles sen. .38, 39
Daw, Rachel .45
Day, Bertie .115, 117, 123
De La Bald, Ledger .162
Dean, Mrs. .53
Defoe, Daniel .42
Derby, Joseph .106
Derby, Richard .48
Dibbe/Dibbs, John .31, 33
Dibbens, Richard .23
Dicker, William .14, 18
Diggs, Jane .48
Direct Windows .167
Dolbery, Elizabeth .31
Dolbery, Richard .31, 32, 33
Dolbery, William .25, 31
Dolby, G. A. .125
Dolphin Centre .167
Dolphin Hotel .162, 163
Dunford, Mr. .71
Dunkirk .139
Durant, John .104
Durell, Aaron .53, 59
Durell, Thomas .73
Durell, Widow .54
Edward IV, King .7
Edward VII, King .111
Edwards, Francis .58
Edwards, John .14
Edwards, Richard .58
Edwin Jones and Co. .138
Efford, Nicholas .33, 39
Electric Theatre .157
Elizabeth I, Queen .13
Emerson, Mary .38
Ensor's .162
Excavations .2, 159, 160, 163
Executions .18, 38
Exhibition of Works of Industry & Art .95, 96
Edwards, John .14
Falkland Square .51, 119, 163, 167
Farewell, Christopher .17
Farmer, Henry .104, 105, 152
Festival of Britain .150
Fever .67, 92
Fiander, Martin .54
Fideler, Richard .4
Field, Mistress .25
Fifty Shilling Tailor .139, 140, 141, 147
Fine Fare .155
Fire .23, 44, 70
Fish Street .53
Flood .54, 138
Food shortages .29, 71, 121, 124, 140
Ford, Bussey .63
Ford, Chris .168
Frampton, William .35
Ford, Madame .138
Franklin, Mary .45
French Horn and Trumpet .65
French Revolution .69
Fricker, John .58
Fricker's Alley .58
Furmage, William .90

Galton, Mary 48
Gambier, Alfred J. 120, 122
Gambier, Evan 115, 117, 120, 124, 125, 132
Garland, Amy 73
Garland, George 73, 77
Garland, Joseph 73
Gas and Coke Company 84
George I, King 46
George II, King 49
George III, King 55
George IV, King 81
George V, King 118
George Inn/Hotel, Longfleet 80, 81
George Inn (new) 57, 58
George Inn (old) . . 25, 28, 31, 32, 33, 35, 37, 38, 45, 46, 48, 54, 55, 58, 60, 61, 63, 109, 110, 116, 130, 135, 144, 149, 153, 156, 157, 159
Gerrard, Neil 162
Gibbon, John 23
Gibbon, Nicholas jun. 23, 29, 31
Gibbon, Nicholas sen. 23, 33
Gibbon, Sidrach 23
Gifford's 123, 143, 147, 152
Gigger, John 48
Gillett, Robert 76
Gillingham, Nicholas 44
Gleed, Richard 54
Globe Alehouse 74
Globe Café 65
Goddard, Cecily 22
Goddard, John 22
Godden, William 63
Gondolier boats 139
Grand Parade 146, 147
Greco's 157, 167
Green, Alice 18, 20
Green, Edward 14, 15, 16, 36
Green, George 13, 96, 134, 152
Green, William 16, 18, 19, 197
Greenwood, Adrian 159
Grist, John 23
Grundy, James 33
Guest, Freddie E. 126
Guest, Lady Charlotte 95
Gyngell, Mr. 78
Hackman, John 58
Haddon, Walter 13
Hall, Anna 65
Hall, Peter 33, 35
Hall Caine, G. R. 133
Hamilton, Augustus 98
Hamilton, Horatio 98, 104, 105
Hamilton, James 85, 87, 98
Hamilton, Julius 87
Hants & Dorset Motor Services Ltd. 135, 153
Harbin, Henry 27
Harrison, John 54
Harvey's 168, 169
Harward, Henry 20
Hastings, Cosmo B. 138
Haviland, Elinor 25
Haviland, James 7, 8, 25
Haviland, Matthew 12
Haviland, William 35
Hawkes, David 141, 151
Hawkes, J.A. and Son . . .94, 113, 120, 123, 131, 136, 141, 152
Hawkes, Joseph Alfred 94, 106, 117
Hawkes, Joseph Charles 106
Hawkes, Victor 141
Hayman, Messrs. 115
Hayter, John 55
Hayward, William 58
Hawkins, Thomas 33
Heckford 33
Henning, Robert 63
Henry VI, King 5, 6
Henry and Co. 145
Hescroff, Mary Ann 92
Hescroff, Mrs. 90
High Street extension 23
High Street properties (modern numbers):
- No. 1 167
- No. 4 .....138, 146
- No. 6 .....20, 146
- No. 8 20
- No. 10 .....20, 56, 115
- No.12 100
- Nos. 12-14 .....11, 12, 20
- No. 15 .....147, 160, 161
- No. 20 113
- No. 21 154
- Nos. 21-27 .....16, 57
- No. 22 114
- No. 25 128
- No. 27 101
- No. 28 147
- Nos. 30-32 .....22, 48
- No. 38 115
- No. 39 93
- Nos. 39-57 159
- Nos. 41-43 25
- No. 43 141
- No. 44 105
- Nos. 47-49 25
- No. 48 92
- No. 52 153
- No. 55 123
- No. 67 .....89, 90, 103
- No. 69 123
- Nos. 69-71 87
- No. 73 25
- No. 76 106
- No. 78 127
- No. 80 136
- No. 81 100,162
- No. 82 .....87, 123
- No. 83 162
- No. 84 139
- No. 87 .....78, 99, 100, 166
- Nos. 87-89 .....42, 42, 66
- No. 89 .....107, 138

Nos. 90-92 . . . . .47, 47
No. 91 . . . . .93, 105, 131
No. 92 145
No. 93 113
No. 94 95
No. 95 61
No. 96 71
No. 99 . . . . .94, 113
Nos. 101 87
No. 102 155
Nos. 103-105 . . . . .44, 166
No. 104 .94, 120, 156, 169
Nos. 105-107 136
No. 107 169
No. 108 167
No. 109 116
Nos. 109-113 50
No. 117 . . . . .141, 152, 169
No. 120 131
No. 121 169
No. 124 153
No. 125 . . . . .86, 97
Nos. 127-129 . . . . .47, 73, 86, 167
No. 130 134
No. 134 . . . . .103, 144, 171
No. 141 . . . . .52, 106
No. 142 156
No. 146 131
No. 151 86
No. 153 167
No. 156 123
No. 180 118
Nos. 180-184 136
No. 181 118
No. 185 109
No. 187 157
No. 189-191 138
No. 203 109
No. 215 113
Hiley, Charles 35
Hiley, Haviland 25, 29, 33, 35
Hiley, Mary 35
Hiley, Mistress 44
Hiley, John 35
Hiley, Mr. 23
Hiley, Peter jun. 35, 38
Hiley, Peter sen. .35, 36, 159
Hiley, Rachel 35
Hiley, William, sen. 25
Hill, Marie 19
Hill, Robert 18
Hill Street (Hell Street) 27, 58, 77
Hillier, William 62
Hindle, Jane 86
Hindle, William 86
Hine, Arthur 117
Hockey, Tom 131
Hollybread, Ann 38
Hollybread, James 38
Holmes, Frank 110
Home and Colonial Stores 116
Hookey, Joseph 54
Hooper, Joan 67
Hopkins, Mrs. 96
Hopkins, Richard Cull 93
Hopkins, Roger 156
Hopkins, Samuel V. 94
Hopwood, Terry 160
Horner, John 55
Horses 28, 29, 37, 64
Hotstuff 166
Houses, 17th century 35, 36, 37
Houses, 18th century 47, 48, 50, 54
Houses, 19th century 101
Houses, 20th century 117
Houses, medieval 2, 7
Houses, Tudor .9, 10, 12, 16
Howard, George 110
Hues, Walter . . . .
Hunter, Rev. Frederick 157
Hussey, S. 95
Hutchings, Herbert 134
Hyde, George .52, 58, 59, 60
Inns 25, 38, 39, 45, 48, 58, 64
International Stores 125
Ivy House 86, 87
Jacobite Rebellion: 1715-1745 . . . . .46, 49
Jacobs and Reeves 167
James II, King 38
Jeffery, John 65, 68, 69, 76, 77
Jeffery, Robert 95
Jenkins, Aubrey 127, 131, 140, 141
John, Augustus 132
Jolliff, Christopher 73
Jolliff, William 54
Jolliffe, Rev. Peter 84
Joyner, Thomas 109, 110, 133, 157
Jubber, Thomas 60
Keat, Thomas 60
Keene, Clarence 124
Keene, George 124
Kemp, James 86
Kemp-Welch, Martin 90
Kentucky Fried Chicken 166
King, James 44
King, John Gerrard .104, 105
King's Arms 38, 45, 54, 64, 70
King's Head . . . 12, 20, 25, 44, 48, 55, 115, 117, 128, 132
King's Cycle Depot 109, 110
Kingland Crescent 153, 154, 155, 157
Kingland Road 135, 143, 154, 158
Knapp, William 52, 53
Knapton, L. S. 123
Knight, Mary 61
Knight, George 90, 90
Knight, William 61
Kyng, Robert 4
Lacy, Edward 104
Lacy, John 76
Ladies Walking Field . . 121, 143, 150, 153, 154, 157
Laglane/Lagland Street 26, 27, 53, 78

Lally, Gwen 150
Lamb, Henry 132
Lamb Inn 33, 37, 54
Lambert family 14
Lambert, Thomas 14, 25
Lankester, John 87, 104
Ledgard, George Welch 84, 99
Ledgard, Louisa 84
Ledgard, Martha 84
Ledgard, Richard 75, 80, 86, 92, 98, 99, 104
Ledgard, Susannah 86, 99
Legg, Mary 67
Legg, John 67
Leland, John 9
Lentcrocks 44
Lester, Benjamin 71, 73
Lester, Benjamin Lester 77, 81, 82
Lester, John 33, 44
Lester, Meshec 57
Lewis, Gerard 49
Library 82, 83, 100, 139
Linthorne, Benjamin .53, 60
Linthorne, Edward 33
Linthorne, John 33
Linthorne, Mary 62
Lion and Lamb Inn 54, 76
Lipton's 99, 104, 114, 116
Listed buildings 150
Littlewood's 161
Llewellin, Miss 114, 151
Lloyd, Alexander 38
Lloyd, Rachel 38, 39
Lloyd, Rebecca 60
Lloyd-Allen, Arthur 158
Lloyd's Bank .166, 167, 168
Loader, Job 103, 104
Lock, Ann 45
Lock, Joan 61
Lock, John 38, 45
Lockyer, Edward 52
London Tavern Inn/Hotel 65, 79, 82, 90, 98, 107, 107, 108, 122, 136, 137, 147
Longfleet . . . 17, 51, 80, 81, 85, 105, 109, 110, 111, 112, 113, 121, 121, 133, 161
Longfleet Congregational Church 118, 134
Longfleet Hotel 136, 162
Looker, John 123
Looker, Nesta 123
Looker's 140, 149
Lovell, Melior 31
Macdonald's 167
Mackrell, Thomas 44
Man, Edward jun. 35
Man, Edward sen. 20
Man, Mrs. 31
Manning, Thomas 76
Marchbank, L. 68
Marks and Spencer 136, 143, 157, 159, 161
Marsh, Sarah 87
Marshall, John 76
Masters, John jun. . . . 41, 49, 50, 53, 58, 59, 60, 73, 77
Masters, John sen. 41
Masters, Sarah 60
Mate, William 77, 90, 100, 102, 104, 117
Matthews, Harry 114, 118
Mawdley, Roger 19
Maypole Dairy 116, 124
McLaine, Mr. 70
Mead, Benjamin jun. .65, 67
Mead, Benjamin sen. .53, 65
Mead, Mary 65
Mead, Melior 65
Meaden, James 54
Melledge, Alice jun. 38
Melledge, Alice sen. 25, 33, 38
Melledge, Elizabeth 34
Melledge, John 25
Melledge, Johnson 25, 27, 31, 33, 38
Mermaid Hotel 158
Mesurers Gap 2, 7, 23
Mesurer, William 8
Midland Bank 130
Miles, Theophilus 99, 106, 124, 131, 152
Miller, Joseph 54
Miller, W. L. and Sons 120, 121, 137, 156
Miller, Leslie 155, 156
Miller, William 58
Milner, George 61
Milner, William 52
Minty, William 34
Monmouth, Duke of .34, 38
Montague Burton's .136, 140
Moore family 77
Moore, Jane 77
Moore, Joseph jun. 76, 89
Moore, Joseph sen. 68, 69, 89
Mothercare 163
Mountjoy, Lord 18
Munday, William 65
Murder 18, 104, 105
Napoleonic War 69, 75
National Provincial Bank 106, 107, 138
Neave, Moses 68
New Orchard 58
New Street 13, 22, 26
Newbery's 167
Newfoundland 9, 33, 37, 39, 41, 42, 43, 49, 56, 60, 65, 71, 73, 77, 78, 99
Newnum, William 54
Nicholas, Prince of Rumania 132
Nicholas, Valentine 34
Norman, Martha 65
North Street 80, 103, 143, 167
Norton, George 105, 106
Nurrey, William 31
Oake, Caroline 86
Oake, Mary 86
Oake, Robert 86
Oake, Timothy 86
Old Orchard 2, 159, 163
Oldmeadow, John 54

Olive, George 60
Olive, Sarah 60
Oliver, John 63
Oliver, Mr. 61
Olympia Café 167
Oven Door Bakery 168
Pageant 150
Palmer, Peter 81
Parade 70, 78, 86, 102
Paradise Street 2
Parliamentary reform 84
Parmenter, Margery 20
Parmenter, Richard 19, 20
Parrot, Thomas 106, 115
Paye, Henry 4
Paye, John 4
Pearce, William 93, 104
Peckett, Thomas 34
Pedestrianisation 163, 164
Penney, George 85, 93, 95
Pepy's 156
Phippard family 43
Phippard, John 48
Phippard, widow 47
Phippard, Captain William 43, 58
Phippard, Sir William 43, 44, 57, 131
Pigs (Piggs) 37, 62
Pitman, Mary 38, 45, 54
Pitney, John 58
Pitt, Mr. 18
Pitwines 17, 23, 27, 40, 53, 133, 154
Pitwines Gas Works 143
Plague 3, 29, 30, 34
Pluddie Lane 58
Plume of Feathers Inn 25, 31, 33, 35, 38, 46, 48, 55
Pococke, Dr. 49
Ponsonby, W.F.S. 81, 82
Poole and Dorsetshire Herald 89, 90, 100, 103
Poole Anti-Tank Island 142, 143
Poole Electric Theatre 117, 119, 124, 133
Poole Museum .82, 137, 170
Poole Pilot 100
Poole Town and County Bank 78, 98
Poole Town Partnership .171
Population 41, 78, 88
Port Mahon Castle Inn 80, 107, 110, 119, 136, 159, 160, 161
Portman Building Society 137
Post Office 88, 106, 131
Prankard, Mrs. 131
Price family 46
Price, Henry 46, 53
Priory 16, 27, 58, 60
Punishment 48
Purdue, Mr. 128
Queen's Head 54
Raid, 1405 4
Railway crossing 102, 110, 125, 137, 143, 146, 149, 150, 154, 159, 162, 163
Railways 90, 101, 102
Randall, James 65
Randall, Joseph 65
Randall, Mr. 46
Rationing 138, 140, 142, 143, 147, 152
Rats 44, 117, 139
Red Cow Alehouse 41, 49
Red Star Coffee Tavern 147, 160
Reeves, Herbert 86
Religion 34, 48, 55, 102, 103, 168
Regent Theatre/Cinema. . . .132, 133, 136, 139, 154, 156, 159, 160, 161
Reyner, Arthur 124
Richards, Thomas 97
Rickman, Tom 95
Riot & disorder 48, 59, 61, 67, 76, 164, 165, 168
Roberts, Thomas jun. .31, 32
Roberts, Thomas sen. .27, 33
Robson, John 14
Rogers, Alfred 123
Rogers, Graham 162
Rogers, widow 34
Rolles, Amey 76
Rolles, John 71, 73
Rolles, Samuel .71, 73, 74, 76
Rolt, John 43
Ropewalks 52
Rose Alehouse 74
Rose, John 48
Russell, Bob . . . .
Ryan, Michael 76
St. Clement Inn 54
St. James' Church 3, 13, 26, 53, 68, 83, 111, 144
St. Paul's Church . . . 83, 84, 85, 98, 99, 111, 156, 157
Salisbury Street 2, 54
Salisbury's 17
Salter family 167
Salter, Thomas 86, 97, 98
Sainsbury's . . . .
Sartin, Horace 120
Saunders and Sons .114, 138
Saunders, Edward 53
Saunders family 113, 114, 115
Saunders, Gilbert 120
Saunders, Herbert jun. .133
Saunders, Herbert sen. 113, 115, 120
Saunders, Mr. 68
Savage, George 53
Scaplen, John 54, 55, 63
Scaplen's Court 1, 7, 8, 9, 10, 25, 32, 55, 128, 129, 130, 134, 137, 149, 151, 154, 163, 165, 170, 171
School 13, 46, 86
Scott, James 70
Scott, Margaret 150
Scriven, John 75
Security cameras 165, 168
Selfe, Henry 95, 99, 100
Seymor, Elizabeth 48
Seymour, H.D. 95
Sharp, Douglas 123
Sharp, Elizabeth 76

Sharp, F.A. 123
Sharp, John 76
Shatford, James 77
Shave, Leslie 123
Shaw, Sid 164
Shean, Mary 87
Sherenham, John 53
Sherring, William 60
Ship Café 156
Ships:
  Amy 64, 68
  Angel 14
  Ann Gallant 14
  Alarm 93
  Arc 31
  Bacchante 93
  Concord 33, 39
  Desire 27
  Diadem 93
  Dolphin 43, 44
  Eagle 42
  Eclipse 93
  Egeria 93
  Elinor 37
  Florinda 138
  Freak 93
  George and Thomas .39
  Happy Returns 37
  Heroine 93
  Hopewell 40
  Jeane 27
  Lark 60
  Lightning 82
  Littleton 60
  Mary 43
  Mayflower 37
  Meteor 82
  Nephraic II 153
  Primrose 27
  Prince 97
  Rachel 37
  Seaflower 27
  Secret 93
  Susannah 27
  Thalia 93
  Thomas Kirk Wright 139
  William 31
  William and Elizabeth 43
  William and Mary 43
Shop opening hours 95, 104, 114, 115, 116
Sibbert, Jonathan 172
Sifrewast, William 14
Simpson, Adam 70
Skinner, John 53, 61
Skinner, widow 53
Skinner's Alley . . . .
Skutt, Allen 37
Skutt, Benjamin jun. 60
Skutt, Benjamin sen. 54, 58, 60
Skutt, Elizabeth 35
Skutt family 54
Skutt, George jun. 33
Skutt, George sen. 27, 29, 31, 32, 35
Skutt, Jane 32
Skutt, Margaret 60
Skutt, Sarah 33
Skutt, William jun. 46
Skutt, William sen. 27, 29, 32, 33, 41
Slade family 99
Slave trade 42, 68, 69
Slum conditions and clearance 127, 149, 154, 159
Smallpox 63
Smith, Abraham 48
Smith and Goodchild 94
Smith, Harry Peace 10, 129, 130, 134, 137, 149, 150
Smith-Asher, Mary 43
Soldiers 27, 69, 70
Soul, T.S. 133
Snook. Caleb T. 109, 110, 121, 133, 152, 157
Society of Poole Men 130, 134
Somerville, Alexander 86
Speed, Gabrielle 141
Spencer, Elinor 19
Spencer, Gerrard 19
Spencer, Gowin 19
Spurrier, Timothy 60
Squibb, Miss 101
Stagg, Mary 46
Standard, James 33
Stanley, Elizabeth 55, 56
Stanley, Richard 55
Stanworth, widow 58
Starre, Clement 20
Steel, Dove 77
Steel, Isaac 77
Stevens, Arthur 123
Stickland, John 76
Stickland, Phillip 56, 65
Stone, Mary 46
Stradlinge, Avice 14
Stradlinge, Edmund 14
Street cleaning 44, 62, 92, 101
Street lighting 84, 147
Street market 164
Street numbering 110, 111, 167
Street surface and repair 18, 24, 40, 117, 138, 163
Street widening 154
Street, Mistress 44
Street, Peter 54, 65
Street, Thomas 65
Strikes 133
Sugar, Christopher 25
Sutton, John 31
Sutton, Richard 48
Sydcombe, Mr. 18
Sydenham, Anna Christiana 89
Sydenham, Elizabeth 89
Sydenham, John jun. 89, 95, 100
Sydenham, John sen. 82, 85, 88, 89, 90, 100

Sydenham, Richard 95, 100
Taverner, William 41, 49
Taylor, Edward 33, 39
Tesco 161, 162, 166
Thatched cottage 16, 45
Theatre 71, 77, 78
Thompson, Sir Peter 49, 54, 61
Thoms, Christian 44
Thoms, Josiah 44
Three Mariners Inn 37
Timothy White's 48, 57, 59, 60, 61, 65, 136
Tito, George 48
Todd, Cecil 137
Tollhouse 80, 110, 130
Topp's Corner 110, 131
Towgood, Matthew 48
Town Arms 37
Town Cellars 2, 3, 4, 7, 8
Town Crier . . . .
Town ditch 5, 40, 49
Town walls 5, 40
Towngate 5, 40, 80
Towngate Lane/Street 27, 51, 58, 63, 79, 80, 110, 112, 163
Towngate Bridge 159
Trams 111, 112, 113, 133, 134, 135
Travers, H. J. .116, 123, 153
Trees 163, 168
Tribbett, James 90, 100
Trustee Savings Bank 167
Turner, Dr. 106
Turner, Mr. 131
Turnpike gate 63
Turnpike Trust 63
Turtle, Robert 84
Tuson's 131
Tyto, David 14
Uvedale, Sir Edmund 21, 22, 48
Uvedale, Sir Francis 21
Uvedale, Lady Mary 22
Vallis, Samuel 71
Victoria, Queen 111
W. H. Smith 163
Wadham, Jane 44
Wadham, Thomas .39, 41, 48
Wanhill, James Manlaws 93
Wanhill, Thomas 93
War Savings Weeks 144, 145
Waring, Charles 100
Water supply 101, 156, 159
Waterman, Ann 80
Watts, William 99
Waugh, Col. 95
Weeks, John 92
Weeks family 92
Welch, Samuel 68, 99
Weld, Mr 93
Wesleyan Church 103, 102, 131
West, Walter 135
Weston, George 58
Weston, Samuel jun. 64, 65
Weston, Samuel sen. 43
Weston, William 47
Wheatley, Col. Mervyn J. 137, 139, 145
Whettle, William 65, 71
White, Joseph 56, 58, 65, 70, 72, 73
White, Mr. 115
White, Samuel jun. 71, 76
White, Samuel sen. 42, 71
White, Samuel third 71, 76
White Bear 38, 45, 46, 58, 60, 64, 127
Whire family 42
White Hart Inn (near Globe lane) 38, 118
White Hart Inn (near Quay) 45, 54
White House Laundry 110, 111, 116, 135
Whiterow, Simon 44
Wilby, G 115
Wiles, John 49
Wilkin's Bakery 162
William IV, King 81
Williams, David 141
Williams, William 31
Wills, Elizabeth 48
Wills, James Joseph 90
Wills, Richard 54
Wilts and Dorset Bank 99, 100, 166
Wimborne, Lord 114
Wimpy 167
Wise, William 54
Witteridge, Samuel 76
Woolworth, F.W. 127, 128, 143, 154
World War I 119, 120, 121, 122, 123
World War II 137, 138, 139, 140, 141, 143, 144, 145, 146
World Stores 141
Yeatman W. H. 117, 152
Young, Spence 57
Zebra Bar 156
Zilwood, Anna Christiana 89

Main Sources

The main sources consulted in the preparation of this book have been lodged for reference, in Poole Local History Centre.